Accessibility, Inclusion, and Diversity in Critical Event Studies

Most early social research into planned events had the effect of broadcasting narratives of dominant cultures and privileged groups. More recently, however, convergences of gender, sexualities, ethnicities, age, class, religion, and intersectional analyses and events studies have started to drive new critical understanding of the impacts of events on non-mainstream, non-majority communities around the globe. This timely book addresses current gaps in the literature surrounding issues of accessibility, inclusion, and diversity in various event landscapes.

Structured into four parts covering the main types of events, the chapters present original topics using innovative methodological approaches. Each chapter employs a case study to illustrate the key intertwining issues in these various experiential realms. Further, the chapters are all cross- or interdisciplinary, drawing on gender, sexualities, cultural, race/ethnicity studies as well as multiple literatures that feed into critical events studies and exploring a variety of global examples.

This significant book opens the path to further research on the role and importance of accessibility, inclusion, and diversity in events environments worldwide. It will be of interest to academics and researchers of critical event studies as well as a number of related social science disciplines.

Rebecca Finkel is an urban cultural geographer and Reader in Events Management at Queen Margaret University, Edinburgh, and a Senior Fellow of the Higher Education Academy. The main focus of her research frames critical events studies within conceptualisations of social justice, equality and diversity, and identity. Her main research interests include resistance to globalisation processes through cultural events, doing gender at festivals, and mapping human rights and international sporting events. Her new research explores the relational wellbeing dimensions of human–animal interactions in events, tourism, and leisure contexts.

Briony Sharp was awarded her PhD in Events Management from Queen Margaret University, Edinburgh, and is currently a Lecturer in Events Management at the University of Huddersfield. Her research examines social impacts from an individual, community, and organisational perspective, and possible social legacy routes from these impacts. Specifically, this includes social engagement initiatives pursued in conjunction with the Glasgow 2014 Commonwealth Games, and the relationship between social capital, community engagement, and potential social legacies. New research investigates innovative methodologies in events with a focus on event volunteering and tourism motivations.

Majella Sweeney is a Senior Lecturer in International Hospitality and Tourism Management at Queen Margaret University, Edinburgh, and a Senior Fellow of the Higher Education Academy. Research interests include small hospitality enterprises, focusing on the host–home relationship and self-identity. Qualitative research methods, specifically visual methods within the hospitality, tourism, and event industry, are another area of interest. Her new research explores hospitality and tourism events with conceptualisations of family inclusion, marginalisation, and accessibility.

Routledge Advances in Event Research Series

Edited by Warwick Frost and Jennifer Laing
Department of Marketing, Tourism and Hospitality, La Trobe University, Australia

Accessibility, Inclusion, and Diversity in Critical Event Studies

Edited by Rebecca Finkel, Briony Sharp, and Majella Sweeney

Routledge
Taylor & Francis Group

LONDON AND NEW YORK

First published 2019 by Routledge

2 Park Square, Milton Park, Abingdon, Oxon OX14 4RN
605 Third Avenue, New York, NY 10017

Routledge is an imprint of the Taylor & Francis Group, an informa business

First issued in paperback 2022

British Library Cataloguing-in-Publication Data
A catalogue record for this book is available from the British Library.

Library of Congress Cataloging-in-Publication Data
A catalog record has been requested for this book.

ISBN: 978-0-815-35082-8 (hbk)
ISBN: 978-1-03-233889-7 (pbk)
DOI: 10.4324/9781351142243

Typeset in Times New Roman
by Integra Software Services Pvt. Ltd.

Contents

PART II
Cultural and political events 79

PART III
Sporting events 165

Contributors

Roaa Ali is a Research Associate at the University of Manchester, Centre on Dynamics of Ethnicity (CoDE). Her research explores the representation of ethnic minorities and the politics of cultural production post-9/11. Roaa completed her PhD at the University of Birmingham and is preparing her thesis for a monograph. Some of her publications appear in the *Research in Drama Education: The Journal of Applied Theatre and Performance, Journal of Arts and Community, Interdisciplinary Perspectives on Equality and Diversity*, and *The Methuen Drama Companion to Theatre and Interculturalism*.

Daniel Barrera-Fernández is Professor at the Faculty of Architecture of the Autonomous University of Oaxaca, Mexico. He is delegate of ATLAS (Association for Tourism and Leisure Education and Research) for Mexico, Central America, and the Caribbean. His research interests focus on urban and cultural tourism, tourist-historic cities, and urban planning in heritage contexts. His doctoral thesis 'Schools of Thoughts in Heritage and Tourist Management of the Historic City', was awarded the Extraordinary Doctoral Award by the University of Malaga.

Marcelo de Castro Haiachi holds a PhD in Human Movement Sciences from the Federal University of Rio Grande do Sul (2017) and a Master's Degree in Human Molecular Science at the University of Castelo Branco (2007). Adjunct Professor of the Federal University of Sergipe. Experience in adapted physical activity, volleyball, and special topics in physical education and health. Coordinator of the ParaSports Project of Sergipe and of selections of the Brazilian Confederation of Volleyball for the Disabled (CBVD). Leader of the research group on Physical Education and Adapted Sports – GPEFEA/ UFRRJ and the research group on Olympic and Paralympic Studies (GPEOP).

Silvestre Cirilo dos Santos Neto holds a PhD in Exercise and Sports Science from Universidade do Estado do Rio de Janeiro (UERJ). His main research interests are sports management, multivariables of sports performance and results, and Olympic and Paralympic studies. Member of Brazilian Association of Sport Management (ABraGEsp). He obtained a fellowship (FP7 Carnival Project) at Coventry University and developed a study on Brazilian

Paralympic Results. He has volunteer experience at World Military, Olympic and Paralympic Games, as well as in Slalom Canoeing competitions. Member of Olympic Studies research group at Universidade do Estado do Rio de Janeiro and the Research Group on Olympic and Paralympic Studies (GPEOP).

Teresa Crew is Lecturer in Social Policy and a HEA Fellow. Her PhD, which was funded by the ESRC, focused on graduate inequalities in relation to class, gender, and place. Prior to this, she co-ordinated the North Wales Gypsy Traveller Accommodation Assessment. Her research interests centre around inequalities in the broad areas of gender, Gypsy Travellers, higher education, and diversity in academia.

Paula Danby is Lecturer in International Tourism Management at Queen Margaret University, Edinburgh. Her research focuses on human–animal relations and experiences within leisure and tourism environments, particularly equestrian tourism. Reflecting upon theoretical insights from human–animal interactional studies, her interests include animal tourism, ecotourism, human–animal relational leisure, and wellbeing. Paula's work explores human–animal interactions for mutual wellbeing.

Vinicius Denardin Cardoso is Professor at State University of Roraima (UERR). Holds a PhD in Human Movement Sciences from the School of Physical Education (UFRGS) and a Master's Degree in Physical Activity Adapted from the University of Porto, Portugal (FADEUP). Graduated in the Physical Education Course of the Federal University of Santa Maria (UFSM). He has experience in adapted physical activity with emphasis on adapted and Paralympic sports. Member of Projeto Esporte Brasil (PROESP-Br), Group of Studies and Research in Physical Education and Sports (GEPEFE/UERR) and of the Brazilian Paralympic Academy (APB).

Michelle Duffy is Associate Professor in Human Geography. Her research includes a critical examination of emotion and affect in creating notions of belonging; and the role of sound, performance, and the body as a means of embodied, emotional, and affective communication. She is joint Editor-in-Chief of *Tourist Studies*.

Asunción Fernández-Villarán Ara holds a BA in Economics and Business Administration and a PhD in Economics and Business Administration (Advanced Management) from the University of Deusto. She currently works as Lecturer at the University of Deusto, where she teaches at the Bilbao campus. She teaches BA courses in Tourism and MA courses in Leisure Project Management and Congress, Events, and Fairs Management. Specifically, she teaches the following subjects on BA courses: Basic Principles of Marketing, Accounting Analysis and Tourism Marketing Management; on MA courses, she teaches: Basic Business Principles of the Leisure Sector and Socio-economic Environmental Analysis. In recent years, she has been working on business management and organisation and tourist destinations, tourism for all, and on innovation in tourism, always pursuing improvement in management. She leads the research group Tourism at Deusto University.

Ailton Fernando Santana de Oliveira holds a PhD in Education from the Federal University of Bahia (2013) and a Master's Degree in Physical Education, Gama Filho University (2007). Adjunct Professor of the Federal University of Sergipe. Experience in physical education, sport, leisure, public policies, diagnosis for sports and leisure, and adapted sports and Olympism. Member of the Research Steering Committee of the Center for the Development of Research in Sports and Leisure Policies of the State of Sergipe. Leader of the research group SCENARIOS – Research Center on Public Policies for Physical Education, Sports, Leisure, and Sport.

Rebecca Finkel is an urban cultural geographer and Reader in Events Management at Queen Margaret University, Edinburgh, and a Senior Fellow of the Higher Education Academy. Main focus of research frames critical events studies within conceptualisations of social justice, equality and diversity, and identity. Main research interests include resistance to globalisation processes through cultural events, doing gender at festivals, and mapping human rights and international sporting events. New research explores the relational well-being dimensions of human–animal interactions in events, tourism, and leisure contexts.

Caroline Gausden is a writer, discursive curator, and visiting lecturer at Gray's School of Art in Aberdeen. She holds a practice-based PhD on Social Art Practice as a Feminist Manifesto. Research interests include the poetics of performative practices at the intersection between radical education and contemporary art. Recent curatorial interventions include a two-year series of events on hospitality for sca-net.org and the reading group, Support Structures, curated in collaboration with Aberdeen-based artist Kirsty Russell. Caroline previously worked as a researcher and manager at CCA, Glasgow, and has published articles for online blogs and journals, including writing on the politics of recorded voice for the *Journal of Archives and Records*.

Emily F. Henderson is an Assistant Professor in the Centre for Education Studies, University of Warwick. She is author of *Gender Pedagogy: Teaching, Learning and Tracing Gender in Higher Education* (Palgrave, 2015), and co-editor of *Starting with Gender in International Higher Education Research* (Routledge, forthcoming). Emily is co-editor of the academic blog 'Conference Inference: Blogging the World of Conferences'. Emily's research lies in the areas of gender and higher education, particularly the production of knowledge about gender; the academic profession, academic mobility and conferences; poststructuralist and feminist theory and research methodology.

Marco Hernández-Escampa is Professor at the Faculty of Architecture of the Autonomous University of Oaxaca, Mexico. He is delegate of ATLAS

(Association for Tourism and Leisure Education and Research) for Mexico, Central America, and the Caribbean. With a PhD in Anthropology and in Engineering, his research interests focus on urban anthropology and heritage conservation and tourism in historic cities. He has participated in several projects about heritage conservation as well as in archaeological research in Mexico and abroad.

Layla-Roxanne Hill is a writer, curator, and researcher. Her areas of interest are found in (de)construction of cultural production, marginality, and Black Scottish lives. Recent contributions and exhibitions include: *Digitalisation of Diasporas: Subverting Misrepresentations* at OSCE, Vienna, and *(Re)imagining Self and Raising Consciousness of Existence through Alternative Space and (Re)imagined Place* at Glasgow International 2018. She is Head of Engagement at investigative journalism platform, The Ferret. In addition, Layla-Roxanne sits on the National Union of Journalists (NUJ) National and Scottish Executive Council(s) and Scottish Trade Union Congress (STUC) Black Workers' Committee.

Ian R. Lamond is Senior Lecturer at Leeds Beckett University. As well as teaching on undergraduate and postgraduate programmes, he has been active in developing critical event studies as an innovative way of approaching the study of events. His research focuses on the theoretical foundations of critical event studies as an emerging sub-field of events studies and exploring its potential scope beyond the traditional frames of reference commonly associated with it, and the aligned field of events management research. He has a specific research interest in events of dissent and the mediation of eventful protest.

Judith Mair is an Associate Professor in the University of Queensland Business School, Australia. Her research interests include pro-environmental behaviour and resilience both in tourism and events, the impacts of events on community and society, consumer behaviour in events and tourism, the relationship between events and climate change, and business and major events. She is joint Editor-in-Chief of the *International Journal of Event and Festival Management*.

Naomi Alice Rodgers is a Berlin-based intersectional feminist activist. Her work is geared towards engaging with feminist movements both locally and internationally, with a focus on anti-pinkwashing activism. Having studied a Master's in Gender Studies at Linköping University, her academic work revolves around research into the occurrence of social segregation and discrimination in social spaces in Berlin.

Ainara Rodríguez-Zulaica has a Bachelor's Degree in Tourism Studies, European Master's in Conference, Event and Exhibition Management, a Master's in International Tourism Management, and a PhD in International and European Studies by the University of Deusto (Bilbao, Spain). Presently, lecturer and researcher at the Tourism Department of the University of Deusto in

Bilbao, Spain. Expert in the following areas: travel agencies, tourism inter-mediation, event management, and industrial tourism. Teaching both on graduate and postgraduate programmes in Tourism and Leisure Studies. Guest lecturer at Haaga University (Helsinki, Finland) in 2002 and 2012, at University of Zealand (Denmark) in 2017, and Queen Margaret University (Scotland) in 2017 and 2018.

Briony Sharp was awarded her PhD in Events Management from Queen Margaret University, Edinburgh, and is currently a Lecturer in Events Manage-ment at the University of Huddersfield. Her research examines social impacts from an individual, community, and organisational perspective, and possible social legacy routes from these impacts. Specifically, this includes social engagement initiatives pursued in conjunction with the Glasgow 2014 Com-monwealth Games, and the relationship between social capital, community engagement, and potential social legacies. New research investigates innova-tive methodologies in events with a focus on event volunteering and tourism motivations.

Zorica Siročić is a doctoral candidate and an external Lecturer in the Depart-ment of Sociology at the University of Graz. She earned a MA degree in political science (Central European University, 2010) and a diploma in political science (University of Zagreb, 2009). Her dissertation project is a study of contemporary feminist mobilisations in Southeastern Europe from a perspective of political sociology.

Francesca Sobande is a Lecturer in Marketing and Advertising at Edge Hill University, Lancashire. Her research addresses issues regarding identity, ideol-ogy, and intersecting inequalities in relation to media and marketplace activity. Francesca's doctoral thesis focuses on the media and online experiences of Black women in Britain, *Digital Diaspora and (Re)Mediating Black Women in Britain*. She is currently co-editing, *To Exist is to Resist: Black Feminism in Europe* (Pluto Press). Francesca has published work in the *European Journal of Cultural Studies* as well as edited collections, including HBO's *Original Voices: Race, Gender, Sexuality and Power* (Routledge).

Gordon Waitt is Professor in Geography at the University of Wollongong, Australia, and Head of the School of Geography and Sustainable Commu-nities. He is an editor of *Annals of Tourism Research*, and former editor of *Tourist Studies*. His work explores the spatial, embodied, emotional, and affective dimensions of tourism.

Trudie Walters is Lecturer in the Department of Tourism at the University of Otago, Dunedin, New Zealand. Her research interests include media represen-tations and individuals' experiences of leisure phenomena, with a particular focus on events and second homes. Trudie is on the World Leisure Organisa-tion Board of Directors, and serves as the Member Engagement Officer on the Board of the Australia and New Zealand Association for Leisure Studies. She is also Associate Editor and Reviews Editor of the journal, *Annals of Leisure Research*.

Keisha Williams studies diversity and inclusion strategies in museums. She has Master Degrees in Art Gallery and Museum Studies from the University of Leeds (2015) and in Visual Arts Management and Curating from Richmond, International American University in London (2017). She has worked with the National Maritime Museum in Greenwich to produce *International Slavery Remembrance Day* and with Battersea Arts Centre as a Young Producer, examining the ways collaborative and co-produced projects can increase diversity, inclusion, and representation in the arts and cultural sector.

Caroline A. Wiscombe has worked in education for 20 years; first in further education, then in higher education, and now back in further education at Exeter College, where she teaches leadership, management, and finance on professional and vocational business programmes. She has embedded events management into the curriculum of the Business and IT Faculty, drawing on previous research, publications, and teaching undertaken at the University of Wolverhampton University, Leeds Beckett University, and the University of Cumbria. Caroline has previously published research about the economic impact as well as the funding, sponsorship, and financial management of events.

Acknowledgements

This book would not have been possible without the contributions from the chapter authors, who so generously took the time and made considerable efforts to report on their research in this emerging area of post-disciplinary study. We would like to thank them for their hard work and look forward to future collaborations that champion positive social change in the critical events field.

Many thanks to the team at Routledge, Emma Travis and Carlotta Fanton, for their continuous support and encouragement.

We consider ourselves fortunate to have a community of strong women to rely on for empowerment and enrichment. Without you, our professional lives would be less rewarding, and our personal lives would be less fun.

Introduction

Rebecca Finkel, Briony Sharp, and Majella Sweeney

Special events are microcosms of society. Because they are temporary and usually bounded by geographic space, they can be considered reflections of or responses to societal norms at the time they take place. As critical events scholars, we can learn a lot about a society by the way people gather and celebrate. By investigating special events, we can learn who and what is important – and unimportant – and how this may manifest itself in everyday life. We can see values and beliefs on display and discern from them the social architecture of the community. Yet, we must also try to understand whose voices are not being heard, whose needs are not being catered for, whose stories are not being told. However, it is only recently that issues of under-representation, marginalisation, and intolerance have begun to emerge in the critical events discourse. Although there has been a recent swell of media attention and public interest in this area, research focusing on non-hegemonic populations as they relate to events environments is still in need of further exploration.

One of the reasons for the paucity of academic literature on these topics is critical events research has only been developing as a scholarly field for just over two decades. In that time, many scholars have analysed broader economic, social, and political issues by situating them in specific event landscapes and evaluating impacts on communities and places. Initially, these impact evaluation studies were mainly focused on the economics of events. Providing 'proof' of return on investment and justification of costs were the *raison d'être* for event researchers until there was a critical 'turn' drawing on geography, sociology and anthropology canons. With the general acceptance of more qualitative approaches, social impacts of planned events on culture, communities, and cities began to gain traction. Most early social research into planned events often had the effect of broadcasting narratives of dominant cultures and privileged groups. However, recent convergences of gender, sexualities, ethnicities, age, class, religion, and intersectional analyses and events, sport, leisure, and tourism studies have started to drive new critical understanding of the impacts of events on non-mainstream, non-majority communities around the globe. This book seeks to contribute to knowledge by addressing current gaps in the literature surrounding issues of accessibility, inclusion, and diversity in various event landscapes.

In developing this book, we took considerable time to contemplate what would be the 'right' themes on which to focus. Was social change too ambiguous? Was equality too abstract? Was including only women's perspectives too specialised? Was disability too limiting (on multiple levels)? We arrived at accessibility, inclusion, and diversity because these terms were deemed broad enough to encompass many of our initial interests as well as provide authors leeway to interpret how their research related to current issues, current events, and current power relationships. Accessibility can be understood in terms of the measures put in place to address participation by those with impairments, both permanent and temporary, as well as both physical and mental, including perceived class and cultural barriers. Inclusion is a ubiquitous term that, we argue, should be more contentious than it is currently considered. Inclusion differs from justice in that the former requires people to participate in society as it is constructed, and the latter requires intervention with a redistributive agenda to achieve equality. Given these nuances, both conceptualisations and applications of social inclusion and social justice can be found woven throughout the chapters of this book. Diversity can be taken to mean individual and community diversity, such as those relating to gender, sexualities, ethnicity, age, religion, and so forth. It also refers to the range of different events being studied. Distinctive events present distinctive issues to explore, and, although this book is by no means exhaustive, it attempts to provide a great deal of variety in order to highlight a myriad of approaches, lessons learned, and possible best-practice solutions.

Although there are some intersections with sport and tourism, critical event studies has been recognised as a subject with its own literatures and approaches, and it is, therefore, unique in its storytelling and experiential narratives. The demand for academic publications focusing on these topics became apparent when the call for chapter abstracts for this book yielded over 30 submissions. This illustrates three key points: 1) many scholars in multiple social science and humanities fields are engaging with critical event studies, not only those in specific 'events' disciplines; 2) there is international research being conducted in this area; and, 3) there are classes being taught in higher education institutions on almost every continent about issues related to accessibility, inclusion, and diversity in planned events contexts. This is very encouraging indeed. Therefore, this book seeks to advance the dialogue and illustrate the importance of evidence-based research for improving scholarship and practice in the events sectors.

As an under-researched area, the chapters not only present original work in terms of topics, but also in theoretical and methodological approaches. All of the chapters can be considered to be cross- or inter-disciplinary, drawing on gender, sexualities, cultural, race/ethnicity studies as well as multiple literatures feeding into critical event studies. Research informing the chapters has been undertaken in different places around the world, so the book is not geographically grounded in one particular country; thus, it explores a myriad of interesting global examples. Intersectional approaches feature in many of the chapters, which is important to improve understanding from multiple perspectives and with multiple voices. Also, auto-ethnography is a technique used in a range of chapters, providing reflective accounts and personal impressions of case study events. As events are temporary, these authors are using scholarly avenues, such as this book, to document and record their experiences in an attempt to give the messages and memories of the events a longer and more impactful existence. In this way, such accounts can help to guide future practice and provide lessons learned for reaching broader audiences and opening up dialogues to obtain greater accessibility, inclusion, and diversity. This also helps to keep the momentum from their events with the goal of driving positive social change.

The sections are structured by the main types of events, such as festivals and fairs, cultural and political events, sporting events, and conferences, which allows for an exploration of a breadth of differing sizes, scopes, locations, and stakeholders. Each chapter employs a case study to illustrate the key intertwining issues in these various experiential realms. Main themes of access, inclusion (keeping in mind its opposite, exclusion), and diversity flow throughout the text, which provides an overall coherence and allows for stronger narratives to be present as well.

Multiculturalism is a key theme of Part I about festivals and fairs. The first chapter by Duffy, Mair, and Waitt examine how the notion of 'encounter' helps to engage with the complex and dynamic processes of community-making at Australian cultural festivals. And although festivals are often supported by authorities to increase tolerance of ethnic diversity, the authors argue that it depends on whose culture is on display, as such festivals may actually be contributing to disharmony and 'othering'. Moving to Mexico in Chapter 2, Barrera-Fernández and Hernández-Escampa analyse the existing accessibility measures at the Guelaguetza Festival in culturally diverse Oaxaca and the perceptions of inclusion of people with reduced mobility. Chapter 3 by Siročić focuses on feminist activist festivals in post-Yugoslav territories in order to contextualise festivals as political tools for women's movements across generations. Turning attention to fairs in Chapter 4, Crew questions whether media accounts of the Appleby Horse Fair in the UK are marginalising for Travellers, who celebrate their traditions at this historic event. The final chapter in this section by Wiscombe discusses the challenges of accessibility at UK agricultural shows in terms of location, logistics, and societal considerations. She found that event organisers prioritise accessibility for human and non-human participation whilst evolving, adapting, and changing to capture the diversity and range of contemporary rural enterprises.

Part II of this book delves into the intertwined cultural and political spheres. Although we originally envisioned this section as addressing solely cultural issues in critical event studies, the authors have used cultural events as a backdrop in order to draw out deeper meanings related to current political issues, including power structures. Chapter 6 by Rodgers explores how electronic dance music (EDM) in Berlin, Germany, became more than just nightclub party events and turned into a political 'movement'. Through an intersectional lens, she deconstructs, and situates within a wider political context, how Berlin's EDM nightclubs promote themselves as safe spaces for people of diverse sexual identities, temporarily suspending social hierarchies and uniting people under one roof; however, the reality often results in segregated ethnic stereotypes informing diversity discourses. From nightclubs to museums in Chapter 7, Williams critically examines current museum events in London, UK, to highlight the presence and experiences of BAME audiences and their dialogues with the arts and cultural sector through co-production and radical trust in order to co-create a more ethnically diverse museum by occupying space and engaging in social activism. Along similar lines, Hill and Sobande showcase in Chapter 8 how people of colour in Scotland remain frequently excluded from institutional creative contexts. This chapter is based on the authors' experiences co-ordinating and participating in an arts and cultural exhibition in Glasgow, Scotland, which highlights the power of words in starting conversations about issues regarding inclusion, exclusion, and resisting marginalisation. Chapter 9 by Ali explores the reticence or receptiveness that both presenter and audience experience in events incorporating the subject of Muslim identity in the UK at three British cultural events. Issues surrounding intercultural exchange, representation, performance, cultural sensitivity, and tolerance are documented in order to define a model of best practice for the delivery of often challenging culturally diverse events. Gausden, in Chapter 10, considers advocacy as performance through an event highlighting the treatment of marginalised Roma communities and the discriminatory practices faced as a result of globalisation processes. Lamond conceptualises events of dissent in Chapter 11 with research on an anti-corruption rally in São Paulo, Brazil. By shedding light on populist movements and protest as event and activism as leisure, the author seeks to provide greater insight into such events of dissent and the political and cultural complexity of participation in such events.

Part III provides a snapshot of sporting events and some accessibility, inclusion, and diversity issues at mega, major, and regional levels. We decided from the outset of this book that sporting events would not be a priority, as there is an already robust body of literature on sport and these topics. Therefore, we aim to emphasise the relevant issues as they relate to events that happen to include sporting aspects. For example, urban mobility issues take centre stage in Chapter 12 by Cirilo dos Santos Neto, Fernando Santana de Oliveira, Denardin Cardoso, and de Castro Haiachi. Their investigation uses the Paralympic Games in Rio de Janeiro, Brazil, as a backdrop. They explain the impacts mega event-led urban regeneration has had on mobility-diverse communities. In Chapter 13, Sharp explores whether engaging in major event volunteering leads to increased wellbeing in a case study of the Glasgow Commonwealth Games in Scotland. The research evaluates the potential for social legacies through volunteer programmes and to what extent this influences wellbeing. On a smaller scale, the next chapter presents research undertaken by Danby and Finkel at the Austin Rodeo in Texas, USA. Framed in post-humanist theory, this chapter seeks to challenge the singular focus around human subjects and prioritises the inclusion of non-humans in co-creating the event landscape, looking beyond human agency and exploring the 'more-than-human' within the human–equine sporting relationship.

Finally, Part IV is framed around research relating to conferences, which is an important but often overlooked research subject. In Chapter 15, Rodríguez-Zulaica and Fernández-Villarán Ara analyse the accessibility of conference centres, in particular the case of the Euskalduna Palace in Bilbao, Spain. They also provide advice in order to adapt conference venues to improve inclusion mechanisms. Chapter 16 features Henderson interrogating the impacts of caring responsibilities on academics' access to and participation at international conferences. Importantly, access in this chapter is conceived of as both the ability to attend conferences and the ability to participate in conferences once there. In keeping with this topic of academic conferences, Walters adopts a case study approach in Chapter 17 based upon personal experiences as co-convenor of an academic association conference in New Zealand. She found that adopting tripartite approaches with regard to physical accessibility, financial accessibility, and cognitive accessibility can facilitate an environment which embraces diversity and fosters inclusion, which has flow-on benefits for all conference delegates. Overall, there is a call for more inclusive interpretations for participation in international conferences, which sit more comfortably at the intersection of accessibility and diversity.

Although there are now more conversations about these topics happening on a multitude of platforms, there is still a need to develop conceptual and empirical research to establish reliable information and capture multifarious accounts about accessibility, inclusion, and diversity in numerous events environments worldwide. This book goes some way to inform these discussions in an effort to improve future scholarship and practice in this exciting, emerging field.

Part I
Festivals and fairs

1 Addressing community diversity

The role of the festival encounter

Michelle Duffy, Judith Mair, and Gordon Waitt

Introduction

We live in a world in which the movement of people is unprecedented; yet, there are significant discrepancies in this mobility. Majority world individuals and communities often need to move in response to local and global challenges, such as political upheaval, human rights abuses, concerns around water and food security, the impacts of climate change, and the desire to seek better outcomes for themselves and their families. In contrast, the mobility of members of the minority world – with the increased wealth, health and life expectancies of its members – is most often tied to lifestyle choices. And while technology has enabled greater connectivity across the globe, this is not without concern. As Fincher, et al. (2014: 3) remind us, in the 'age of migration' (Castles and Miller 2009), the question of whether some urban inhabitants' ethnic and racialised identities are stigmatised, trivialised, valued, or recognised in relation to others, is a crucial element of social justice in the city.

Questions are again being raised about the strength of social cohesion in western nations, such as contemporary Australia (e.g. Forrest and Dunn 2010), particularly with regard to so-called radicalisation of disaffected youth (Grossman and Tahiri 2015). However, diversity has broader meaning than simply that of ethnic, cultural, or national identity. Identity and notions of belonging are also constituted through particular ideas within a society about gender, class, sexuality, age, and able-bodiedness, which in turn construct an individual's and community's feelings of inclusion and connectedness or exclusion and alienation. In terms of social justice, 'managing' diversity raises issues about social cohesion and belonging because we need to consider group and community rights and how these relate to individual rights and freedoms. This can be problematic in liberal democratic societies because of an emphasis on individual rights rather than community rights (Capeheart and Milovanovic 2007). Thus, when considering belonging, we are also concerned with the ways in which power is embedded within the relations between people as well as with place.

One popular strategy for creating and/or re-affirming a sense of community has been to generate festival events that serve to create a sense of shared identity and belonging in ways that can encompass difference. What underpins such festivals is the desire to promote social cohesion through discourses of an official 'imagined' community; yet, some scholars argue that tension and debate – perhaps better conceptualised as agonism (Mouffe 1994) – play an important role in acknowledging the heterogeneity of contemporary life and thus retain the potential to transform democratic politics. Nonetheless, questions as to who has a right to be a part of 'the community' continue.

The starting point for the ideas presented in this chapter is the work of Fincher and Iveson (2008: 146, 175), who argue that the encounter facilitates a "social differentiation without exclusion" where "unscripted encounters" offer opportunities to experience the diversity of communities. Many local governments seek to lessen potentially divisive responses to difference and demonstrate a commitment to creating a welcoming, inclusive and accessible community, often through the creation and staging of community festivals. However, Fincher and Iveson (2008: 146) suggest that the festival offers a means to facilitate exploration and experimentation in the design of our communities, which requires "planning for disorder". They argue we need to pay attention to the "importance of small-scale, casual and unpredictable encounters" (Fincher and Iveson 2008: 146) because it is through fostering encounters with difference and diversity that we can start to address injustice and inequality.

This chapter draws on data from a range of case study communities and festivals. Each case study employed mixed-qualitative research methods that help uncover how the festival may provide opportunities for such unpredictable encounters. The key methods included semi-structured interviews with key organisers and event participants alongside participant observation. Semi-structured interviews offered possibilities to access the sets of ideas that informed the events through the sharing of stories; whereas, participant observation allowed the researchers to access the experiential dimensions of events that are often beyond words. A combination of discourse, narrative, and affective analysis was employed to interpret what these may mean for thinking about ways to enhance social connectedness and inclusion.

'Managing' diversity

Inherent in the development of policy discourse around diversity are questions as to who has the right to the place of the city (Lefebvre 1991; Purcell 2002). Lefebvre (1991) argues that social justice requires a radical rethinking of the city: that the right to the city is embedded within occupying and participating in the life of the city, and is not an intrinsic right associated only with the ownership of property and capital. As Purcell (2002: 102) points out,

> under the right to the city, membership in the community of enfranchised people is not an accident of nationality or ethnicity or birth; rather it is earned by living out the routines of everyday life in the space of the city.

Therefore, the city is not simply a passive stage on which social life unfolds; rather, the city is constituted through civic, material, cultural, and social processes. Underpinning much of the literature examining social relations in public space is a focus on how a proximity to strangers in this shared space may facilitate some understanding and acceptance of otherness (as observed in work on cosmopolitanism, hospitality, new urban citizenship, and urban planning; see for example, Amin 2002; Bell 2007; Iveson 2007; Laurier and Philo 2006; Wilson 2011). Policies that seek to manage diversity have approached this by attempting to "manage public space in ways that build sociality and civic engagement out of the encounter between strangers" (Amin 2008: 6). Managing difference through processes that seek to construct a sense of community has in some instances reframed social cohesion and connectedness as "as a logical 'solution' to a growing number of social ills and/or the 'target' of urban policy interventions" (MacLeavy 2008: 541). However, critiques of such a formulation of policy argue that this approach pathologises difference, and, rather than enabling or encouraging diversity, this framework actually reproduces and disguises relationships of power.

A "geographies of encounter" has focused on documenting how individuals negotiate social diversity, urban difference, and prejudice in everyday life (Wilson 2016). However, as Wilson (2016) points out, there has been little critical examination as to how the concept of *encounter* is mobilised in policy and practice, apart from the notion that "low-level sociality and banal everyday civilities have enduring effects" (Valentine and Sadgrove 2012: 2050; see also Laurier and Philo 2006). In this framework,

> [t]he freedom to associate and mingle in cafés, parks, streets, shopping malls, and squares is linked to the development of an urban civic culture based on the freedom and pleasure to linger, the serendipity of casual encounter and mixture, the public awareness that these are shared spaces.
>
> (Amin 2002: 967)

Yet, as Amin goes on to discuss, this framing of chance encounters in the public sphere is problematic. Visibility and proximity may encourage interaction because of a pragmatic need to accommodate difference, but this does not then translate into respect for others (Valentine 2008). While unscripted encounters may encourage certain forms of civil behaviour (Buonfino and Mulgan 2007), this is not the same as generating respect for difference or for greater openness to diversity (Gawlewicz 2015). Hence, simply being co-present in public space fails to lead on to challenging individual and community assumptions about certain individuals and groups, and thus enable communities to reconcile various notions of difference (Amin 2002; Duffy and Mair 2018).

Nevertheless, a common approach to addressing such ideas about diversity in public space has been through the hosting of community festivals, where it is hoped that opportunities to engage with difference within the relatively 'safe' framework of a festive event may lessen potentially divisive responses to difference and demonstrate a commitment to creating a welcoming, inclusive, and accessible community. Thus, festivals are significant to a politics of

belonging because of the ways in which they are utilised as a common framework for community celebration and for reinvigorating notions of a shared
community (Duffy and Mair 2018; Jepson and Clarke 2015). Part of the challenges
of incorporating festivals into policy is that within this framework, the term
'community' is popularly understood as being those people, usually of a specific
locale, who share a set of values and social relations characterised by personal
connections. The community festival is a common framework for reinvigorating
notions of a shared community, wherein difference may be celebrated but the focus
is on commonality (Jepson and Clarke 2015). The official discourse of those
groups controlling the festival operate to produce an 'imagined' community, which
the festival is then planned to encapsulate and promote. In this framework, the
imperative of community-oriented festival is localism – that is, a celebration of the
unique qualities of people and place forged by histories and geographies (del
Barrio, et al. 2012; Duffy and Mair 2018; Jaeger and Mykletun 2013; van Winkle,
et al. 2014) or in generating new place-based forms of identification (Lewis and
Dowsey-Magog 1993; Picard 2015).

Yet, while the concept of community is central to policy and planning
approaches, such frameworks in practice need to contend with often markedly
high social difference that produce sites of "throwntogetherness" (Massey 2005:
11). What is meant by *belonging* or *social connectedness*, therefore, raises
important questions about how we understand community. As Massey (1994:
121) explains, the identity of a community or a place is about "the specificity of
interaction with other places." However, feelings of attachment to a community
is not simply about being and remaining in place. Rather, belonging creates a
sense of connection in particular ways or to particular collective identities, and
these attachments and identities are embedded within the narratives that people
tell about themselves as a community (Yuval-Davis 2006). That said, such
notions of belonging can also be problematic because of the sorts of identities
or social relations invoked by a festival theme (Cornish 2015; Jodie 2015).
Festivals are, therefore, complex sites of community building. In considering
the role festivals may play in the process of individual and collective belonging, we need to acknowledge that communities are not homogenous. Possibilities for conflict arise from competing narratives that inform who (and what)
constitutes a place or a community. In addition, as Young (2008: 4–5) argues,
we need to critically explore the relationships between planning practice and
the dimensions of culture that inhere in communities and their ways of life, in
history and intangible heritage, and in environments. In the absence of this,
planning may continue to languish in political, ethical, and strategic terms,
while culture continues to exhibit heightened diversity and dynamism and a
rising potential tapped by the cultural economy and exploited in the processes
of cultural commodification.

Young (2008) cautions us as to the increasing commodification of culture and
its incorporation into planning practice, particularly as this often fails to capture
the complex, dynamic, and subtle nature of what culture is. He also points to
disparities in terms of whose culture is valued, noting a "global pattern" that

generally favours white, middle-class, male, heterosexual, urban, and settler culture over that of less powerful groups including women, sexual minorities, Indigenous groups, non-urban communities, and those cultures arising out of diverse and intercultural groups (Young 2008: 7). In the ways these patterns of cultural hegemony shape the distribution of power, these unequal relations are most often re-inscribed in social and material relations that serve to reinforce social injustice (Young 2008).

A potential means for planning and policy to critically engage more with encounter is to consider social, cultural, and material relations in terms of experience so as to reconfigure engagement and participation. Research in this area suggests that rather than framing the festival in terms of spectatorship, wherein a detached audience observes the performance of difference (Hage 1998), organisers would be better to explore the role of sociability, conviviality, excitement, and encounter within festival (O'Grady and Kill 2013). Drawing on Bourriaud's *Relational Aesthetics* (1998), O'Grady and Kill (2013: 278) suggest conceptualising the encounters that occur at festival events as examples of a "relational performance", which, they argue, "requires dialogue, interaction, or audience intervention to make it work... its emergence within the festival space gives it a particular contextual dimension which is related intimately to how festival-goers experience the festival space both physically and psychically."

In this framing, the festival performance is no longer the focus; rather, its purpose is to catalyse encounters (O'Grady and Kill 2013). This then means that those who attend a festival "become co-authors of their own festival experience rather than merely consumers of a pre-packaged product" (O'Grady and Kill 2013: 279). Such a framing of festival participation is important in policy and planning given that, increasingly, the focus in some fields of festival research is for a better understanding of the influences and effects of the festival event as it spills out beyond its temporal and spatial boundaries, a process called *festivalisation* (Cremorna 2007; Roche 2011; Yardimci 2007).

Festivalisation processes draw on collective understandings and practices of space, time, and agency that are then deployed so as to shape communal notions of identity and belonging (Roche 2011). This, in turn, means that festivals, rather than transcending the everyday, are now examined for the ways they are intimately embedded within the public sphere as normative, and, at times, transformative processes (Giorgi and Sassatelli 2011). As such, festivals are recognised as political mechanisms that help constitute individual feelings of acceptance and belonging within an imagined, collective sense of community (Duffy and Mair 2018). Festivals are often planned as a way to represent a community; however, the festival space is never fixed, but rather comprised of informal and formal unfolding relations. Consequently, the festival space may be simultaneously a site of social inclusion and exclusion. As demonstrated by the body of festival literature discussed, it is not enough simply to bring people together for any positive outcomes to ensue. Instead, festivals must be planned and managed in ways which provide those attending opportunities to actively share in generating the festival atmosphere through both the formal and informal interaction which takes place.

Discussion

Our research on community festivals over recent years has identified a number of findings that bear out the difficulties associated with using festivals instrumentally to achieve local government policy aims. Each of the following examples highlights specific challenges. First, communities are not homogenous. Therefore, it is important not to expect festivals to be able to bring disparate elements of a community together without explicit efforts to make this happen. For example, Pakenham, now a satellite suburb of Melbourne, Victoria, hosts the Yakkerboo Festival, which was created in the 1970s. The format is relatively similar to many small community festivals and has not changed substantially since it was first established. It includes a street parade, street market, funfair, fireworks, art show, and twilight carnival. Our research (Duffy and Mair 2018) shows that while Pakenham and its surrounds have changed substantially in recent years, mostly through peri-urban housing developments on the outskirts of Melbourne, the festival remains broadly representative of a particular set of ideals, traditions, and values associated with the farming community for whom Pakenham remains a country town. We found divergent views between "official" takes on how a local community is represented through cultural performance, and the "on the ground community" view of participants (Duffy and Mair 2018). By maintaining the festival and its traditions exactly as they are, despite the changing demographics and cultural economies of Pakenham, there is a danger that organisers are unintentionally excluding or marginalising new residents. Of course, for new residents, it may be the case that becoming involved in community traditions is a low priority. And it may be for some new residents that they do not wish to forge a connection with this existing display of community, given that it reflects another time and place. The format of the Yakkerboo Festival, rather than providing an opportunity for dialogue and debate between members of the old and new communities in Pakenham, appears to reproduce an imagined or ideal community. Our conclusions to this research suggested that in towns undergoing rapid social transformation, festivals offer a time and place where ideas of community may be negotiated and actively questioned, rather than a celebration of ideal notions of the past (Duffy and Mair 2018). We suggest that such interaction allows community members to move beyond simple encounter to a form of exchange, not necessarily commercial in nature, but a process whereby those involved can acknowledge the encounter (Duffy and Mair 2018).

Second is the paradox of difference. Multicultural festivals are one common tool used by local authorities to attempt to promote social harmony and celebrate ethnic diversity. The aim is often to encourage new migrants to maintain their culture of origin and, indeed, to showcase their heritage and cultural traditions to those in majority group(s). It is hoped that by doing so, negative attitudes and prejudices displayed by majority group(s) towards those in the minority can be reduced, if not eliminated altogether. However, whilst such aims are laudable, nonetheless multicultural festivals, by staging and portraying new cultures as 'the other', may work towards social divergence rather than cohesion. Take for example our research on Experience! The Casey Multicultural Festival hosted annually in Berwick, a small town in the City of Casey, located in the outer south-east of Melbourne, Victoria. Census detail in 2016 reports that Berwick residents have a diverse cultural ancestry, with over a quarter of residents born in non-English speaking countries. The City of Casey chose to stage a multicultural festival to encourage residents to build community capacity and build confidence in community associations to display their cultural identity and to celebrate difference. The festival has free entry to underscore the aim of inclusion. The festival is generally well received and well attended by residents, thus suggesting that the Council has been relatively successful in achieving its aim of allowing attendees to experience diversity (Duffy and Mair 2018).

However, it is important to recognise that social cohesion is much more than just being present. The ever-present danger of the multicultural festival is how cultures become represented by drawing on selective elements of the past, including clothes, food, songs, or dance. Jupp (2002) reminds us in his critique of the portrayal of cultural diversity festivals as "spaghetti and polkas". How particular ethnic groups are portrayed may result in the festival space becoming a site of exclusion where one or more segments of the community feel that they are not welcome. Additionally, the choice of cultures included in the festival, and the way these cultures are portrayed, can lead to questions such as 'whose traditions are we keeping alive?', and 'whose interpretation of history and tradition are we privileging?'. Our conclusions from Experience! The Casey Multicultural Festival suggest that multicultural festivals are conceived as a way to manage difference; yet, by their very nature, they emphasise such differences. Simply staging a festival with diverse cultural elements seems to rely on a very simplistic interpretation of the power of the encounter with difference. Despite facilitating encounters between diverse peoples and between majority and minority groups, without express efforts to build harmony and acknowledgement of difference, multicultural festivals alone are unlikely to achieve a more socially inclusive society (Duffy and Mair 2018).

The paradox of difference is central to our research on music festivals. An example of this is our conclusions from the Four Winds Festival, a classical music festival held biannually in Bermagui, New South Wales (Waitt and Duffy 2010). We argued for the importance of examining the role of sound at music festivals in creating individual and collective identities. While recognising the importance of the representational qualities of music in celebrating identities (for example, national anthems), in this project, we sought to engage with the embodied and pre-cognitive dimensions of sounds and their role in generating a sense of belonging. This project was underpinned by the notion that sounds possess certain powers and qualities that enable personal and social things to 'happen'. Equipped with audio and video recorders, our aim was to map the power of sounds at the Four Winds Festival in helping constitute place-based social relationships. Enveloped by sound worlds, our participants revealed how the affective and emotional agency of festival sounds dissolved personal boundaries that then contributed to a sense of belonging and heightened their sensitivity towards a responsibility for Indigenous notions of country. That said, our Four Winds Festival research also pointed towards how the organisation and attendance at festivals brought an increased awareness of classed, educational, and financial divides in a coastal community, embedded within inward amenity-led migration predominantly from Melbourne since the 1980s. These issues are given further consideration in the next section.

Festival attendees are differentiated along social lines of difference including age, class, education, gender, and sexuality. How festival spaces bring to the fore class and differences in educational opportunities is often illustrated through those festivals aligned to the arts, particularly book and classical music festivals. Another example of such a case relates to the Clunes Book Festival, held annually in Clunes, Victoria, around one hour's drive north of Melbourne. Gold was discovered there in the late 19th century; however, once gold mining ceased, the town gradually succumbed to rural decline, high unemployment, and an ageing population, similar to other small rural towns in Victoria and elsewhere (Duffy and Mair 2018). Inward migration to rural areas, known in Australia as 'tree changing', is a relatively common phenomenon used to characterise the movement of financially secure and tertiary-educated middle classes from urban into rural areas, who are often referred to, derogatorily, as the 'latté set' (Duffy and Mair 2018). In Clunes, an association of 'tree changers' was formed, Creative Clunes, which proposed a rural renewal programme that would be based on cultural development in general and books in particular. The focus on cultural activities has become a popular strategy to attract the so-called 'creative classes' into economically depressed areas, who then help initiate regeneration through a cultural economy. The Clunes Book Festival has proved successful in its community renewal program, as it has enhanced artistic and culture life in the region, stimulated tourism, and contributed to building community capacity (Duffy and Mair 2018).

When considering questions of the role of festivals and inclusivity, Clunes provides an interesting case study. Instead of empty shops and a dwindling population, Clunes now has cafes, bars, bookshops, and a reinvigorated sense of community (Duffy and Mair 2018). Yet, whose place is this? Does this newly regenerated outpost of the city, with its bookshops and wine bars, continue to be the place that the original members of this former agricultural community hold dear? Echoing the findings of Overvåg and Berg (2011), there are certainly long-term residents who feel unhappy with the crowds attracted by the book festival, and even some who may not be entirely comfortable with the new direction that the town is taking (Duffy and Mair 2018). The tension is conceptualised by Overvåg and Berg (2011: 419) as relating to people "sharing the same spaces, but using them for different purposes". Furthermore, as Driscoll (2016: 11) notes, book-related events "carry a sense of social distinction", and perhaps even overtones of snobbery. The creation of a book festival, and the ensuing designation of Clunes as an International Book Town, certainly has the potential to interrupt the "settledness" (Milbourne 2007) of rural places. Lavenda (1992: 76) notes that festivals are recognised as inherently about "people celebrating themselves and their community in an 'authentic' and traditional way, or at least emerging spontaneously from their homes for a community-wide expression of fellowship". The introduction of a festival by a group of new residents may be seen as counter to this definition of festivals. Nevertheless, our conclusions show that rural festivals such as the Clunes Book Festival contribute significantly to maintaining rural livelihoods and allowing different ideas of community and belonging to co-exist, albeit uneasily (Duffy and Mair 2018). Nonetheless, the encounter here, between classes and between long-term rural residents and tree changers, goes far beyond a simple meeting during a one-off festival and has developed into a relatively inclusive social and economic exchange that has benefited the town and all its residents.

Conclusion

In this chapter, we have paid critical attention to the predominant goals of social cohesion and community building that are ascribed to a range of festivals. Importantly for local councils and other stakeholder groups, festival events are one of a small range of community development tools available to local authorities working on limited budgets (Getz 2013), and many have invested substantial resources with the expectation that positive outcomes for local communities will be delivered. As our work to date demonstrates, festivals offer a way to increase meaningful social interactions (Argent and Smailes 2007). If generated and shared successfully, these social interactions can contribute to the social, civic, or economic wellbeing of individuals and communities (Duffy and Mair 2018; Halpern 2005). As Fincher and Iveson (2008) argue, we can start to address injustice and inequality through fostering encounters with difference and diversity. Festivals are fundamentally about encounter in its broadest sense; these are events and periods of time in which people meet and interact. Yet, as Hage (1998) has pointed out, the festival structure and intent can be critiqued because of the ways in which the festival is embedded within policy that is interpreted as 'managing' diversity. In terms of social justice, 'managing' diversity raises issues about group and community rights and how these relate to individual rights and freedoms. Our research demonstrates how the festival may provide opportunities for those unpredictable or "unscripted" (Fincher and Iveson 2008) encounters that may enhance social connectedness and inclusion. What we have found is that, while difference and diversity can prove challenging, these festival encounters are nevertheless significant to the vibrancy of life in communities.

Questions for discussion

1. How does the notion of encounter help to engage with the complex and dynamic processes of community-making at events?

2. Why does the spatiality of events matter if organisers seek to better understand events as a mechanism that may work towards building a shared sense of community?
3. If the goal of such events is to create a sense of community, how might the differing and often contested narratives of a community's past be addressed?
4. What role can festivals play in the establishment of greenfield communities?

References

Amin, A. (2002). Ethnicity and the multicultural city: living with diversity. *Environment and Planning A*, 34(6), 959–980.

Amin, A. (2008). Collective culture and urban public space. *City*, 12(1), 5–24.

Argent, N. and Smailes, G. (2007). The amenity complex: towards a framework for analysing and predicting the emergence of a multifunctional countryside in Australia. *Geographical Research*, 45(3), 217–232.

Bell, D. (2007). The hospitable city: social relations in commercial spaces. *Progress in Human Geography*, 31, 7–22.

Buonfino, A. and Mulgan, G. (2007). *Civility Lost and Found*. London: Young Foundation.

Capeheart, L. and Milovanovic, D. (2007). *Social Justice: Theories, Issues and Movements*. London: Rutgers University Press, 77–92.

Castles, S. and Miller, M. J. (2009). *The Age of Migration*. 4th ed. New York: Guilford Press.

Cornish, H. (2015). Not all singing and dancing: padstow, folk festivals and belonging. *Ethnos*, 81(4), 1–17.

Cremorna, V. A. (2007). Introduction: the festivalising process. In T. Hauptfleisch, S. Lev-Aladgem, J. Martin, W. Sauter, H. Schoenmakers (eds.) *Festivalising! Theatrical Events, Politics and Culture*. Amsterdam: Rodopi, 5–13.

Del Barrio, M. J., Devesa, M., and Herrero, L. C. (2012). Evaluating intangible cultural heritage: the case of cultural festivals. *City, Culture and Society*, 3(4), 235–244.

Driscoll, B. (2016). Local places and cultural distinction: the booktown model. *European Journal of Cultural Studies*, https://doi.org/10.1177/1367549416656856.

Duffy, M. and Mair, J. (2018). *Festival Encounters: Theoretical Perspectives on Festival Events and Social Cohesion*. London: Routledge.

Fincher, R. and Iveson, K. (2008). *Planning and Diversity in the City: Redistribution, Recognition and Encounter*. London: Palgrave Macmillan.

Fincher, R., Iveson, K., Leitner, H., and Preston, V. (2014). Planning in the multicultural city: celebrating diversity or reinforcing difference? *Progress in Planning*, 92, 1–55.

Forrest, J. and Dunn, K. (2010). Attitudes to multicultural values in diverse spaces. *Space and Polity*, 14(1), 81–102.

Gawlewicz, A. (2015). Beyond openness and prejudice: the consequences of migrant encounters with difference. *Environment and Planning A*, 48(2), 256–272.

Getz, D. (2013). *Event Studies*. Oxford: Routledge.

Giorgi, L. and Sassatelli, M. (2011). Introduction. In G. Delanty (ed.) *Festivals and the Cultural Public Sphere*. London: Routledge, 1–11.

Grossman, M. and Tahiri, H. (2015). Community perceptions of radicalisation and violent extremism. *Journal of Policing, Intelligence and Counter Terrorism*, 10(1), 14–24.

Hage, G. (1998). *White Nation: Fantasies of White Supremacy in a Multicultural Society*. Annandale, NSW: Pluto Press.

Halpern, D. (2005). *Social Capital*. Cambridge: Polity Press.

Iveson, K. (2007). *Publics and the City*. Oxford: Blackwell Publishing.

Jaeger, K. and Mykletun, R. J. (2013). Festivals, identities, and belonging. *Event Management*, 17(3), 213–226.

Jepson, A. and Clarke, A. (eds.) (2015). *Routledge Advances in Events Research Book Series: Exploring Community Festivals and Events*. Oxford: Routledge.

Jodie, G. (2015). Examining the cultural value of festivals. *International Journal of Event and Festival Management*, 6(2), 122–134.

Jupp, J. (2002). *From White Australia to Woomera: The Story of Australian Immigration*. Cambridge: Cambridge University Press.

Laurier, E. and Philo, C. (2006). Possible geographies: a passing encounter in a cafe. *Area*, 38, 353–363.

Lavenda, R. (1992). Festivals and the creation of public culture: whose voice(s)? In I. Karp, C. M. Kreamer, S. D. Lavine (eds.) *Museums and Communities: The Politics of Public Culture*. Washington, D.C.: Smithsonian Institution Press.

Lefebvre, H. (1991). *The Production of Space*. Cambridge, MA: Blackwell.

Lewis, L. and Dowsey-Magog, P. (1993). The Maleny 'fire event': rehearsals toward neo-liminality. *The Australian Journal of Anthropology*, 4(3), 198–219.

MacLeavy, J. (2008). Managing diversity? 'Community cohesion' and its limits in neoliberal urban policy. *Geography Compass*, 2(2), 538–558.

Massey, D. (1994). *Space, Place and Gender*. Cambridge: Polity Press.

Massey, D. (2005). *For Space*. London: Sage Publications.

Milbourne, P. (2007). Re-populating rural studies: migrations, movements and mobilities. *Journal of Rural Studies*, 23, 381–386.

Mouffe, C. (1994). For a politics of nomadic identity. In G. Robertson (ed.) *Travellers' Tales*. Oxford: Routledge, 106–113.

O'Grady, A. and Kill, R. (2013). Exploring festival performance as a state of encounter. *Arts & Humanities in Higher Education*, 12(2–3), 268–283.

Overvåg, K. and Berg, N. G. (2011). Second homes, rurality and contested space in eastern Norway. *Tourism Geographies*, 13(3), 417–442.

Picard, D. (2015). The festive frame: festivals as mediators for social change. *Ethnos*, 81(4), 600–616.

Purcell, M. (2002). Excavating Lefebvre: the right to the city and its urban politics of the inhabitant. *GeoJournal*, 58, 99–108.

Roche, M. (2011). Festivalisation, cosmopolitanism and European culture: on the socio-cultural significance of mage-events. In Giorgi, L., Sassatelli, M., and Delanty, G. (eds.) *Festivals and the Cultural Public Sphere*. Oxford: Routledge, 124–141.

Valentine, G. (2008). Living with difference: reflections on geographies of encounter. *Progress in Human Geography*, 32(3), 323–333.

Valentine, G. and Sadgrove, J. (2012). Lived difference: a narrative account of spatiotemporal processes of social differentiation. *Environment and Planning A*, 44(9), 2049–2063.

Van Winkle, C. M. and Woosnam, K. M. (2014). Sense of community and perceptions of festival social impacts. *International Journal of Event and Festival Management*, 5(1), 22–38.

Waitt, G. and Duffy, M. (2010). Listening and tourism studies. *Annals of Tourism Research*, 37(2), 457–477.

Wilson, H. (2016). On geography and encounter: bodies, borders, and difference. *Progress in Human Geography*, 41(4), 451–471.

Wilson, H. F. (2011). Passing propinquities in the multicultural city: the everyday encounters of bus passengering. *Environment and Planning A*, 43(3), 634–649.

Yardimci, S. (2007). *Festivalising Difference: Privatisation of Culture and Symbolic Exclusion.* Florence: European University Institute.

Young, G. (2008). *Reshaping Planning With Culture*. Aldershot: Ashgate.

Yuval-Davis, N. (2006). Belonging and the politics of belonging. *Patterns of Prejudice*, 40(3), 197–214.

2 Inclusion of people with reduced mobility in festivals

Perceptions and challenges at the Guelaguetza Festival, Mexico

Daniel Barrera-Fernández and
Marco Hernández-Escampa

Introduction

Many cities worldwide organise festivals and cultural events to attract tourists, promote their distinctiveness, increase the local economy, and enhance quality of life. Events are particularly attractive because cities that are not known by other resources such as heritage or leisure attractions, can promote themselves and become competitive tourist destinations by such means. However, during the process of events organisation, inclusion of local residents as a whole or particular groups of them is sometimes not taken into account. Especially focusing on people with disabilities and people with reduced mobility in general, there are few studies regarding their perception of inclusion. The present research aims at adding further discussion on this topic focusing on the case study of the Guelaguetza Festival in Oaxaca, Mexico.

Accessibility in the urban environment is a concept that evolves hand in hand with the increase of the perceptions and tolerance of society as a whole towards diversity and its increasing demand. Thus, it is difficult to offer a general definition that could be acceptable in every different context, from countries where this topic has become central in a context of fast aging, to regions where this debate is at a very early stage. The Convention on the Rights of Persons with Disabilities (United Nations 2006: 9) defined accessibility as the measures "to enable persons with disabilities to live independently and participate fully in all aspects of life". The Convention includes measures that States shall take to advance accessibility and that are related to accessibility in festivals and events, such as those related to the right of being included in the community (art. 19), personal mobility (art. 20) and especially participation in cultural life, recreation, leisure and sport (art. 30), where it stated that States Parties should promote access to places for cultural performances or services, such as theatres, museums, cinemas, libraries, and tourism services.

The previous definition focuses on disabilities, which are defined by the World Health Organization (2017) as,

an umbrella term, covering impairments, activity limitations, and participation restrictions. An impairment is a problem in body function or structure;

an activity limitation is a difficulty encountered by an individual in executing a task or action; while a participation restriction is a problem experienced by an individual in involvement in life situations.

The concern about accessibility was included in *New Urban Agenda* 2016 (United Nations 2017), the document meant to guide urbanisation and its global challenges for the next 20 years. Its innovation is the mention of accessibility as a collective good that benefits all, as an integral component of good policy to achieve inclusive and sustainable urban development.

Accessibility has become a priority at a global level, taking into account that by 2050 it is expected that about 6.25 billion people will be living in urban centres, 15% of whom will be persons with disabilities (United Nations Department of Economic and Social Affairs 2014). Nowadays, it is estimated that there are over one billion persons with disabilities worldwide (United Nations 2016). In Mexico, it is considered that 6% of the total population is disabled (Instituto Nacional de Estadística y Geografía 2016).

Since the publication of the Convention on the Rights of Persons with Disabilities, the concept of 'people with disabilities' has given way to broader definitions such as 'users with varying abilities' and, focusing on the built environment, 'persons with reduced mobility (PRM)'. Thus, accessibility has been recently defined as "a feature or quality of any physical or virtual environment, space, facility or service that is capable of accommodating the needs of users of varying abilities or disabilities to understand, get access to or interact with" (United Nations 2016: 6).

Speaking of physical barriers within the built environment, the concept of persons with reduced mobility is the broadest one because it covers not only people with motor, visual, intellectual, and hearing impairments, but also everyone facing any difficulty to move. In Mexico it includes pregnant women, babies and children under five years old, people older than 60 years old, persons with obesity grade III, people with temporary lesions, and people who attend them. The consideration of persons with reduced mobility means taking into account around 40% of the total Mexican population (Consejo Nacional de Población 2015).

As previously stated, there is a gap in academic literature about inclusion and participation of people with reduced mobility in festivals and events. Research shows that accessibility is the main environmental barrier to participation in arts and cultural events (Milligan, et al. 2014). Doshi, et al. (2014) developed a checklist for organisers of conferences to make events more accessible to people with disabilities. This proposal was focused on conferences and convention centres and has been the basis of the questionnaire applied in this research for visitors and organisers of the Guelaguetza Festival 2017 in Oaxaca, Mexico, which needed certain adaptations because our case study combined a festival venue, the Cerro del Fortín auditorium, and performances in the public space. Liu (2014) analysed three dimensions of socio-cultural impacts of Liverpool 2008 European Capital of Culture which could contribute to the enhancement of quality of life, namely participation in cultural activities, accessibility and inclusion, and enhancement of a sense of place and local identity. In relation to accessibility, the focus was given to the use of public space, initiatives designed to assist people in attending the main programme of events and dedicated transport, following a previous approach developed by Palmer (2004). Milligan, et al. (2014) included in their research individuals with disabilities, managers of cultural organisations, caregivers and health care providers, and other stakeholders, finding that there is a limited awareness about accessibility among residents and managers of cultural organisations. This approach has been considered in this research as explained below.

The Guelguetza Festival: the major indigenous event in Mexico

In order to understand the Guelaguetza Festival, some contextual information is required. Mexico is located in the southern portion of North America and it represents the union of two major biogeographical zones. Due to the high number of species present in the country, it is considered a mega-diverse one (Cantu, et al. 2004). Mexico's cultural diversity is equally prominent. A seat for the development of ancient civilisations, further contact with other areas of the world has historically increased cultural complexity in the country. (Fuentes and Reyes 2000). The state of Oaxaca is located to the south and it is the most diverse Mexican area, both naturally and culturally (Poole 2007; Robson 2007).

The modern state of Oaxaca has been divided in eight regions, each one defined by geographical and cultural traits (Ordóñez 2000). The Central Valley region is seat to Oaxaca City, capital of the homonymous state. This region historically has ruled over the rest of the regions and provides an astonishing archaeological sequence since ancient times to the present (Marcus 1990; Brumfield and Fox 2003; Flannery and Marcus 2005). The historic city of Oaxaca and the associated archaeological site of Monte Albán are included in the UNESCO World Heritage List. The introduction of western culture during colonial times indeed changed the ancient social structures; however, syncretism and resistance eventually created new cultural results. Just to give an idea of cultural richness in Mexico, it can be mentioned that besides Spanish and other introduced languages, eleven linguistic families are still spoken in the country, six of them in Oaxaca (Martin, et al. 2011).

Guelaguetza is a Zapotec word which means 'to share' or 'to cooperate'. The precedents of the contemporary festival can be traced back to pre-hispanic times. The Central Valleys of Oaxaca had been inhabited by a number of ethnic groups, most notably the Zapotecs and later the Mixtecs. These societies flourished until the Mexicas, also known as Aztecs, conquered the region in the 15th century. This later group founded Huayxácac, which is the precedent of contemporary Oaxaca City, as a military base to control the region. According to historic sources, the Aztecs established a cult devoted to the dual or bisexual god/goddess of the corn called Centéotl. The ceremonies possibly took place in a nearby hill nowadays known as Cerro del Fortín (Hill of the Small Fortress), which has been since those times seat to the Guelaguetza (Lizama Quijano 2006; Flores-Marcial 2015).

After the Spanish establishment in the region, the cult of Centéotl was substituted by the Catholic figure of the Carmen Virgin which is venerated on 16 July. It was established that the nearest two Mondays to that date would be festive, called *Lunes del Cerro* (Mondays of the Hill) (Oaxaca State Government 2015). The modern version of the Guelaguetza was established in 1932 (Lizama Quijano 2006). The main structure of the festival is framed by the two consecutive festive Mondays. The scene for this event is the auditorium at Cerro del Fortín. On both of these days, a woman, representing the ancient deity Centeótl, opens the festival. After that, dance and music representing each of the regions of Oaxaca are performed in a long-lasting sequence displaying the cultural diversity of Oaxaca as a whole. Gifts are thrown to the audience representing both ancient offerings and colonial tribute. On both Saturdays prior to the festive Mondays parades pass through the city as invitations to the main festivities. In general, the Guelaguetza accounts for almost two weeks of continuous spectacles both in the city and on the sacred hill. Gastronomy and handicrafts are also offered to visitors in the form of special events. The Guelaguetza is considered a major indigenous festival in Mexico, also one of the most important ones on the American Continent, attracting a great number of visitors to Oaxaca each year.

Research methods

The objective of the research was to analyse the existing accessibility measures in the Guelaguetza Festival and the perception of inclusion of people with reduced mobility. In order to achieve this objective, questions regarding accessibility were put to the general public, public administration officials and attendants with reduced mobility. This information was completed with the architectural analysis of the main venue and direct observation during the performances and parallel activities. The following research methods were used:

1 Application of the Event Experience Scale methodology for visitors' perception

The Event Experience Scale (EES) measures the experience of people attending events, focusing on mood and emotion. The scale was developed by Tilburg University in 2012. In 2014 an international team called ATLAS Event Experience Research Project was created with the aim of applying the scale and comparing the results at events from different countries. The aims of the project are to provide a platform for comparative research on events worldwide; to improve the knowledge of events, their visitors and their impacts; to develop a database as a research resource and benchmarking tool for cultural and sporting events; and to produce case studies of best practice in events development, marketing and research. In Mexico this scale has so far been applied at the Festival Internacional Cervantino in Guanajuato (Barrera-Fernández and Hernández-Escampa 2017) and at the Guelaguetza.

In the case of the Guelaguetza, a survey incorporating EES was carried out interviewing 164 people between 17 and 29 July 2017, coinciding with the celebration of the festival. The survey was carried out in the main festival venue at the Cerro del Fortín auditorium before the Monday performance (Lunes del Cerro), and in public spaces where parallel activities took place during festival days, namely Oaxaca's city centre before the street parade, El Llano park and La Danza square. Of the respondents, 48% were female, 51% were male and 1% did not specify their gender; 84% were Mexicans, 11% of which were from Oaxaca and the rest from other states in Mexico, especially Mexico City, Baja California Sur and the State of Mexico. Among foreigners, one half were from the USA, followed by people from Canada, Argentina and Spain. On average, groups of visitors were made up of three adults and two children.

The surveys needed some adaptations for the purpose of this research. A specific question was included asking about how respondents, no matter if they have disability or not, evaluated different aspects of the festival, including accessibility for people with reduced mobility.

2 Architectural analysis of measures to grant accessibility and barriers to accessibility in the Guelaguetza auditorium

An analysis was carried out during the celebration of the festival at its main venue from an architectural point of view. Since in Oaxaca there is no updated comprehensive technical regulation on building measures on accessibility, the current Handbook of Technical Regulations on Accessibility from Mexico City (Government of Mexico City 2016) was considered to assess the accessibility of the auditorium from the public space and inside the facilities.

3 Interviews with public administration officials and qualitative textual analysis of policy reports

Interviews with officials from the City Council, the State's Secretary of Tourism, the State's Secretary of Culture and the State's Secretary of Mobility were conducted to gather information on measures to grant accessibility that have been implemented in the festival. In addition, policy reports on the festival's organisation were collected; of particular interest is the Guelaguetza's Organisation Handbook (Oaxaca State Government 2015).

4 Direct observation

The research group attended the major performance at the auditorium and several parallel activities in public spaces during festival days to observe accessibility measures, barriers to accessibility, participation of people with reduced mobility and staff attitudes. Participant observation included interviews with staff members regarding specific measures and procedures to allow attendance by people with different disabilities.

5 Application of a checklist on accessibility measures

As mentioned above, Doshi, et al. (2014) elaborated a checklist for organisers of conferences in indoor venues to make the event more accessible to people with disabilities. This checklist (see Table 2.1) was simplified, reordered and adapted

Table 2.1 Checklist of accessibility measures asked of officials and people with reduced mobility.

Venue	Guelaguetza auditorium
	City centre
	El Llano park
	La Danza square
	Other
Dissemination before the event	Texts in braille
	Printed materials in large print and good contrast
	Audio narration
	Sign language interpreter
	Subtitles in real time
	Accessibility symbols included in leaflets
	Websites meet accessibility standards
	Specific contact information
During the celebration of the event	Texts in braille
	Materials in large print and good contrast
	Hearing aid devices
	Audio narration
	Sign language interpreter
	Subtitles in real time
	Accessibility symbols included in leaflets
Accessibility of the place	Accessible transport to get to the venue
	Accessible parking
	Access for wheelchairs
	Access for wheelchairs through the main entrance
	Dedicated signage
	All areas accessible or people available to offer assistance
	Elevators, where available, have accessible buttons
	Reserved spaces for wheelchairs
	Reserved spaces for wheelchairs located in all sitting areas
	Aisles are wide enough
	Good lighting
	Good visibility of the stage from a wheelchair
	People with hearing disabilities have dedicated seats near the stage
	Accessible toilets nearby and well signed
	Electrical cables or cords are covered
	Hearing aid devices are arranged when requested
	Accessible public telephones
	Guide dogs are allowed to enter
	Pavement lines or changes in floor textures
	Glass signage
	Direction and areas signage
	Signage is simple, bright and colourful
	Stage is accessible and adapted for performance of people with reduced mobility
Staff	Staff given training in needs and requirements of people with different disabilities
	Staff provide information on accessible toilets and emergency exits
	Staff have clearly visible clothes
	Staff know how to proceed in case of emergency

to the particular features of the Guelaguetza, the Mexican classification of disabilities and the usual technical measures existing in Mexico to grant architectural and urban accessibility.

Officials of the public administration and people with reduced mobility attending the Guelaguetza Festival 2017 answered the checklist. Its application was useful to measure perception on accessibility by people who need specific measures and by officials who are responsible to grant them.

Analysis and perceptions of the accessibility of the Guelaguetza Festival in Oaxaca

When general people answered about their opinion on different aspects of the festival, accessibility did not appear to be an issue of concern. Something different occurred when the group of persons with reduced mobility expressed themselves about the same topic. Such contrast in responses is seen in Figure 2.1. There was a significant difference depending on the origin of the respondent. Local people were more aware of the problem of accessibility, probably because they may have

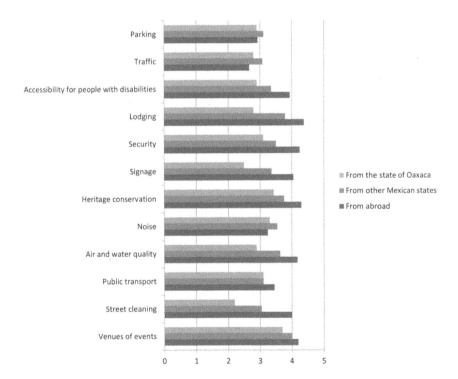

Figure 2.1 Perceptions of general attendants about some features related to the festival. In the scale 0–5, 0 means 'very negative' and 5 'very positive'.

Source: by the authors.

experienced a temporal disability themselves or have noticed the difficulties that this group of people have to face. Furthermore, there are some aspects of the festival indirectly related to accessibility that make general visitors aware. For example, tourists from abroad value traffic negatively, Mexican visitors notice problems in street cleaning, and local attendants perceive signage and street cleaning negatively. All these topics are seen as barriers to accessibility.

From the architectural analysis of the Cerro del Fortín auditorium, it can be concluded that its major challenge is to solve the access to the public space. Nowadays, attendants have to walk along the Pan-American road before arriving at the main entrance. People wait for hours in long queues, exposed to vehicles passing at high speed (see Figure 2.2). This is a major problem both for the general public and particularly for people with reduced mobility. Nevertheless, a public car park has recently been built which includes devoted parking lots for people with disabilities, and it is connected by an accessible bridge to the auditorium. Thus, the difficulty of arriving by car has been partially solved but people who arrive on foot or with a wheelchair are still in need of a solution. In addition, public transport is not adapted for wheelchairs, so this is another pending issue. Once in the auditorium there are adapted toilets, and people with reduced mobility can get assistance from staff (see Figure 2.3). People in wheelchairs can access the auditorium and specific places for them are located at the rear of the auditorium, as a result with less visibility. Electrical cables or cords are covered and although there is signage throughout the venue, it is not adapted for people with disabilities.

Figure 2.2 People going to the auditorium are unable to cross the Pan-American road safely. Source: Photograph by the author.

Figure 2.3 Staff help people with wheelchairs to move to their reserved seats and around the auditorium.

Source: Photograph by the author.

The public administration has developed a number of initiatives to increase accessibility over the years. Nowadays, people are offered printed materials in large print and good contrast, and audio narration. According to the officials' answers, signage, lighting and visibility are correct for people with reduced mobility and the stage is accessible and adapted for performance. The staff in the different venues are given training on the needs and requirements of people with different disabilities; they provide information on accessible toilets and emergency exits; they have clearly visible clothes; and they know how to proceed in case of an emergency.

The organisation of the festival focuses on three areas, each of them divided into a number of committees. The Legal-Administrative Area includes the committees of Administration, Legal, General Services, and Ticketing. The Logistics Area covers the committees of Credentials, Attention to Delegates, Staging, Opening Ceremony, Tourist Information, Welcoming, and Security. The Area of Promotion and Marketing is divided into the committees of Communication, Design, Sponsors, Promotion, Merchandising and Public Relations. Some of these committees play key roles in granting accessibility to the event, but, according to interviews and information provided, there are no specific requirements for staff working in the organisation committees regarding needs of people with reduced mobility, and specific initiatives for these persons are not stated.

The research group attended the main performance in the auditorium and some parallel activities. Pictures were taken and the direct observation served to highlight some initiatives that have been included to make the visit of people with reduced mobility easier, as well as those needing improvement.

Finally, people with reduced mobility that attended the Guelaguetza in 2017 were asked about their perception of the festival's accessibility. Respondents have different disabilities, thus each one responded very differently according to their particular needs. Most people agreed that the staff help people with special requirements once they arrive at the auditorium and when they are looking for their seats or want to go to the toilet. However, arriving at the auditorium is significantly difficult for people with reduced mobility because, according to their answers, there is no adapted public transport, not enough dedicated car parking, and slopes and floor materials are unsuitable for wheelchairs.

Conclusions

There is a gap in academic literature regarding inclusion and participation of people with reduced mobility at festivals and events. However, granting accessibility for them is needed when the goal is to achieve more sustainable and socially valued events. This is even more in the context of an aging population and where increasing accessibility measures would have a positive impact on the population which ranges from 15% (United Nations Department of Economic and Social Affairs 2014) if we focus only on persons with disabilities, to 40% (Consejo Nacional de Población 2015) if we consider people with reduced mobility.

From this case study of the Guelaguetza in Oaxaca there are some conclusions that could be useful for the organisers of similar festivals elsewhere. The general public does not perceive barriers to accessibility any more than they notice other aspects that affect their experience of the festival. The organisation lacks specific policies on accessibility and this topic has not become central yet. However, improvements have been made in the last years. People with reduced mobility consider these measures to be still far from their needs. Staff at the festival do as much as they can to facilitate the attendance and participation of people with specific needs but there are still major physical and organisational barriers to making the Guelaguetza a truly inclusive event. Collaboration among stakeholders needs further development and more research in this field is needed to put accessibility of people with reduced mobility at the centre of events and festivals organisation.

Further studies are needed to draw conclusions or design proposals in urban and architectural terms. However, direct experience shows that major faults exist. Located on a hill, the auditorium lacks a big enough plaza to receive visitors. At the end of the festival, people are forced to exit directly onto a highway, resulting in chaotic scenes, let alone danger for people. Some basic accessibility measures have appeared gradually, but major adaptations are still needed.

Questions for discussion

1. What are the urban planning or legal reasons why universal design in the public space is still unapplied in some relevant Latin American public spaces?
2. How is it possible to socialise this need in order to achieve people participation and better results?
3. What kind of policies are needed to assess and guarantee the progress of the needed transformations?

References

Barrera-Fernández, D. and Hernández-Escampa, M. (2017). Events and placemaking: The case of the Festival Internacional Cervantino in Guanajuato, Mexico. *International Journal of Event and Festival Management*, 8(1), 24–38.

Brumfield, E. M. and Fox, J. W. (eds.). (2003). *Factional Competition and Political Development in the New World*. Cambridge: Cambridge University Press.

Cantu, C., Wright, R. G., Scott, J. M., and Strand, E. (2004). Assessment of current and proposed nature reserves of Mexico based on their capacity to protect geophysical features and biodiversity. *Biological Conservation*, 115(3), 411–417.

Consejo Nacional de Población. (2015). *La situación demográfica de México*. Mexico City: Consejo Nacional de Población.

Doshi, J. K., Furlan, A. D., Lopes, L. C., Delisa, J., and Battistella, L. R. (2014). Conferences and convention centres' accessibility to people with disabilities. *Journal of Rehabilitative Medicine*, 46, 616–619.

Flannery, K. V. and Marcus, J. (2005). *Excavations at San José Mogote 1: The household archaeology*. Vol. 1. Ann Arbor: University of Michigan Museum.

Flores-Marcial, X. M. (2015). *A History of Guelaguetza in Zapotec Communities of the Central Valleys of Oaxaca, 16th Century to the Present*. PhD thesis, University of California Los Angeles.

Fuentes, J. M. L. and Reyes, A. L. (2000). *Historia general de México*. Mexico City: Grupo Editorial Patria.

Government of Mexico City. (2016). *Manual de normas técnicas de accesibilidad*. Mexico City.

Instituto Nacional de Estadística y Geografía. (2016). *La discapacidad en México, datos al 2014*. Mexico City: Instituto Nacional de Estadística y Geografía.

Liu, Y. (2014). Socio-cultural impacts of major event: Evidence from the 2008 European capital of culture, Liverpool. *Social Indicators Research*, 115, 983–998.

Lizama Quijano, J. (2006). *La Guelaguetza en Oaxaca: fiesta, relaciones interétnicas y procesos de construcción simbólica en el contexto urbano*. Mexico City: CIESAS.

Marcus, J. (ed.). (1990). *Debating Oaxaca Archaeology*. Vol. 84. Ann Arbor: University of Michigan Museum.

Martin, G. J., Camacho Benavides, C. I., Del Campo García, C. A., Anta Fonseca, S., Chapela Mendoza, F., and González Ortíz, M. A. (2011). Indigenous and community conserved areas in Oaxaca, Mexico. *Management of Environmental Quality: An International Journal*, 22(2), 250–266.

Milligan, N. V., Nieuwenhuijsen, E. R., and Grawi, C. L. (2014). Using a participatory action strategic approach to enhance accessibility and participation in arts and cultural events: Results of four focus groups. *Disability and Health Journal*, 7, 105–113.

Oaxaca State Government. (2015). *Manual de Organización. Guelaguetza*. Oaxaca.

Ordóñez, M. J. (2000). El territorio del estado de Oaxaca: una revisión histórica. *Investigaciones Geográficas*, 42, 67–86.

Palmer, R. (2004). *European cities and capitals of culture: Study prepared for the European Commission*. part 1. Brussels: Palmer-Rae Associates.

Poole, D. (2007). Political autonomy and cultural diversity in the Oaxaca rebellion. *Anthropology News*, 48(3), 10–11.

Robson, J. P. (2007). Local approaches to biodiversity conservation: Lessons from Oaxaca, southern Mexico. *International Journal of Sustainable Development*, 10(3), 267–286.

United Nations. (2006). *Convention on the Rights of Persons with Disabilities*. New York.

United Nations. (2016). *Good Practices of Accessible Urban Development. Making Urban Environments Inclusive and Fully Accessible to All*. New York.

United Nations. (2017). *New Urban Agenda 2016*. Adopted at the United Nations Conference on Housing and Sustainable Urban Development (Habitat III) in Quito, Ecuador, on 20 October 2016.

United Nations Department of Economic and Social Affairs. (2014). *The World Urbanization Prospects*. New York.

World Health Organization. (2017). Health topics: Disabilities. Available at www.who.int/topics/disabilities/en/.

3 Do-it-yourself or going professionally?

On the different potentials of community inclusion through gendered festivals in the post-Yugoslav space

Zorica Siročić

Introduction

A booming literature on social events reflects the rise in the number of festivals globally since the 1990s (overviews in Finkel, et al. 2013; Getz and Page 2016; Lamond and Platt 2016). Bennett, et al. (2014) use the term, "festivalisation of culture" to capture the spread of festivals as well as the accompanying diversification of their programme forms, audiences, and types. Being a ubiquitous form of social participation, festivals attract the attention of social scientists and policy analysts for their impact on local communities (Jepson and Clarke 2013). Festivals as platforms for socialisation and celebration can strengthen community identities, promote diversity and inclusion, but can also perpetuate the use of exclusionary and hegemonic practices that strengthen groups in power (Clarke and Jepson 2011).

In the hands of excluded and/or marginalised groups, festivals may become a repertoire of contentious politics or dissent that challenge dominant identities, practices, and norms. This chapter treats events that are labeled as feminist, women's, and LGBTQ as examples of cultural repertoires of contention used by social movements to challenge, subvert, or destabilise hegemonic norms of gender and sexuality (examples of similar festivals in Browne 2011, 2009; Gamson 1997, 1996; Markwell and Waitt 2013; Richards 2017). The history of gendered festivals in Southeastern Europe begins in 1984 when the "first European lesbian and gay film festival" took place in Ljubljana, Slovenia (Kajinić 2016: 59; Richards 2017: 41). This festival is still running and has together with the lesbian and gay (LG) movement outlived the succession of Yugoslav countries. The Slovene Office for Gender Equality initiated the City of Women ten years later, a festival to promote women-made contemporary art. Since the late 1990s, from initially two festivals, to the time of writing this chapter, the number of festivals labeled as feminist, women's, and LGBTQ rose to more than 20 or, as some activists put it, feminist politics "festivalised" (see Table 3.1). Some of these events have seen more than ten annual editions, while others would vanish after the first or second year. Case studies on the regional queer festivals demonstrate the political relevance and the subversive character of the festivals' content for a particular context (for example, Dioli 2011; Hvala 2010; Kajinić 2012). Nonetheless, comparative studies of diverse festivals or those considering their common impact across different levels are missing. This chapter addresses the identified literature gap by examining how do organisers of activist festivals include the local community in their programmes; how do they include their activist community; and is there a trade-off in reaching both levels? Whereas, the shared political values and advancement of the movement's goals define the first community and not necessarily the territory, building on Staggenborg's (1998) understanding of social movement community, the latter describes spatial units that encompass diverse groups and actors including those that do not necessarily share movement's values or do not actively advance movement's goals.

The ethnographic research (2015–2017) on self-identified women's, feminist, and LGBTQ festivals in the post-Yugoslav territory indicates that activist festivals organised on do-it-yourself (DIY) principles proved to work best for building and sustaining an activist community and the inclusion of new participants ("reaching in") (Mansbridge 1986: 178), while professional (selective) art festivals have stronger potential in reaching the broader audience in local community ("reaching out") (ibid.), serving the movement indirectly. The effect proved to be in a reverse relation to the size of the existing activist, academic and (sub)cultural offer of the given local context: the most heterogeneous audience could be found in the smallest communities. The chapter bridges social movements and critical event studies as the findings illustrate models of best practice and lessons learned with respect to event accessibility, inclusion, and diversity on the level of activist and local communities.

Theoretical framework

Festivals as platforms for socialisation and celebration can boost a sense of community belonging through an atmosphere of spontaneity, unity, and festive spirit (Jepson and Clarke 2013). Yet, as Jeong and Almeida Santos (2004) emphasise, festivals are not spontaneous events. To set one up, a group of organisers plans the programme, targets the desired audience, chooses venues, and can be considered for that matter as gatekeepers controlling processes of inclusion and exclusion in the communities. The existing studies of the festivals and other social events revealed the crucial role that organisational and programme management plays in contributing or hindering social inclusion and promotion of community diversity in terms of gender, sexuality, ethnicity and abilities (see in Allison and Hibbler 2004; Finkel 2009, 2010; Gamson 1996; Laing and Mair 2015).

The explicitly activist or political festivals differ from similar events for having a connection to the broader activist community, hence the community that is based on shared political values and goals. The organisers of activist or political festivals choose the programme and the content in accordance with the political agenda. The political festival can be understood as an arena for "socially marginalised groups [to] express discontent and challenge the established order through symbolic revolutionary acts; [... as] resistance to the dominant social order" (Jeong and Almeida Santos 2004: 641). In other words, the festival can be understood as one of the action repertoires of an activist community to disrupt and destabilise hegemonic order by, for instance, using "pre-figurative" political practices (Eleftheriadis 2015) and/or acting subversively as a form of a "contra-public" in a local community (Hvala 2010).

In addition, festivals and other cultural repertoires have the potential of transforming random individuals and groups into an activist community. The cultural events create affective bonds, social networks, and generate the sense of collective identity (Staggenborg 2001; Tilly and Tarrow 2015: 125). Besides generating and/or strengthening the community, cultural events nurture political conciseness and interpersonal bonds in phases of social movement's abeyance (Staggenborg 1998). Consequently, the role and the potential of the activist festivals in promoting diversity needs to be analysed with respect to two levels, the activist community and the local community; and, across two dimensions, the diversity of included participants and ideas. Sometimes, diversity promotion on both levels causes strategical contradictions that Mansbridge (1986: 178) describes as a tension between "reaching in" and "reaching out". To affect the desired change, a movement should include as many people as possible, but to build a devoted core that would sustain the movement in the long run, it should prompt a sense of exclusivity ('us' vs. 'them'). In the former case, activists would use a festival for an external mobilisation and inclusion of the local community; whereas, in the latter case, the festivals would be directed inwards to internally consolidate the activist community.

The research on the role of festivals for the processes of collective identity construction revealed opposing tendencies (Browne 2009, 2011; Eder, et al. 1995; Gamson 1997, 1996; Richards 2017). On the one hand, findings indicate that activists used festivals to nurture the sense of unity and collective identity which often depended on the use of exclusionary practices and norms to keep the movement relatively homogeneous. In this case, activists relied on the organisational and entrance policies to filter the access of participants and ideas that might challenge the settled power relations and collective identities. The Michigan Womyn's Music Festival stirred academic and activist contro-versies, as its organisers created boundaries based on biologically deterministic principles. Namely, festival entrance policy was based on the 'womyn-born womyn only' credo that had it roots in politics of lesbian, radical and separatist feminism.

On the other hand, activists can treat a festival as part of the broader scholarly and activist postmodern and queer political trends to contest ideas of stable identities (for example, women or gay) (Gamson 1995; Markwell and Waitt 2013). Unlike the "category-supportive political strategies" that depend on stable collective identities (Gamson 1995: 391), festival organisers can use "decon-structive cultural strategies" (ibid.) to challenge, push, and subvert the identity boundaries of the settled communities by including diversity of ideas and participants in the activist narratives and circles.

The post-Yugoslav feminist and LGBTQ festivals are an analytically intriguing example, as most of them combine elements of both cultural as well as political strategies of the gendered festivals already in their announcements and programmes (see Table 3.1). In addition, they stretch across different local settings and use a variety of programme formats and organisational practices through which the impact on inclusion and promotion of community diversity can be observed. This chapter examines how the formal status of the group in charge of the activist festival and the programme selection criteria affects the potential of a festival to contribute to the diversity of people and ideas on two levels: 1) in the activist communities; and, 2) in the local communities.

Research methods

The methodological principles of grounded theory and situational analysis (Charmaz 2014; Clarke 2003; Mattoni 2014) that rely on abductive logic of simultaneous collection, coding, mapping, and analysing of data guide this chapter. The selection criteria encompass events that are self-identified as women, feminist, and LGBTQ taking place across post-Yugoslav terrain. Most of the relevant empirical material comes from three sources. Firstly, direct and participant observation of festivals in 2015 and 2016 ('o' in Table 3.1). Secondly, from the 24 semi-structured and problem-centered interviews that were conducted with the festivals' initiators, programme selectors, and organisers identified by targeted sampling ('i' in Table 3.1). The actors were asked about the motivation, interest, and first experiences in activism, organisation of a festival, and the broader activist and local scene. The interviews lasted on average 52 minutes; they were anonymised and, except for two interviews in English, they were conducted in the interviewees' native languages and transcribed word for word. Additional sources include conversations with 34 attendees during the festivals without recording them. The notes of these conversations together with those of observations were taken afterwards. Thirdly, programmes, press-clippings, and other accompanying festival materials (badges, posters, flyers, etc.) of each festival are included in the study ('p' in Table 3.1).

Findings and discussion

Besides the first two festivals in the sample, the Ljubljana LGBT Film Festivals and the City of Women that were launched in 1984 and 1994, respectively, the rest of the festivals appeared after 2000. Their organisers were dominantly members of the post-Yugoslav millennial generation that came of political age after 2000 alongside the women's and LG movement that consolidated during the transitional 1990s. The interviews show that the "different views of the common struggle" (Mansbridge 1986: 185) and a perceived closure of the settled movement made engagement of the millennial generation through the existing groups less likely. The activists staging small festivals acquired their first political experiences in different activist and sub-cultural scenes (for example, punk and

Table 3.1 Organisational and programme variations in post-Yugoslav 'women', 'feminist' and 'LGBTQ' festivals.

	Name	Time and place	Self-identification and goals (p)
DIY	Red Dawns (i) (o)	2000 – Ljubljana, SI	"International feminist and queer festival [that] celebrates our lives and redefines public space [to] make it accessible for creativity and socializing of women on our own terms: in a non-hierarchical, non-exploitative and anti-capitalistic manner."
	Girlz are Weird (i)	2002–2007 Kutina, CRO	Women's music festival; "[intended] primarily for women, transgender people and anyone who finds a safe space for creative expression and social engagement".
	Anarchofem Fest (i)	2005, 2007 MC & CRO	Festival of anarchofeminist action and politics.
	Queer Belgrade	2004 – occasionally Belgrade, SR	"[Festival's goal is] cooperation and empowering people […] through entertainment and promoting queer politics [by creating] a space to overcome the closed boxes of homo- or hetero-sexuality […] radical politics linking all aspects of oppression."
	FemFest (i)	2006–2007 Zagreb, CRO	Festival of feminist theory, art and activism.
	Girl Power Fest (i)	2008–2009 Koprivnica, CRO	Festival of female creativity.
	Feminae Extra. (i)	2009 Split, CRO	"Festival of female creativity, artistic and cultural female scene [the aim is to] create artistic and cultural female scene in Split and an interdisciplinary collective […] of all those who are interested in gender issues."
	Wild Hags) (i)	2013 – Cerkno, SI	"[Festival] gives priority to creators […] who reject stereotypical ideas about women and violate unwritten rules about 'normal' […] defends the equality of all women – including those who have not been born as women – and a fairer world for everyone: women, men and children."
	Blasfem (*)	2017 Banja Luka, BH	Women's art and activism festival; "[…] promotes women's rights, raises awareness, speaks about feminism trans-generationally, trans- historically and regionally".
	Homo, Festa! (*)	2016 – Porec, CRO	LGBT Festival; "[…] raises awareness in the local community on needs and obstacles of LGBTQ people."

(Continued)

Table 3.1 (Cont.)

	Name	Time and place	Self-identification and goals (p)
DIY plus	PitchWise (i) (o)	2006 – Sarajevo, BH	Women's art and activism festival; "[aims to] take the neglected public space and transform it into a meeting place that brings together socially engaged artists, activists, theoreticians, feminists [...]".
	VoxFeminae (i) (o)	2007 – Zagreb, CRO	"An international transdisciplinary festival; [...] enhances the visibility of women's creativity and actions by removing it from existing templates and presentation methods."
	BeFem (i) (o)	2009 – Belgrade, SR	"BeFem wants to deconstruct stereotypes about feminism and encourage new generations to engage in activism [...]."
	FemiNis (i)	2010 – Nis, SR	Festival of feminist activism and art; "a feminist space for connecting, empowering, acting, associating activists, theoreticians, artists, fellow citizens [...] linking and empowering young feminists".
	First & Female (i) (o)	2013 – Skopje, MC	Women's art and activism festival; "a space for creative expression, exchange of information and knowledge [...]".
	The LGBT Film Festival (*)	1984 – Ljubljana, SI	"Non-competitive film festival focusing on international gay and lesbian cinema."
	Merlinka (*)	2009 – regional	Festival focused on LGBTQ+ cinema.
Professional Selective	City of Women (i) (o)	1994 – Ljubljana, SI	"An international festival of contemporary art"; "present [...] mainly women's authorship".
	Queer Zagreb	2002 – Zagreb, CRO	Festival aims to affirm queer art as relevant artistic expression.
	FemArt (i)	2013 – Pristina, KO	Women's art and activist festival

(*) Blasfem and Homo, Festa! were organised for the first-time in 2016 and it remains to be seen in which direction the groups in charge may develop the event. The LGBT Film Festival and Merlinka seem to be in terms of the programme closer to selective art festivals, and in terms of the organisation to DIY plus versions.
(i) Data is collected by using semi-structured and problem-centered interviews with the festivals' initiators, programme selectors and organisers. (o) Data is collected by direct and participant observation of festivals (2015/2016).
(p) Translations of the excerpts are made by the author of this paper based on the available festivals' programmes and media announcements.
(-) The festivals whose last edition was the year in which this paper was prepared (2017).

hardcore punk, anarchist and alter-globalisation movements, anti-regime protests) and/or through education (sociology, literature, gender studies). The spread of similar events on the international and national stage provided a setting for learning about the potentials that festivals offer.

For feminists, a particularly influential event was the Ladyfest (Olympia, USA, 1999) which raised the voice against gender inequality and sexism in creative industries, and against the widespread gendered physical and psychological abuse. The Ladyfest organisers continued the ideas previously articulated by the Riot Grrrls movement (see Rosenberg and Garofalo 1998). The Ladyfest is a part of action repertoires of contemporary and third wave feminist politics (for example, Dean 2010; Dean and Aune 2015; Evans 2015). The initiators and organisers of post-Yugoslav feminist festivals were familiar with these events by being a part of transnational grassroots networks, by reading international fanzines and blogs, by visiting them or by acquiring first-hand experiences as employees or volunteers on various local festivals.

In particular, the members of the millennial "creative" and "artistic precariat" (Bain and McLean 2013; de Peuter 2014) could use this form to connect professional expression and activist dedication. The "creative precariat" (de Peuter 2014) is a critical reference to the concept of "creative class" (Florida 2003). The people organising festivals in the sample work in occupational spheres such as technology, entertainment, journalism, and arts, but they are far from being the well-paid labour segments that governments would consider to be the force of urban renewal. On the contrary, the local governments antagonise or are suspicious of the politicised cultural and art sector. These activists/artists have several jobs on short-term contracts for unstable positions and insecure income (see Beck 2000 on flexibility, self-employment, and "short-termism"). They resist the commodification of the culture while simultaneously epitomising the typical features of post-Fordist creative industries:

> juggling multiple short-term 'projects'; blurring the boundaries of work and non-work time; [...] producing monetary value from knowledge, symbols, or other-wise intangible resources; [...] personally funding perpetual education upgrades; [...] performing work without a guarantee of compensation; assuming responsibility for maintaining a steady flow of paid work and, hence, on a job search without end; and willingness to put the passion for the work ahead of the size of the pay.
>
> (de Peuter 2014: 264)

Goals

The millennial activists used the festival as a platform to create and/or to redefine public space as free from sexism, misogyny, and homophobia, as it can be read from their self-identified goals (see Table 3.1). Yet, some placed emphasis on providing the space for expression of women-made art (for example, Girl Power Fest, Girls are Weird, City of Women), while others promoted art content, forms and practices which explicitly aim at disrupting gender-based expectations in creative industries and society in general (for example, Red Dawns, Wild Hags, Queer Belgrade). Therefore, the festivals are an explicit link to the broader political agenda of the feminist movement fighting against marginalisation of women as political and creative subjects. The grassroots feminist collectives share with the women's movement the conviction that feminist politics is necessary to fight widespread gendered oppression and constraints of creativity through gender hierarchies; yet, they circumvent the political or institutional means and/or have no access to it, so they act through cultural ones. With the contra-cultural and sub-cultural groups (for example, punk, anarchist) they share the conviction that their goals can be achieved through alternative organisational practices outside of the conventional institutions but are confronted with the (unwritten) standards that belittle female and queer contributions on sexist grounds. As its initiators aim at challenging power relations and hegemonies (Clarke and Jepson 2011) in the society in general, but also inside the existing contra-cultural and activist circles, the festivals can be understood as the indicators of movements within the movements.

Programme forms and organisational practices

The most salient organisational feature of the early millennial festivals is the dedication of their organisers to do-it-yourself (DIY) principles. DIY ethics or as Bain and McLean (2013: 99) put it "DIO" or "do-it-ourselves collectivism" draws on punk subculture, grassroots, and anarchist politics. The advocates of DIY principles consider these as a resistance against consumer society, state authority, and commodification of art and culture (Biel 2012; Collective, et al. 2012). Characteristic features of DIY-based activism include organisation of skill-sharing workshops, life in autonomous spaces, and an aim for a high degree of self-sufficient lifestyle (ibid.). Informal collectives, contra-cultural, and sub-cultural groups rather than registered and professionalised groups usually practise DIY principles to sustain the groups, but also to produce the zines and the magazine, as well as to set up the protests, the concerts, or other political and cultural repertoires.

Some festivals are dedicated to one form only, which usually corresponds to one art form, such as the film or performative arts (for example, Ljubljana LGBT Film Festival, City of Women, Queer Zagreb, Merlinka). Others explicitly link art to activism by combing several forms of each (for example, PitchWise, Vox Feminae, FemiNis, First & Female). These combined art-activist festivals usually mix several types of programme including: 1) workshops; 2) discursive forms (forums, discussions, panels, lectures); 3) art forms (performative arts, visual arts, music, film, literature); 4) comedy (stand-up, cabaret); 5) entrepreneurship (sale of arts and crafts); and, 6) leisure (clubbing). While workshops, forums and leisure/clubbing are by definition inclusive, programme forms such as the lectures and arts have the potential to include, but also to transmit their message from a position of authority.

To summarise, besides having distinctive goal orientations, the festivals in the sample differ in terms of their place in a matrix that crosses the organisational and selection practice (DIY, informal collectives vs. professionalised, registered groups) with the programme forms (single form, specialised programme vs. multiple forms, combined programme). In the first version, marked here as 'DIY only', the programme is mostly a combination of art and activism, but it can be dedicated to one form only which is particularly pragmatic in the beginnings. The organisers, usually gathered as informal collectives, understand DIY consequently and ideologically; they cover the expenses through volunteering work, benefit concerts, or sale of self-made accessories (for example, Red Dawns, anarchofeminist festivals, Girlz are Weird). The second version here denoted as 'DIY plus' encompasses usually a combined art-activist programme, but organisers understand DIY principles complementary, pragmatically, and do not hesitate to engage in external fundraising as formally registered organisations. For such groups, a festival is usually one of many activities in their activist repertoires (for example, PitchWise, VoxFeminae FemiNis, First & Female). The third version encompasses 'professional selective' festivals that usually present an art programme, and usually specialise in one art form. An art director or programme selector leads a team of organisers, and the preparation of the festival is usually the main activity of the group behind it. The content and the performers are selected based on institutionally set art standards, not only for sharing the activist commitment (for example, City of Women, Queer Zagreb, FemArt). It is important to emphasise that these variations are based on practices which tend to dominate in festival organisations. Thus, these are not stable and fixed types, but are merely analytical orientations that could be identified at the time of writing and which in some respects may overlap (see (*) in Table 3.1).

Strong in reaching in to the activist community, weaker in reaching out to the local community: 'DIY only' festivals

The interviewees recalled that the motive and the idea to initiate a small DIY feminist festival came from a little guerrilla group that draw some graffiti in the town. In the words of Person4,

> We did not overthink the concept. We worked on the principle of what would interest us. It was great that some people from the region would come, that we would recognise someone generationally close to us who does similar things, and to get to know each other, to see each other.

The DIY principle proved to be encouraging organisationally, as such events do not require advanced logistics, material equipment, working space, or familiarity with administration. The participants perceive the work based on DIY principles as a counterpoint to the hermetic language and constraining templates of presentation characteristic for academia or the art scene. The DIY style enables experimentation and treats the work as an open signal for those that can recognise congruence with their own sentiments and ideas. The low-threshold, creative approach, play and fun (Shepard 2011, 2010) encouraged new people to the politics of feminism.

In the collectives that are organising the festival, actors reported to rotate the tasks within the team following principles of horizontality. Besides setting the stage, organisers of such events are (often) performers and/or actors themselves. For acquiring different skills, taking over diverse roles and familiarising themselves with the gender studies knowledge, many of the participants remain connected to the politics of the movement as active contributors. Yet, as Person3 reports, there are some problematic aspects of DIY practices:

> [organising] was really exhausting and it was quite chaotic [. . .]. We were all volunteers, [which means that] you are struggling with the garbage before the concert, with the garbage after the concert, with the cleaning, with the sound engineers, with the equipment, you know with this nonchalant approach [. . .] the reason why I perhaps quit with the organisation was the fact that this place started to collapse physically. I remember that on the last concert some pipe broke and it stank horribly. I had a look at that space and realised how I no longer have the nerves for that.

The lack of resources and of stable logistics paired with unpaid work and unclear division of labour make 'DIY only' festivals organisationally fragile (see Table 3.1). For that matter, many DIY festivals may not endure long enough to be recognised in the local context.

In terms of content, DIY festivals, particularly smaller ones, are not under the pressure to attract wide audiences that would justify external grants. They have the freedom to experiment with the content, pushing and challenging narratives, norms and practices of the established activist community. In this disruption of the settled community culture, the participants often discursively "stretch" and "bend" (Lombardo, et al. 2009) the queer frame in making engagement "radical, inclusive, [and that] connects all kinds of politics" (Queer Belgrade in Table 3.1). Thus, the DIY festivals have the potential for reaching out to the broader circles of the local community and including new members of the activist community as active contributors. Yet, if DIY as an organisational principle is understood in the strict ideological terms, there might be a trade-off between activating the activist community and communicating with the local context. An event can have an impact on the former in transnational terms (for example, feminist anarchist networks) but remain detached from the immediate local environment. This happens when the content is too specific, and the staging venue, aesthetics, and networks of acquaintances are strongly associated with specific sub-cultural groups.

Potential for reaching both activist and local community: 'DIY plus' festivals

Some interviewed organisers expressed how they do not understand DIY in ideological terms and as a goal itself, but as an opportunity to set activist events in motion where the circumstances do not allow other forms. Person7, organising a festival attended by a heterogenous audience, described the process of making the programme "by relying on our instincts: let's do that, that would be great for our town, people would recognise that".

In such contexts, groups take 'DIY' as an auxiliary (and/or necessary) organisational principle, which is usually accompanied with the openness of the programme towards its nearest surrounding. The organisers of such events that are marked here as 'DIY plus' festivals combine art and activist forms in the programme. Besides volunteers, the people employed in organisations that initiate the festival organise the event. People working on the programmes are usually not professionals in film, theatre, music, or visual arts, but are attracted to festivals for the possibilities of creative expressions and transmission of political messages and knowledge through cultural forms.

Organisers that orientate the programme to the needs and the pulse of the local environment tend to acquire public institutions for the festival's staging venue, advertise the event in conventional media, place substantial parts of the programme during hours compatible with professional and private obligations; and, in some instances, these events offer services and programmes for children. The programme usually offers different participatory workshops which are adapted to the local context.

The activists in 'DIY plus' festivals still tend to have horizontal division of labour and (usually) rotate the tasks within the team. Though they are not engaged to such degree as protagonists in comparison to 'DIY only' programmes, the 'DIY plus' festivals also allow activists-organisers to express their creative and intellectual agency. The festivals provide a counterpoint to the everyday routinised practices of bureaucratic work in non-governmental organisations (NGOs). Though still unstable and insecure, the work in the registered organisations makes groups less volatile to external changes in comparison to 'DIY only' collectives.

Potential for reaching out to the local community, weaker in reaching in to the activist community: 'professional selective' festivals

Some interviewees share the agenda of challenging hegemonic norms of gender relations and sexuality, but express this dedication primarily through art. Person23 describes the motivation for staging the festival in the following words:

> I wanted to do a festival that was not converting already converted ones [...]. This is not a festival about activists and their gathering, or some people that do art. I wanted to celebrate art, but quality art that speaks for itself, but in the same time contains important messages.

Illustrative of such a professional selective approach is the organisers' aim to go beyond the social movement's community building to reach out the broader audiences that would appreciate the artistic arrangements besides the political message. The programmes in the selective professional festivals are based on a set of art standards which means that such festivals may not include many participants in the role of active contributors. Yet, they are important both for the activist community and the local community. They might bring ideas that the activists can use in their political agendas or in challenging settled activist culture. While most of the visitors may not become activists, they will be affected on an epistemological and on an ideational level through exposure to novel content. The selective professional festivals are organisationally more resilient for relying on paid and specialised staff.

Interaction of festivals and the local context

Responding to the question of how other politically left-oriented activists react to their programme, one of the organisers and performers (Person13) in a festival located in a prolific activist, cultural, and academic environment:

> I don't notice them on our events. I did notice some people from the academic scene, those left-intellectuals would visit some lectures we orga-nise, but that they would visit our festival...I doubt that, not really, I don't know if we have time enough to follow each other's events.

Though one might expect that festivals taking place in an environment that cherishes a tradition of progressive politics of gender and sexuality attract a diverse audience, it is the other way around. In such places, groups specialise in different aspects of such politics. In contexts with prolific production of cultural and educational content, as well as in the contexts characterised by a vivid sub-cultural and cultural scene, the offering tends to specialise, and so the audience tends to fragment and homogenise.

The organisers of festivals in small communities with the less prolific cultural offering and/or activist scene, in the words of Person22, recognised the advantage of their setting:

> The possibilities for going out, having a party, or visiting some event are limited. But as there is little going on, every weekend there is just one thing, you either go or don't go, there is no other choice. In that sense this minus of having only few things happening is good for us. Because people show up that wouldn't otherwise visit such performances, discussions or films, as they find it yucky, or they even might be against it.

Such festivals are organised in shared and public venues where they are often the only programme that occurs this month or week. Consequently, the festivals organised in small communities, both DIY and professional, attracted more heterogeneous audiences, defined as attracting people of diverse demo-graphic and lifestyle characteristics. This increased the potential of familiarising people with feminist ideas and LGBTQ activism who would otherwise avoid such content.

Conclusion

Festivals proved to be infrastructurally accessible tools for activists in making their own agenda visible and attracting supporters. This form has enabled the creation of the communities that build on the content and organisational practices that they perceived not to be represented in the institutionalised mechanisms for gender equality or the non-governmental sector (for example, queer theory, 'artivism', and anarchist feminism); or to bring subversive politics of gender and sexuality in places that previously lacked such content. Such an inexpensive form easily spread across different localities which made festivals the most salient tactical form of post-Yugoslav feminist and LGBTQ millennials.

Generally, this chapter demonstrates that festivals can improve accessibility, inclusion, and diversity inside the movements as well as, in case of feminist and LGBTQ groups, promote these values on the outside in the local communities. The festivals enabled inclusion of activists of diverse generational and ideological backgrounds in the settled social movements. As a form of community-oriented and participatory engagement, festivals made the politics that challenges hegemonic norms of gender and sexuality more visible in the local environment.

The organisational practices and the programme selection criteria were shown to be important factors in influencing the possibility of using festivals equally effectively on both fronts. In short, while DIY activist festivals 'reached in' to diverse members as active contributors, the professional-selective art festivals 'reached out' to familiarise the broader audiences with the movement's ideas. To gain deeper insights into this topic, future studies are required that consider the changes of these practices over time and that take into account other factors such as the festivals' content, the impact they have on the local communities, and question the interaction of festivals with other social movements, institutionalised state mechanisms, and academic knowledge production.

Questions for discussion

1. How can activists use festivals to consolidate the movement's core, strengthen affective bonds, and collective identity through the shared sense of exclusivity in festivals, and, at the same time, communicate their ideas and knowledge with the broader audience?
2. What are the strengths and what are the weaknesses of different organisational and programme models of activist festivals (DIY festivals, DIY plus, and professional selective festivals)?
3. Which organisational and programme-related festival model seems to be appropriate for a local context that lacks previous activist, academic, and/or art traditions that challenge dominant norms of gender and sexuality?

46   *Zorica Siročić*

References

Allison, M. T. and Hibbler, D. K. (2004). Organizational barriers to inclusion: Perspectives from the eecreation professional. *Leisure Sciences*, 26(3), 261–280.

Bain, A. and McLean, H. (2013). The artistic precariat. *Cambridge Journal of Regions, Economy and Society*, 6(1), 93–111.

Beck, U. (2000). *The Brave New World of Work*. Cambridge, MA: Polity Press.

Bennett, A., Taylor, J., and Woodward, I. (eds.) (2014). *The Festivalization of Culture*. Surrey: Ashgate.

Biel, J. (2012). *Beyond the Music: How Punks are Saving the World with DIY Ethics, Skills, and Values*. Portland, OR: Microcosm Publishing.

Browne, K. (2009). Womyn's separatist spaces: Rethinking spaces of difference and exclusion. *Transactions of the Institute of British Geographers*, 34(4), 541–556.

Browne, K. (2011). Lesbian separatist feminism at Michigan Womyn's Music Festival. *Feminism & Psychology*, 21(2), 248–256.

Charmaz, K. (2014). *Constructing Grounded Theory* (Introducing Qualitative Methods). 2nd ed. London: Sage Publications.

Clarke, A. and Jepson, A. (2011). Power and hegemony within a community festival. *International Journal of Event and Festival Management*, 2(1), 7–19.

Clarke, A. E. (2003). Situational analyses: Grounded theory mapping after the postmodern turn. *Symbolic Interaction*, 26(4), 553–576.

Collective, D. S., Goldman, E., De Cleyre, V., Dunbar-Ortiz, R., and Freeman, J. (2012). *Quiet Rumours: An Anarcha-Feminist Reader*. 3rd ed. Edinburgh: AK Press.

Dean, J. (2010). *Rethinking Contemporary Feminist Politics*. Basingstoke: Palgrave Macmillan.

Dean, J. and Aune, K. (2015). Feminism resurgent? Mapping contemporary feminist activisms in Europe. *Social Movement Studies*, 14(4), 375–395.

Dioli, I. (2011). *Belgrade, Queeroslavia*. OBC Transeuropa. www.balcanicaucaso.org/eng/Areas/Serbia/Belgrade-Queeroslavia-92030.

Eder, D., Staggenborg, S., and Sudderth, L. (1995). The national women's music festival: Collective identity and diversity in a lesbian-feminist community. *Journal of Contemporary Ethnography*, 23(4), 485–515.

Eleftheriadis, K. (2015). Organisational practices and prefigurative spaces in European queer festivals. *Social Movement Studies*, 14(6), 651–667.

Evans, E. (2015). *The Politics of Third Wave Feminisms: Neoliberalism, Intersectionality, and the State in Britain and the US*. Basingstoke: Palgrave Macmillan.

Finkel, R. (2009). A picture of the contemporary combined arts festival landscape. *Cultural Trends*, 18(1), 3–21.

Finkel, R. (2010). 'Dancing around the ring of fire': Social capital, tourism resistance, and gender dichotomies at Up Helly Aa in Lerwick, Shetland. *Event Management*, 14(4), 275–285.

Finkel, R., McGillivray, D., McPherson, G., and Robinson, P. (eds.) (2013). *Research Themes for Events*. Wallingford: CABI.

Florida, R. (2003). *The Rise of the Creative Class: And How It's Transforming Work, Leisure, Community and Everyday Life*. Melbourne: Pluto Press.

Gamson, J. (1995). Must identity movements self-destruct? A queer dilemma. *Social Problems*, 42(3), 390–407.

Gamson, J. (1996). The organizational shaping of collective identity: The case of lesbian and gay film festivals in New York. *Sociological Forum*, 11(2), 231–261.

Gamson, J. (1997). Messages of exclusion: Gender, movements, and symbolic boundaries. *Gender and Society*, 11(2), 178–199.

Getz, D. and Page, S. (2016). *Event Studies: Theory, Research, and Policy for Planned Events*. London: Routledge.

Hvala, T. (2010). The red dawns festival as a feminist-queer counterpublic. *Monitor ISH*, 12(1), 7–107.

Jeong, S. and Almeida Santos, C. (2004). Cultural politics and contested place identity. *Annals of Tourism Research*, 31(3), 640–656.

Jepson, A. and Clarke, A. (2013). Events and community development. In: R. Finkel, D. McGillivray, G. McPherson, P. Robinson (eds.) *Research Themes for Events*. Wallingford: CABI, 6–18.

Kajinić, S. (2012). Regional queer or queering the region? In: S. Mesquita, M. Katharina Wiedlack, K. Lasthofer (eds.) *Import-Export-Transport: Queer Theory, Queer Critique and Activism in Motion*. Vienna: Zaglossus.

Kajinić, S. (2016). The first European festival of lesbian and gay film was Yugoslav: Dismantling the geotemporality of Europeanisation in Slovenia. In: B. Bilić (ed.) *LGBT Activism and Europeanisation in the Post-Yugoslav Space: On the Rainbow Way to Europe*. London: Palgrave Macmillan, 59–80.

Laing, J. and Mair, J. (2015). Music festivals and social inclusion – The festival organisers' perspective. *Leisure Sciences*, 37(3), 252–268.

Lamond, I. and Platt, L. (eds.) (2016). *Critical Event Studies: Approaches to Research*. London: Palgrave Macmillan.

Lombardo, E., Meier, P., and Verloo, M. (eds.) (2009). *The Discursive Politics of Gender Equality: Stretching, Bending, and Policy-Making*. Routledge/ECPR Studies in European Political Science 59. London: Routledge.

Mansbridge, J. J. (1986). *Why We Lost the ERA*. Chicago: University of Chicago Press.

Markwell, K. and Waitt, G. (2013). Events and sexualities. In: R. Finkel, D. McGillivray, G. McPherson, P. Robinson (eds.) *Research Themes for Events*. Wallingford: CABI, 57–68.

Mattoni, A. (2014). The potentials of grounded theory in the study of social movements. In: D. della Porta (ed.) *Methodological Practices in Social Movement Research*. Oxford: Oxford University Press, 21–42.

de Peuter, G. (2014). Beyond the model worker: Surveying a creative precariat. *Culture Unbound: Journal of Current Cultural Research*, 6(1), 263–284.

Richards, S. (2017). *The Queer Film Festival: Popcorn and Politics*. London: Palgrave Macmillan.

Rosenberg, J. and Garofalo, G. (1998). Riot Grrrl: Revolutions from within. *Signs*, 23(3), 809–841.

Shepard, B. H. (2010). *Queer Political Performance and Protest: Play, Pleasure and Social Movement*. Routledge Advances in Sociology 41. New York: Routledge.

Shepard, B. H. (2011). *Play, Creativity, and Social Movements: If I Can't Dance, It's Not My Revolution*. Routledge Advances in Sociology 57. New York: Routledge.

Staggenborg, S. (1998). Social movement communities and cycles of protest: The emergence and maintenance of a local women's movement. *Social Problems*, 45(2), 180–204.

Staggenborg, S. (2001). Beyond culture versus politics: A case study of a local women's movement. *Gender & Society*, 15(4), 507–530.

Tilly, C. and Tarrow, S. (2015). *Contentious Politics*. Oxford: Oxford University Press.

4 Appleby Fair for all

Teresa Crew

Introduction

The events industry is a key driver of the UK government's 'growth agenda', as it is estimated that festivals, fairs, and other cultural events will bring in approximately £1.4 billion to the UK economy by 2020 (All Party Parliamentary Group. UK Events Industry 2013). Such events also have socio-cultural impacts, that is, enhanced community identity, celebration of culture, and individual pride through participation. Community events such as fairs are pivotal dates on the annual calendars of small towns and villages, and part of a new wave of specialist tourism (Jepson and Clarke 2013). The Appleby Fair, held annually in the week of the second Wednesday in June, is a major cultural gathering for the Gypsy Traveller community and attracts visitors who come to witness horse sales and the tradition of washing horses in the river. Billed as the biggest traditional Gypsy Fair in Europe, it attracts 10–15,000 Gypsies and Travellers and upwards of 30,000 other visitors. A common story is that the event traces its history back to James II, who, in 1685, granted a royal charter allowing a horse fair near the River Eden. Although the Charter only permitted the holding of a two-day fair or market on the second Thursday in April, the present fair is now held on a different date and in a different location (Eden District Council 2008). This chapter draws upon observations and interviews during Appleby Fair in 2017 to examine the commonalities of meanings for a selection of stakeholders. The first part of this chapter situates Appleby Fair in event studies, with a particular focus on the rural nature of the event, and how the mainstream media portray Travellers. Following a brief outline of research methods, the chapter discusses the common themes found when speaking to visitors, locals, and Gypsy Travellers at Appleby Fair.

The study of events

Critical event studies is an interdisciplinary field that encompasses definitions and types of events and events logistics. The discipline draws mainly from business management (Getz 2007), but as events involve people, sociology has some specific themes of interest. For instance, rural sociology highlights how small communities may be vulnerable to the social disruption caused by sudden large influxes of new residents (ibid.). This is especially apparent in the small town of Appleby-in-Westmorland in Cumbria, England, which has a population of 2,500 prior to the fair, rising to up to 50,000 during one week in June annually. Empirical studies of local festivals mainly point to the economic benefits; however, less is said of those in smaller communities, with their more limited resources, which may struggle to cope, specifically in terms of accommodation, infrastructure, and essential services. Arrivals of new residents, especially if they are from different cultural backgrounds, inevitably have an impact on the homogeneity of the community – even if the event is for a short time (Potter, et al. 2004). Incidentally, as Gypsies and Travellers are outnumbered at Appleby Fair, there are some who feel that this is destroying the cultural aspects of the fair (Eden District Council 2008). Holloway's (2005: 356) geographical research with residents of Appleby gives further texture to this. In interviews, the "true Gypsy" is judged as disappearing, being replaced by the "hanger on". The former being "nice people", the latter classed as responsible for any increases in criminal activity (Holloway 2005: 359).

Media representation of the Traveller community is laden with stereotypes. Often, they are represented as menacing invaders, vagabonds, and thieves; or, they are depicted as quaint people with horse drawn carriages. Amnesty International (2012) evaluated all newspaper coverage relating to Scottish Travellers over a four-month period. Specific stereotypes featured strongly: 38% of the articles made some connection to criminality while 32% referred to dirt and hygiene. Richardson's (2014) research examining political comment on the behaviour of the Roma population in Sheffield found similar keywords: migrants (n186), immigrants (n135), benefits (n81), rioting (n80), and tensions (n71). Holloway (2004) mapped newspaper coverage of Appleby Fair during 1945–1969, a period which saw intense debate about the future of the fair. When the future of the fair was not in doubt (late 1940s until the early 1960s), the discourse focused on Appleby Fair being "a traditional, centuries-old gathering" (Holloway 2004: 154). However, Holloway did note rumblings of discontent with the less traditional aspects, such as "modern dress and chrome-rimmed trailers" (ibid.). When the future of the fair was under threat (mid- to late-1960s), familiar themes re-emerged, including Travellers being portrayed as dirty, disruptive, and disease ridden. Today, the mainstream media has less explicit references to dirt or disease. This could be attributed to the dedicated work of Billy Welch, the 'Head Gypsy', who represents Gypsy Travellers, alongside the public sector and voluntary organisations who have been involved in co-ordinating the annual event for the last six years. Yet, concerns are still raised about animal welfare and antisocial behaviour (Multi-Agency Strategic Co-ordinating Group 2018), the emphasis always being on the behaviour of Gypsy Travellers rather than the huge numbers of non-Travellers who visit the event.

Research methods

The aim of this study was to understand the meanings that Gypsy Travellers, locals, and visitors attributed to the event. Two qualitative methods were used. Conversational interviewing, an approach used to generate data through talking about specific topics with participants in an informal way (Conrad and Schober 1999), was deemed suitable for capturing data in a noisy and fast-moving event. Participant observation was also employed, as it is an unobtrusive way to elicit a deeper understanding of the social dynamics of audiences (Mackellar 2013). Appleby Fair is booked up a year in advance, so the author visited the event on a day trip via coach on the Saturday, one of the busiest days. The strategy was to observe activities, and when the opportunity arose, speak to potential respondents. Table 4.1 outlines details of respondents.

Spradley's (1980) nine dimensions of descriptive observations: space, actors, activities, objects, acts, events, time, goals, and feelings were used to analyse the data.

One of the limitations of the study is that the sample was one of convenience and was conducted within the author's own geographical proximity and may not be representative of the whole population of Appleby Fair.

Appleby Fair: setting the scene

Appeby Fair is not an organised event in the contemporary sense, and, as such, there is no set programme. Most activities take place on either Fair Hill, the main Gypsy campsite, with some catering and trade stands (see Figure 4.1). More recently, Market Field, opened up by a local farmer several years ago, has also become an area for trading and catering. It is estimated that 50% of people who actually stop at the fair stay on Fair Hill. The rest stay on the surrounding privately owned fields (Connell 2015).

Stalls in both fields sell fine china and cut glassware as well as adult and children's clothes alongside horse bridles and cast iron cooking pots. The 'Gypsy way of life' is also represented by many fortune tellers, palm readers (see

Table 4.1 Description of respondents.

Group	Description of group
Visitor group one	Two couples, two men and two women
Visitor group two	Three women in cafe
Visitor group three	Woman sat on a wall
Visitor group four	Woman in MacMillan van
GT group one	Three young men with their horses at the river
GT group two	Three women, three children near the fortune stand
GT group three	Two women in a cafe
Local group one	Man and woman walking up to fields
Local group two	Woman in a cafe
Local group three	Man and woman running cafe
Local group four	Man and woman near 'flashing lane'
Local group five	Man running a burger van

Figure 4.1 Fair Hill.
Source: Photograph by the Author.

Figure 4.2) and music stalls, alongside traders making and selling pegs from elderwood. There are many fast food stalls mainly frequented by visitors.

Although most Irish Travellers are Roman Catholics and Romani Gypsies would describe themselves as Christians, Quarmby (2014: 1) talks of a

Figure 4.2 One of many fortune tellers at Appleby Fair.
Source: Photograph by the Author.

pentecostal revival, "where in a reversal of roles, Gypsy Travellers are seeing themselves as the preachers of the truth who want to heal the world as broken by a lack of faith". The march pictured in Figure 4.3 demonstrates the traditional with the modern as the young girl is taking a selfie of the march.

Figure 4.3 A religious march.
Source: Photograph by the Author.

Horse trading takes place at the 'flashing lane', the crossroads on Long Marton Road (see Figure 4.4). This is where horses are shown by trotting up and down the lane at speed. The 'flashing lane' is not suitable for anyone of limited mobility due to the risks associated with horses travelling at speed.

Figure 4.4 Horse-trading on 'flashing lane'.
Source: Photograph by the Author.

An iconic location on the River Eden often appears in local and national newspaper coverage of the event (see Figure 4.5). During the event, many of the horses are taken down to 'the Sands', near the town centre and beside the River Eden in a centuries-old traditional washing routine.

Findings and discussion

Events provide moments of collective meaning-making with the "creative activities of individuals and the constraining and empowering forces of social structures" (Li, et al. 2017) occurring simultaneously. Respondents were asked, 'What does Appleby Fair mean to you?'. Three common themes emerged:

- Gypsy Traveller culture
- business opportunities
- tradition versus commercialism.

Gypsy Traveller culture

A major aspect of the culture is travelling, seen as the 'ideal' way of life, as many have an aversion to bricks and mortar. This is done either as a single family unit or in

Figure 4.5 Horse-washing in the River Eden.
Source:Photograph by the Author.

a group, and is often related to work, visiting family, or attending weddings and funerals. Successive governments have brought in legal restrictions on nomadism, so Gypsy fairs such as Langley, Wickham, and Appleby are important to the culture, as they act as a meeting place for friends and family (Bhopal and Myers 2008).

Respondents talked of how attending the fair played an important role in maintaining their culture: "Appleby is the Traveller holiday, we always come here" [GT1]. All spoke of their excitement of meeting up with their extended family and friends: "Already I'm seeing people I've not seen all year. I won't see them until next year, or until a wedding" [GT2].

One respondent reported that it was the only time that they saw their family "as they [the respondent] live in bricks and mortar accommodation" [GT3]. Responses varied according to gender. Gypsy Traveller young men laughed as they referred to Appleby as being the place to: "find a wife" [GT1]. As gender relations are often characterised by patriarchy (Powell 2013), the young women respondents were not quite as explicit, instead talking about "meeting friends". Their mothers were more candid: "the men like trotting the horses in the water to show off their muscles; the girls like to walk up and down with their friends to catch a boys eye – in a respectable way mind!" [GT2]. Casey (2014) supports this idea of respectability, as Gypsy Traveller young women's lives are strictly monitored by their mothers, but they are normally allowed to start seeing boys and 'courting' when they were about sixteen. The expectation is they would meet their future husband at social events like Appleby Horse Fair (ibid.).

Travellers tend to have large 'extended' close-knit families where the man is the head of the family, and the woman is considered the heart. They often marry young and are reported to be respectful to their older relatives. Traditional gender roles are maintained with women being involved with the home and their extended family networks, and men feature more in the public sphere (Travellers Aid Trust 2009). There were clear examples of gender segregation at Appleby Fair amongst the older generation. Men were either in social groups with other men or helping their family/extended family display their horses by racing them up and down the 'flashing lane'. This was expected, as a positive correlation exists between doing physical jobs and gender roles. Several young men in research by Greenfields (2008) refer to work in terms of what the older men in the family did.

Walking around Appleby Fair, Gypsy Traveller women still have domestic responsibilities, such as keeping their van clean, but they spend parts of the day walking around the fair with children and extended members of the family. A common thread in interviews with Gypsy Traveller women was about the familial bond between mothers and daughters. The relatively unchanging family structures common to the majority of Gypsy Travellers means that there is an exceptionally high level of contact between mothers and daughters on a daily basis (Rogers 2015). GT group three, who described themselves as being older mothers, mentioned that whilst they look forward to Appleby Fair so they can see their wider family, the main pleasure they got from being there was spending time with their daughters and grandchildren away from everyday life. Despite gender segregation amongst older members of the family, there was evidence of some egalitarian gender roles, as men were also involved in childcare. But this was linked with the passing on of "Gypsy knowledge" [GT3]. Observations supported this: young girls working with their fathers to display the horses, and another father instructing his daughter to listen while he sold a horse. Although in the main, Traveller parents tend to encourage daughters to consider gendered professions/courses such as care work and training in personal services, for example, hairdressing or beauty therapy (Greenfields 2008).

Visitors and locals, in various ways, referred to their own participation as: "Taking part in and understanding more about an unfamiliar culture" [Local1]. As one local interviewee pointed out: "Appleby is like a fast track introduction to Gypsy Traveller life" [Local4]. All respondents (both local and non-Traveller visitors) reported having some prior knowledge or understanding of Traveller culture, citing examples such as travelling and close ties to family.

"My mum lives near a site and has no trouble. They helped her no end when she was unwell" [Local3]. Gypsy Travellers often return to the same spots in Appleby. For one local respondent, this has led to tentative friendships: "They've parked on my drive for years, I look forward to seeing them" [Local1]. A local tradesman discussed the ongoing business relationship they had through their shared appreciation of horses, pointing out: "They are nothing like what you think. They are very polite, always say thank you sir to my dad" [Local4]. A further Local who talked of his dealings with the community described how at one time he did not like the fair, but: "the more time I've spent with them [Gypsy Travellers] the more I like the fair and Travellers. Yes, it's messy and loud, but its great for the local area. If you are 'good' with them, they are 'good' with you" [Local3].

Interviews with locals were particularly positive, as they support anecdotal findings from Hirst and Crew (2013) that the longer the Travellers live in or visit a local community, the less likely they are to experience discrimination. This is perhaps surprising given the institutionalised prejudice and mistreatment Travellers face (Cemlyn, et al. 2009), which often means that developing mutually beneficial relationships can be challenging (Ryder 2011). It is notable that this is an under-researched area, as whilst there is a plethora of research on social exclusion and Gypsy Travellers, there is little (if any) examination of friendships between local communities and Gypsy Travellers.

Business opportunities

Throughout its history, it is clear that Gypsy Travellers see Appleby Fair as a place to do business. Buying a horse has its own ritual. Buyers are supposed to stand next to the horse they are interested in until the owner appears. There is a tradition of haggling: the buyer slaps the seller's palm with each bid, getting faster and faster. When they agree on the deal, the seller grabs the buyer's hand (Quarmby 2013). The horse trading starts as early as 8am, continuing into the early evening. Horses are raced and trotted up and down the 'flashing lane' to allow prospective buyers to assess their form and fitness. Listening to snippets of conversations, visitors appeared to be potential horse buyers but talked of the horses being "overpriced for the tourists". One bystander spoke of liking Appleby to buy horses: "I know that [well-known family] will be there and he gives me a good deal."

Despite the general emphasis on Gypsy and Traveller culture being male-dominated (Travellers Aid Trust 2009), there was a parallel economy where the younger women ran stalls selling antiques and traditional clothes and ran mobile beauty salons, while matriarchs charged for the ancient craft of fortune telling (Quarmby 2013).

Special fairs or events are often critical to local economies. Direct economic impact can be created as visitors increase their demand for goods and services at shops, restaurants, and hotels. There is often an increase in the output of those services, as producers react to meet increased demands (direct effects), and this has a knock-on effect where there is an increase in demand on their suppliers (indirect effect) (Niemczyk and Seweryn 2014). Although the fair itself is not a commercial enterprise as such (for example, it is not ticketed), it brings a great deal of trade to the town during the event and puts Appleby onto the tourist map. This can be seen to have year-round benefits for the town (Holloway 2005). Focus groups were held with Appleby residents in 2008, the majority of which owned local businesses. Most said that they did "very well out of the fair", but also said that they "would not be sorry if they never saw another one". The suggestion being that Appleby, as a town, benefited most, but many felt that profits were offset by other related costs (Eden District Council 2008). This is understandable, as local businesses may have to employ extra staff or make temporary alterations to their premises to cope with increased demand (Holloway 2005). Annual research by the Multi-Agency Strategic Co-ordinating Group (MASCG) is mainly quantitative, focusing on familiar themes of statistics on crime, animal cruelty, and cost. Statistics on recorded crime and incidents where owners of animals were given advice or assistance has gone down since the creation of the Co-ordinating Group. In 2017, the Co-ordinating Group developed greater links with local Police forces, local authorities as well as the Residents' and Travellers' Forum. An increased social media presence (daily updates via the website, Facebook, and Twitter) and daily meetings with community representatives from the resident and Traveller communities meant that the focus could be on the fair and its opportunities, as opposed to negative media coverage.

Appleby previously had a reputation of 'shutting up shop' when the fair came to town, but there were packed cafes and, to a lesser extent, pubs in the town that were open all day, alongside local catering vans on the main field when this research was being conducted. Potentially, this is due to the work of the Co-ordinating Group, as they reportedly work closely alongside restaurants, takeaway establishments, and licensed premises to listen to their concerns (MASCG 2018). However, there is no recent qualitative data to support this. Speaking to a local trader running a catering van, the business opportunities were clear: "I can understand that for someone who doesn't run a business they might be against it [the fair], But from a business point of view, from a tourist point of view, the fair brings us a lot" [Local5]. This view was also supported by a café owner: "It can be hard to cope with sometimes but we do a good business in the café. The fair pays my rent for the year" [Local3].

Walking around Appleby, business opportunities were not confined just to cafes and takeaway vans, as some locals used their back gardens to sell refreshments and advertised their drive for parking. MASCG (2018) shows the total external cost for the 2017 operation was £230,090, but the issue of financing remained a key issue for the future in order to reduce the cost to the tax payer. Yet, there also needs to be an attempt to calculate (if there has not already been an attempt) and promote the revenue that Appleby Fair brings. This is important, as Richardson (2006) who found "mess" and "cost" were two key themes that gripped the media and political debate on Roma and accession from new EU countries ten years ago. Rarely, if ever, do positive aspects of Travellers receive attention, and, as such, as the 'other' their voices are seldom heard and often misunderstood. The concentration by MASCG on how much money and time it costs the locality as opposed to what Travellers bring can further feed fear and paranoia and exacerbate community conflict.

Tradition versus commercialism

The interplay between the community associated with the event and that of those who host the event can contribute to the long-term sustainability of an event. Research by Acton (2007) reminds us that the majority of the villagers in Horsmonden supported the continuation of the annual horse fair in opposition to the local council decision to close the fair. Such acceptance by the local stakeholders enhances the potential for fairs such as Appleby to sustain itself. Attempts were made by local people to ban the event in the 1960s. However, as a further example of collective political action by Gypsy Travellers (ibid.), the Boswells, a respected Romani family, set up a defence committee to save the fair (Kendrick 2010). Further local concerns in the early 2000s led to Eden District Council commissioning research to gain an understanding of the views of stakeholders. The Cumbria Constabulary Survey (2002) surveyed respondents, 43% of whom were aged over 60. Respondents were most satisfied with the business income that the fair brought to the town as well as the publicity the town received. The Economic Impact Report (Jura Consultants 2004), which interviewed visitors and local traders, highlighted organisational issues. The Brough Fair Consultation (Appleby Fair Review Group, 2007) consisted of fourteen Gypsies and Travellers interviewed during Brough Horse Fair in September 2007. Over half of the travellers were very satisfied with the Appleby Fair experience; yet, there was great sympathy for the residents and the effects the fair may have on them. As such, Travellers talked of holding a meeting with residents of Appleby during the fair, the aim being to share concerns with residents, listen to their concerns, and develop a more mutual understanding (Eden District Council 2008). This led to the implementation of the aforementioned MASCG. Finally, an informal discussion took place with Irish Traveller Representatives, where concern was expressed about the increasing numbers of 'non-authentic' people allowed on the site. For instance, it was reported that only about 20% of the traders were Gypsies and Travellers. As Travellers were beginning to be outnumbered by visitors, the feeling was this was destroying the cultural, social, and economic aspect of the fair.

Events generate revenue and create jobs, but tourism can have negative impacts on the authenticity of cultural events, a modern urban lifestyle where 'everything is for sale' can play a part in destroying indigenous values and traditions. This view was supported when speaking to Gypsy Travellers and locals. For the Travellers there were concerns about Appleby Fair and cultural dilution: "There are more gorgers [non-Travellers] than us. It's not a Traveller horse fair anymore" [GT1]. As Holloway (2005) notes, in recent years, the fair has seen considerable changes with horse trading being overtaken by a growing market trade (see Figure 4.6.). Of concern was the amount of of 'gorger' traders: "They take over, theres too many stalls, we don't want them" [GT2]. Another Traveller talked of how: "Twenty years ago, Travellers would sell bridles or some china to each other. There isn't a need for anything else" [GT1]. There was also anger that some contentious cultural aspects of the fair were kept out of sight. A young Traveller bemoaned the lack of bare knuckle fighting, mentioning the "boxing booth that used to be up on the field"[GT1].

Local participants also worried about how the fair had changed: "It is a shame for the genuine Gypsies that these chavs turn up and ruin it for those that are there as Travellers!" [Local3]. This view was also supported by one local who had the same family "park" every year: "The traditional Gypsies who stay with me are very nice and are appalled by the way their lifestyle has been co-opted by those who are not willing to observe their own strict codes of behaviour and honour" [Local1]. These comments support Mayall's (1988) research on "inauthentic" others, where one becomes obsessed with identifying characteristics as an essential stage in identifying a separate "race" (cited in Powell 2007). The romantic myth, developed in the late nineteenth century, was that "Gypsies live in and off the country in harmony with nature" (Holloway 2005: 389). This outdated view ignores that Gypsies Travellers are now more likely to live in a house than a caravan.

As the previous section outlined, visitors came along to the fair to understand more about Gypsy Traveller culture. Speaking to visitors about their experiences, there was confusion when asked if their experience was 'authentic', it was just accepted that it was. They felt that if they saw or interacted with Travellers, then they were experiencing the culture. This view is unsurprising, as Ravenscroft and Matteucci's (2003) study of the San Fermin Festival in Pamplona, Spain, found that the cultural understanding shown by tourists was low. If there has been little interaction with a specific culture, as is likely the case of Gypsy Travellers, authenticity is likely to be judged in a positive manner. Chhabra, et al. (2001), who studied the Highland Games staged in the United States, found that visitors generally saw them as "authentic", even though the games involved a high degree of staging and took place far away from its original cultural roots in Scotland. Locals were more likely to quibble over authenticity, referring back to Appleby Fairs gone by. The overall consensus when speaking to the Traveller community at Appleby Fair indicated

Figure 4.6 'Gorger' trading stalls at the fair.
Source: Photograph by the Author.

that the very presence of outsiders shifts the construct of the fair from celebration to spectacle, from production to consumption, and Travellers from subject to object. How to meet the desires of the different stakeholders remains the unanswered question for now.

Conclusion and moving forward

This small-scale research study set out to investigate the meanings of Appleby Fair for both locals and a variety of visitors (including the Traveller community) and has shown commonalities: 1) it represents Gypsy Traveller culture; 2) it presents an opportunity for business; and, 3) it raises shared concerns over tradition versus commercialism. The study differs from existing research in so much that it generally portrays Appleby Fair as less of an invasion, but more of a friendly takeover. Concerns were raised that Gypsy horse fairs may be evolving to the point that they are losing their sense of authenticity. Future research of a comparison study with other Gypsy Traveller fairs, such as Selby Horse Fair, Kenilworth, or Wickham Horse Fair, would be useful to highlight if this is particular to Appleby Fair. Despite being time-consuming to negotiate access and build relationships, Finkel and Sang's (2016) participatory research approach is recommended to ensure that Gypsy Travellers are included throughout the research process.

From Hogmanay in Edinburgh to Bonfire Night in Lewes, Britain is home to a range of excellent festivals and events throughout the year. Yet, the discourse of such events is becoming more about those who wish to preserve the traditional culture of the event and those who advocate change.

Questions for discussion

1. In what ways is Appleby Fair a representation of Gypsy Traveller culture?
2. What effects are visitors having on the fair?
3. How can relationships between diverse stakeholders be negotiated at fairs?
4. In these changing times, can Appleby Fair be sustained as a 'Gypsy fair'?

References

Acton, T. (2007). Human rights as a perspective on entitlements: The debate over gypsy fairs in England. In M. Hayes and T. Acton (eds.) *Travellers, Gypsies, Roma: The Demonisation of Difference*. Newcastle: Cambridge Scholars Press.

All Party Parliamentary Group. UK Events Industry. (2013). *Inquiry Report into The International Competitiveness of the UK Events Industry*. London: House of Commons.

Amnesty International. (2012). *Caught in the Headlines: Scottish Media Coverage of Scottish Gypsy Travellers*. New York.

Appleby Fair Review Group. (2007). Brough Fair Consultation. In Eden District Council Housing and Communities Panel. *Appleby Fair scrutiny review: Final report*. Penrith: Eden District Council.

Appleby Fair Strategic Group (2017). Appleby Fair 2017 Evaluation Report. www.appleby fair.org/sites/default/files/attachments/ApplebyFairEvaluationReport_2017.pdf.

Bhopal, K. and Myers, M. (2008). *Insiders, Outsiders and Others: Gypsies and Identity*. Hertfordshire: University of Hertfordshire Press.

Casey, R. (2014). 'Caravan wives' and 'decent girls': Gypsy-Traveller women's perceptions of gender, culture and morality in the North of England. *Culture, Health & Sexuality*, 16, 7.

Cemlyn, S., Greenfields, M., Whitwell, C., and Matthews, Z. (2009). *Inequalities Experienced by Gypsy and Traveller Communities: A Review*. Research Report no. 12. London: Equality and Human Rights Commission.

Chhabra, D., Healy, R., and Sills, E. (2001). Staged authenticity and heritage tourism. *Annals of Tourism Research*, 30(3), 702–719.

Connell, A. (2015). *Appleby Gypsy Horse Fair: Mythology, Origins, Evolution and Evaluation*. Kendal: Titus Wilson & Son.

Conrad, F. and Schober, M. (1999). Conversational interviewing and data quality. *Proceedings of the Federal Committee on Statistical Methodology Research Conference*.

Cumbria Constabulary. (2002). Cumbria Constabulary Survey. In Eden District Council Housing and Communities Panel. *Appleby Fair scrutiny review: Final report*. Penrith: Eden District Council.

Eden District Council. (2008). *Housing and Communities Panel*. Appleby Fair Scrutiny Review. Penrith.

Finkel, R. and Sang, K. (2016). Participatory research: Case study of a community event. In I. Lamond and L. Platt (eds.) *Critical Event Studies: Approaches to Research*. London: Palgrave Macmillan.

Getz, D. (2007). *Event Studies: Theory, Research and Policy for Planned Events*. Oxford: Butterworth-Heinemann.

Greenfields, M. (2008). *A Good Job for a Traveller? Exploring Gypsy and Travellers' Perceptions of Health and Social Care Careers. A Report for Aim Higher South East*. Buckinghamshire: New University.

Hirst, D. and Crew, T. (2013). *Gypsy and Traveller Accommodation Needs Assessment*. Cardiff: Welsh Government.

Holloway, S. (2004). Rural roots, rural routes: Discourses of rural self and travelling other in debates about the future of Appleby New Fair, 1945–1969. *Journal of Rural Studies*, 20, 143–156.

Holloway, S. (2005). Articulating otherness: White rural residents talk about Gypsy-Travellers. *Transactions of the Institute of British Geographers*, 30, 351–367.

Jepson, A. and Clarke, A. (2013). Events and community development. In R. Finkel, D. McGillivray, G. McPherson, P. Robinson (eds.) *Research Themes in Events*. Walingford: CABI.

Jura Consultants. (2004). Economic Impact Report. In Eden District Council Housing and Communities Panel. *Appleby Fair scrutiny review: Final report*. Penrith: Eden District Council.

Kendrick, D. (2010). *The A to Z of the Gypsies (Romanies)*. Maryland: Rowman & Littlefield.

Li, J., Moore, D., and Smythe, S. (2017). Voices from the 'heart': Understanding a community- engaged festival in Vancouver's Downtown Eastside. *Journal of Contemporary Ethnography*, 1–27. doi: 10.1177/0891241617696808.

Mackellar, J. (2013). Participant observation at events: Theory, practice and potential. *International Journal of Event and Festival Management*, 4(1), 56–65.

Mayall, D. (1988). *Gypsy-Travellers in Nineteenth Century Society*. Cambridge: Cambridge University Press.

Multi-Agency Strategic Co-ordinating Group (MASGG). (2018). *Appleby Fair 2017 Evaluation Report*. Penrith.

Niemczyk, A. and Seweryn, R. (2014). Consumption of specific tourist products – The value of participation in mega-event and its influence in shaping visitor loyalty to a destination. *Journal of International Studies*, 7(1), 109–121.

Potter, J., Cantarero, R., Yan, W., Larrick, S., and Ramirez-Salazar, B. (2004). A case study of the impact of population influx on a small community in Nebraska. *Great Plains Research: A Journal of Natural and Social Sciences*, 716. http://digitalcommons.unl.edu/cgi/viewcontent.cgi?article=1713&context=greatplainsresearch.

Powell, R. (2013). Loic Waquant's 'ghetto' and ethnic minority segregation in the UK: The neglected case of Gypsy-Travellers. *International Journal of Urban and Regional Research*, 37, 1.

Quarmby, K. (2013). *No Place to Call Home: Inside the Real Lives of Gypsies and Travellers*. London: Oneworld Publications.

Quarmby, K. (2014). *Romani Pilgrims: Europe's New Moral Force*. London: Newsweek Insights.

Ravenscroft, N. and Matteucci, X. (2003). The festival as carnivalesque: Social governance and control at Pamplona's San Fermin Fiesta. *Tourism, Culture and Communication*, 4(1), 1–15.

Richardson, J. (2006). An examination of the treatment of Gypsies and Travellers: Human rights in an expanding Europe? *Paper presented at the ENHR Conference 'Housing in an Expanding Europe: Theory, Policy, Participation and Implementation'*, Ljubljana, Slovenia.

Richardson, J. (2014). Roma in the news: An examination of media and political discourse and what needs to change. *People, Place and Policy*, 8(1), 51–64.

Rogers, C. (2015). *Beyond Bereavement: The Impact of Bereavement on the Resilience of Children and Families. Today's Children – Tomorrow's Parents*.

Ryder, A. (2011). *Gypsies and Travellers and the Third Sector*. Third Sector Research Centre. Working Paper 63. www.birmingham.ac.uk/generic/tsrc/documents/tsrc/working-papers/working-paper-63.pdf.

Spradley J. (1980). *Participant Observation*. Fort Worth: Cengage Learning.

Travellers Aid Trust. (2009). A grant-makers guide to supporting gypsies and travellers. www.travellersaidtrust.org/pdfs/grantmakersguide.pdf.

5 Agricultural shows

The challenge of accessibility

Caroline A. Wiscombe

Introduction

There is a rich tradition of events throughout many counties (Bowdin, et al. 2006). Events are temporary organised occasions which stem from a process of planning and management that bring together people and location in a meaningful way (Getz and Page 2016). Events can be described by typology, for example special events, mega-events, festivals, hallmark events, cultural events and community events. However, they can also be described by size, scope, form (such as music, art or sport) and setting (Bowdin, et al. 2006; Getz and Page 2016; Robinson, et al. 2010).

Agricultural shows are events steeped in rural life and history. They are complex cultural phenomena which depend on the surrounding communities to support the agricultural show through:

- volunteering to help plan and run them;
- competing in a range of classes, showing produce, animals or equipment;
- paying to attend;
- involving sponsorship, donation or membership.

If an event is described as accessible, then it is assumed it is easy for people to reach or get into. If something is accessible to people, upon which events depend, they can easily use or obtain it. Accessibility is a term which has become usually associated with disability (Church and Marston 2003; Connell and Sanford 2001; Rimmer, et al. 2005) and, more recently, with technology (Adam and Kreps 2009; Annable, et al. 2007; Ellis and Kent 2011). Defining accessibility for events is important and helps move away from stereotypical assumptions. This empirical research stretches our understanding and definition of the term accessibility to include both human and non-human participation at events and festivals celebrating rural life or located in rural locations. The research does include accessibility issues for people (participants, spectator and volunteers), but also those for animals, agricultural machinery, trade stands, entertainment, hospitality and technology (Farrington and Farrington 2005; Getz 2009; Holloway, et al. 2010; Velaga, et al. 2012).

The research for this chapter is rooted in analysis of data from three agricultural shows and is embedded in ethnographic approaches. It does not seek to analyse the shows and their effect on social processes (Anderson 2003; Holloway 2004), but rather aligns with Gray (2010) in seeking how the "logistics of design" (Handelman 1998) push forward our knowledge, and, in this case, our understanding of contemporary events management.

Agricultural shows

Agricultural shows are manifestations of rural life in the UK and include county shows, county fairs, and other agricultural events at a local, regional, county, and national level (Gray 2010; Holloway 2004). They are public events, charging admittance fees, showcasing everything associated with the land: animals, food, equipment, skills, and, in many instances, leisure and recreational pursuits (Henryks, et al. 2016). Holloway (2004) suggests that agricultural shows are part of a sector strategy to re-image farming with the convergence of farmers and the farming community, allowing agricultural societies to use the opportunity to stage manage encounters between them and non-farmers. Interviews and observations used in this research did not encounter such sardonic approaches and resulting negative connotation of manipulation. Instead, the research shows agricultural shows are honest representations of agribusiness and environmental practices in the rural communities they represent. The events themselves are changing to adapt to the diversification encountered amongst those farming cultures and the farming community, and, with the agricultural associations representing them, are doing much more than simply repositioning in relation to gaining increased consumption (Allen and Watson 2017; Hart 2017; MAS 2017; Watson 2017).

Agricultural shows are key sites of knowledge exchange (Goulet 2013), and the atmosphere created suggest that farmers and the providers of products and services to them use these occasions to make contacts and relationships which, because of the rural nature of farming, may otherwise be difficult (Rychen and Zimmermann 2008). Discussions and informal meetings are a common facet in sharing best practice amongst the farming community (Fisher 2013). For some external visitors, smaller agricultural shows can appear as if they are simply an opportunity for farmers to meet and have a drink (Gray 2010); yet, the "rural buzz" they create (Thomas 2016) spreads wider than the showground. Thomas (2016) reports that 22% of people who watched coverage of the Royal Welsh Show are based outside the UK, and the spread of social media extends the potential for horizontal (farmer to farmer) and vertical (farmer to consumer or farmer to supplier) knowledge exchange through initial interactions at the showground.

Agricultural shows continue to evolve to capture the diversity and range of rural enterprises which have been forced to adapt and change; for example, the Anglesey Show in Wales has said to have "developed, adapted and grown to fit the changes in society" (AAS 2018) and provides a link between the Welsh farming community and local tourism needs. Their success can be measured in numbers of visitors, which have grown from around 20,000 to 60,000 over the last 50 years. However, the sustainability of overall event support (which is very dependent upon volunteers) and continuity of agricultural shows as a phenomena also appear to be important measures.

Case study research

Three agricultural shows have formed the basis of this case study research each having different location issues, transport facilities, price points, expected number of visitors and attractions which the event organisers need to plan for. The background of these will be provided for contextualisation of the findings from the empirical research based on ethnography and participant observation.

Ennerdale and Kinniside Show

Ennerdale and Kinniside Show (E&KS) is held in rural Cumbria; it is a hub, as a community and cultural occasion attracting hundreds of competitors and visitors to its one day event. It is described by its show secretary as a traditional family show which is accessible and benefits from an ideal location (Whitehaven News 2016). E&KS began its life in association with the local primary school thus education is embedded in its core ethos. However, the show occupies a bespoke spatial configuration which like many other very rural events, such as the Appleby Horse Fair, captures a specific unique cultural heritage and representation of agricultural activities which appears to be more to do with the local community than education of visitors (Gray 2010); yet, many tourists attend, particularly if the weather is good.

The showground is accessed via tiny lanes which lead to the remote location of Kinniside, near Ennerdale Water, in the isolated valley of Ennerdale. It offers a range of competitions and attractions including horse shows, fell runners, hound trails, poultry showing, vintage tractor displays and car enthusiasts. It also hosts a uniquely regional sport as part of its show, that of Cumbrian wrestling. There is no public transport to the venue, with the nearest bus routes stopping very irregularly some three miles away and in 2018 entry to the one-day show cost £5 per adult with children under 12 attending free. There are no concessions. The showground is open to the public from 9am with parking available in nearby fields and spectators run to hundreds, rather than thousands, of visitors.

The Melplash Show

The Melplash Show (MS) was founded in the 1840s and began as a ploughing competition between different villages. The Melplash Agricultural Society Ltd, a charitable company limited by guarantee, was formed from the success of those early ploughing matches. The MS is held on the third Thursday of August each year and attracted 18,000 visitors in 2016 (Bol 2016). The Melplash Show Society is a registered charity with the aim of "promoting and improving agriculture and horticulture in West Dorset for the public benefit" (MAS 2018a). Visitors, as well as the local community, visit the show year after year with tourists planning their holidays to coincide with show day.

The Melplash Showground is accessed via a number of trunk roads with regular bus routes to mainline railway stations at Dorchester and Weymouth. Described by the show secretary as "a great opportunity to showcase West Dorset and it is a real celebration of agriculture" (Hart in Bol 2016), the show is the major income stream for the Melplash Agricultural Society (MAS), thus allowing it to meet its charitable aims with bursaries of over £10,000 being paid to ten agricultural students (MAS 2016).

Ticket prices for the 2018 show are £16 (£14 if bought online in advance) with those under 16 admitted free. A number of free services are offered to those travelling to the event; bus travel is offered by a local company from local towns and villages, park and ride services from locally provided car parks, and at-the-show parking, with identified disability bays within a few hundred yards from the main entrances. Mobility services (scooters and wheelchairs) are provided via a third-party service which can be booked and paid for in advance. The showground is open to the public from 8.30am until 6pm on show day (MAS 2018b). There is a limited telephone signal and no Wi-Fi provided to trade stands or the public although the show secretary's tent receives signal for the purposes of social media monitoring and synching competition results (Wiscombe 2017).

The Devon County Show

The Devon County Show (DCS) was first run in 1872 with an attendance of 25,000 people. In 2015, it was estimated that over 100,000 people attended whilst it regularly attracts 90,000 spectators across its three-day programme of activities. In 2014, it faced difficulties caused by the weather and was forced to close down for the first time in its 119-year history because of safety concerns following vehicles being trapped in its parking facilities (BBC 2014). Across its three show days, the 150-acre showground is packed with a vast array of animals, farm equipment, entertainment and goods and services targeting agricultural, regional and tourist communities. The bus stop is right outside the showground with regular public transport into the city of Exeter which provides excellent transport links to other parts of the South West and to other more urban locations such as Bristol. Parking at the showground is free and has been a major investment in land allocation, time, and planning (see Figure 5.1), and, whilst extra shuttle buses operate from Exeter Bus Station to the showground throughout the three days, charges are payable directly to the bus company.

Pricing is more complex than at either of the other two shows. Ticket prices accommodate one-day visits and three-day passes, which are linked to full membership of the Devon County Agricultural Association. One-day tickets for adults are £21 on the day or £19 if purchased in advance. Over-60s are offered

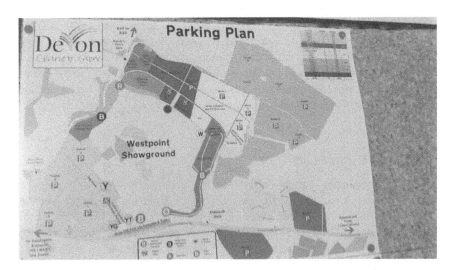

Figure 5.1 Map showing extensive parking arrangements at Devon County Show.
Source: Photograph by the author.

concessionary prices per day, and special deals on Thursday and Friday. Prices for children (under 16) also vary according to the day of the visit. However, on Saturday, one adult can take two children in for free. On all days, those under five years old go free. Wheelchairs and disability scooters can be hired from a third-party service. Wi-Fi and phone signals are readily available (DCAA 2017a).

The role of the agricultural show is extensive and can be vital for rural economies. It seeks to provide education, knowledge exchange, and a showcase for the rural community. DCS suggests that its three-day event is planned to capture "all things Devon" (Allen and Watson 2017) and showcase the county; "it is a gigantic shop window for local agriculture, horticulture, food and drink, rural crafts, and forestry" (DCAA 2017b), which, in 2018, also includes consideration of the coastline in which the county sits. The show also plays a real role in tourist attraction, where the media surrounding it brings visitors to the area. The focus is on fun learning rather than education (Allen and Watson 2017), as it introduces a wide range of visitors to the six huge arenas which display food and drink, flower and garden displays, crafts, country life, trade stands offering a wealth of goods, and lots of traditional entertainment.

Agricultural shows come in a range of sizes, but each has accessibility issues in terms of location, logistics and societal considerations for people, animals, equipment and machinery; for example, human and non-human participation at DCS in 2017 included visitors plus 450 stewards, 800 trade exhibitors, 70 student helpers, 1,000 horse exhibitors entered into 1,400 classes of competition, 1,400 head of sheep and nearly 600 cattle. In addition, there were 90+ angora goats, alpacas, goats, pigs, poultry, cavies (a type of rodent), and bees. MS saw cattle, horse, donkeys, pigs, ferrets, vintage tractors and a vast range of crafts and handicrafts facilitated into the showground alongside a parade of foxhounds and beagles, the 'Stampede Stunt Company', cookery demonstrations, and falcons; the only thing missing was the poultry due to an outbreak of avian flu earlier in the year. At E&KS, there was an equally eclectic, though smaller, mix of horses, dogs, hounds, sheep, handicrafts, photography, artwork, flowers, vegetables and produce including bread, scones and preserves together with wrestlers and fell runners.

Findings and discussion

Human participants in agricultural shows are challenged by a wide range of accessibility issues including price, location, travel, culture, and internet access at the showgrounds, which create events management challenges for show organisers (see Figure 5.2). For human participants, price, culture, and, for some, organisational structures cause accessibility issues not shared by non-humans.

Location, parking, travel, access, and egress also resonate as key accessibility issues for non-human participants, whether they are there to enter competitions or to be part of a show exhibit (see Figure 5.3).

Bio-security practices and animal husbandry are absolutely vital for all animals and livestock to stop the spread of endemic and exotic diseases, but they also have an impact on humans due to the potential of cross-contamination of zoonotic viruses. Legislation to control spread of such disease and appropriate animal husbandry are perceived barriers for some participants; yet, the safety and security of all show-goers are paramount.

MS, DCS, and E&KS all utilise rural areas. DCS is the only site that is only used for shows and events all year round and, thus, has some infrastructure, including electricity. Even so, it is a blank canvas into which everything else needs to be structured. MS and E&KS fields are predominately used for livestock or other agricultural use, for example crops, and, thus, a substantial amount of equipment, goods, services, and supplies are essential to make the fields accessible to human and non-human participants. In addition, the fields need to be cleared of animals 28 days before the event due to bio-security legislation.

Supplies include providing electricity, toilets, food, drink, furniture, agricultural housing, animal feedstuffs, cash, and marquees. Therefore, as well as considering location, price, travel, parking, access, and egress at the showground, the event organisers need to ensure co-ordination of all other facilities. In doing so, accessibility issues for participants gain a contextual significance different to that of other events which may take place in purpose-built stadia or arenas.

The spatial use of the surroundings has an impact on availability of the internet, and, thus, technology, including its adoption and adaptation, needs to be considered by event organisers when planning, running, organising, and marketing the shows. Even at DCS, signal access is weak and unpredictable despite the office network in use; thus, in the running of the show, the traders'

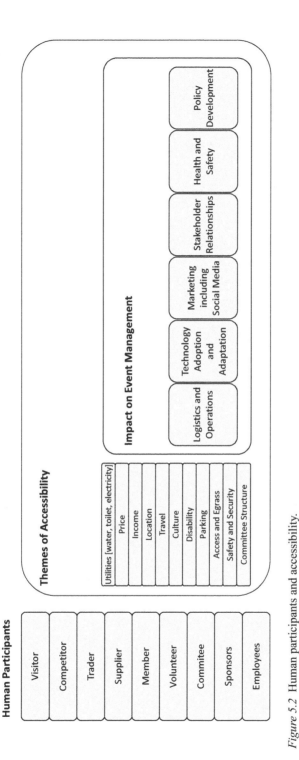

Figure 5.2 Human participants and accessibility.
Source: by the authors.

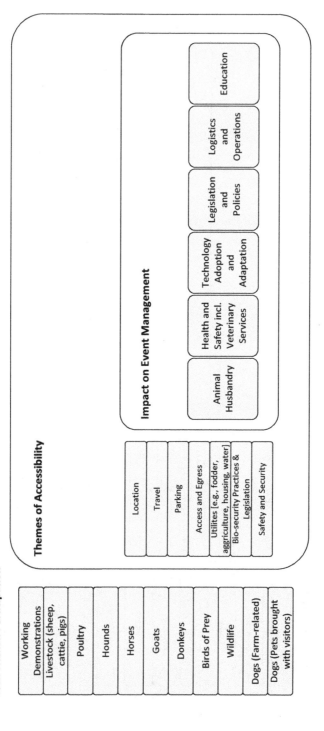

Figure 5.3 Accessibility issues for non-human participants.
Source: by the authors.

ability to use credit card machines – or even mobile phones at EK&S – and the adoption of interactive technology at the grounds becomes a challenge. Information boards which might be linked to show apps are currently not possible to push the format and interaction for the shows further.

In today's technological age, this lack of internet access is a clear challenge for event organisers as they strive to market via social media and improve their product experience and accessibility. Yet, social media has become an important facet of MS and DCS marketing campaigns. Twitter, Facebook and Instagram are all important mediums for the marketing and promotion of the events. Indeed, as of January 2018, MS has 3,576 followers on Twitter and DCS 15,000. This is especially important because many potential visitors interact via electronic devices in many aspects of leisure activity; for example, payment for goods and services is expected via contactless whilst entry to the show might be expected via barcode rather than a physical ticket. Also, biosecurity practices can be enhanced using technology to track animal movements. This year, DCS adopted technology to track the entry of the sheep to the showground using their ear tags.

Finally, this chapter began by challenging the definition of accessibility as not just being about disability; yet, this group of visitors cannot be ignored. Given almost one in five people in the UK have a disability, which equates to around 13.3 million people (DLF 2018), it is part of the challenge for event organisers to ensure that their provision is accessible to the disabled population. Examples from these three agricultural shows include:

- A mother with an autistic son who was worried about paying the £16 entrance fee for herself to accompany her charge, who may then need to leave within an hour or two.
- Those confirming that disabled parking arrangements were close enough to the showground.
- An adult carer whose adult charge's benefit payments could not cover both entrance fees.
- A member who wanted to access the members pavilion needed to drive into the showground, but could not do so by the morning deadline. A golf buggy was used to collect them from the main car park.

These queries were dealt with on a one-to-one basis and each provided with appropriate access solutions. Whilst many organisations appear to have difficulties in providing access for the disabled, this individual approach to understanding the problems and providing solutions creates a caring and responsive approach which appears to be very much appreciated by the visitor. In addition, using this approach, the agricultural show organisers show a commitment to meeting the requirements of the Equality Act 2010 which requires reasonable adjustment to be made to ensure accessibility (CAB 2018).

At both DCS and MS, those with mobility disabilities are guided via the webpage and the show office to the provision of scooters, wheelchairs, and other aids supplied via a third party for hire at the showground. At these venues, the specialist supplier has gained specific quality marks for its equipment, which makes for a safe and secure day out for the visitor and a clear logistical solution for the event manager. It was found that a wide range of stakeholders including the community, utility companies, authorities (police, traffic, and Department of the Environment, Food, and Rural Affairs), accommodation providers, specialist services, local and regional government officers, sponsors, and suppliers work together with show staff and volunteers to deliver an accessible event experience for all participants.

Conclusion

The size and scope of issues which relate to accessibility at agricultural shows should not be underestimated. They provide huge logistical and operational challenges partly because agricultural shows are, by their very nature, held in some very inaccessible locations. Many large shows, such as the DCS, have moved to bespoke showgrounds, but others, such as MS and E&KS, are homed in the rural fields and the geographical landscapes they seek to represent. This brings accessibility issues of transport, parking, and, indeed, roads to both human and non-human participants.

The shows are challenging for the surrounding areas, bringing with them congestion and interference in daily lives, if only for a short time. Other societal considerations include the external observation of an inaccessible culture which agricultural associations are fighting to break down and, in many ways, succeeding. Moving toward publishing their charitable aims more widely, and indeed their expenses, would help attract new populations to understand the pricing strategies adopted which can appear expensive. Breaking down some of the cultural barriers would help to drive up membership which in turn provides such excellent value for money.

Increased use of science is clearly evident in the control of animal disease, and technology greatly assists this. However, availability of technology in rural areas is limited; until all geographical areas, including rural fields, are supported by high speed broadband networks, some aspects of technology are limited. This includes the use of social media marketing on the day and the use of technology to enhance animal biosecurity. Currently, apps and other tools cannot be integrated into the shows to enhance the product for today's leisure market, and at MS and E&KS, all trading on the showground has to be in cash, rather than using online payment methods. Transversely, the shows that have adopted online booking systems can sell tickets via the web but then have to use other face-to-face, including cash, outlets to accommodate their varied marketplace.

Agricultural shows hum with excitement; the "rural buzz" defined by Thomas (2016) can be heard all around the grounds. The planning, organising, and knowledge needed to run such events are enormous, and the logistics and operations complex. Human interaction and communication is imperative in dealing with such a wide range of issues across such a multifaceted range of stakeholders, and, thus, accessibility continues to evolve within agricultural shows allowing more and more people to experience their vibrancy.

Acknowledgements

With thanks to: Devon County Agricultural Association and the Devon County Show staff and volunteers; Ennerdale and Kinniside Show and the wider Ennerdale Community; Melplash Agricultural Association and the Melplash Show staff and volunteers.

Questions for discussion

1. How could technology further aid accessibility when connectivity in rural locations is still a major problem?
2. Mobility scooters and electric wheelchairs are causing some health and safety issues as their use at agricultural shows are growing. What solutions to this problem could you suggest, whilst not limiting access to disabled visitors?
3. The agricultural show committees have a unique and complex role in organising, planning, and running their events due to the eclectic mix of stakeholders and participants. What skills and characteristics do you think they need over and above those of other event organisers?

References

AAS. (2018). Anglesey agricultural show: A brief history. www.angleseyshow.org.uk/en/the-society/history.

Adam, A. and Kreps, D. (2009). Disability and discourses of web accessibility. *Information, Communication & Society*, 12(7), 1041–1058.

Allen, O. and Watson, E. (2017). *Interview on the Planning, Organisation, Management and Control of Devon County Show*. Exeter: Devon County Show Offices. 1 December.

Anderson, K. (2003). White Natures: Sydney's royal agricultural show in post-humanist perspective. *Transactions of the Institute of British Geographers*, 28(4), 422–441.

Annable, G., Goggin, G., and Stienstra, D. (2007). Accessibility, disability, and inclusion in Information Technologies: Introduction. *The Information Society: An International Journal*, 23(3), 145-147.

BBC. (2014). Safety concerns cancel Devon County Show's final day. www.bbc.co.uk/news/uk-england-devon-27538140.

Bol, D. (2016). Record Crowds visit Melplash Show 2016 for 'celebration of agriculture'. *Bridport & Lyme Regis News*. www.bridportnews.co.uk/news/14705629.PICTURES__Record_crowds_flock_to_Melplash_Show_2016_for__celebration_of_agriculture_/.

Bowdin, G., O'Toole, W., Allen, J., Harris, R., and McDonnell, I. (2006). *Events Management*. London: Routledge.

CAB. (2018). The Equality Act 2010: duty to make reasonable adjustments for disabled people. www.citizensadvice.org.uk/law-and-courts/discrimination/what-are-the-different-types-of-discrimination/duty-to-make-reasonable-adjustments-for-disabled-people/.

Church, R. L. and Marston, J. R. (2003). Measuring accessibility for people with a disability. *Geographical Analysis*, 35(1), 83–96.

Connell, B. R. and Sanford, J. A. (2001). Difficulty, dependence, and housing accessibility for people aging with a disability. *Journal of Architectural and Planning Research*, 18(3), 234–242.

DCAA. (2017a). Devon County Show – Frequently asked questions. www.devoncounty show.co.uk/frequently-asked-questions.

DCAA. (2017b). Devon County Show – homepage. www.devoncountyshow.co.uk/.

DLF. (2018). Key facts provided by the Disabled Living Foundation. www.dlf.org.uk/ content/key-facts.

Ellis, K. and Kent, M. (2011). *Disability and New Media*. London: Routledge.

Farrington, J. and Farrington, C. (2005). Rural accessibility, social inclusion and social justice: Towards conceptualisation. *Journal of Transport Geography*, 13(1), 1–12.

Fisher, R. (2013). 'A gentleman's handshake': The role of social capital and trust in transforming information into usable knowledge. *Journal of Rural Studies*, 31 13–22.

Getz, D. (2009). Policy for sustainable and responsible festivals and events: Institutionaliza-tion of a new paradigm. *Journal of Policy Research in Tourism, Leisure and Events*, 1(1), 61–78.

Getz, D. and Page, S. J. (2016). *Event Studies: Theory, Research and Policy for Planned Events*. London: Routledge.

Goulet, F. (2013). Narratives of experience and production of knowledge within farmers' groups. *Journal of Rural Studies*, 32 439–447.

Gray, J. (2010). Local agricultural shows in the Scottish Borders. *The Journal of the Royal Anthropological Institute*, 16(2), 347–371.

Handelman, D. (1998). *Models and Mirrors: Towards an Anthropology of Public Events*. London: Berghahn books.

Hart, L. (2017). *An Invitation to the Melplash Show Office for Preliminary Research Discussions*. Bridport: Melplash Show Office. 5 July.

Henryks, J., Ecker, S., Turner, B., Denness, B., and Zobel-Zubrzycka, H. (2016). Agricul-tural show awards: A brief exploration of their role marketing food products. *Journal of International Food & Agribusiness Marketing*, 28(4), 315–329.

Holloway, I., Brown, L., and Shipway, R. (2010). Meaning not measurement: Using ethnography to bring a deeper understanding to the participant experience of festivals and events. *International Journal of Event and Festival Management*, 1(1), 74–85.

Holloway, L. (2004). Showing and telling farming: Agricultural shows and re-imaging British agriculture. *Journal of Rural Studies*, 20(3), 319–330.

MAS. (2016). Annual report and financial statements for the year ended 31 October 2016. http://apps.charitycommission.gov.uk/Accounts/Ends01/0001130201_AC_2016 1031_E_C.PDF.

MAS. (2017). *Interviews and Observations*. Bridport: Melplash Agricultural Society. 20–26 August.

MAS. (2018a). About the Melplash Agricutural Society. www.melplashshow.co.uk/about/.

MAS. (2018b). Melplash show 2018 – Tickets. www.melplashshow.co.uk/tickets/.

Rimmer, J. H., Riley, B., Wang, E., and Rauworth, A. (2005). Accessibility of health clubs for people with mobility disabilities and visual impairments. *American Journal of Public Health*, 95(11), 2022–2028.

Robinson, P., Wale, D., and Dickson, G. (2010). *Events Management*. Oxford: CABI.

Rychen, F. and Zimmermann, J. B. (2008). Clusters in the global knowledge-based economy: Knowledge gatekeepers and temporary proximity. *Regional Studies*, 42(6), 767–776.

Thomas, G. (2016). The Royal Welsh Show: Facilitating rural buzz. *Regional Studies, Regional Science*, 3(1), 428–436.

Velaga, N. R., Beecroft, M., Nelson, J. D., Corsar, D., and Edwards, P. (2012). Transport poverty meets the digital divide: Accessibility and connectivity in rural communities. *Journal of Transport Geography*, 21, 102–112.

Watson, E. (2017). *Introductory Discussion about the Proposed Research*. Exeter: Devon County Show Office. 5 July.

Whitehaven News. (2016). It's showtime at Ennerdale. www.whitehavennews.co.uk/news/ Its-showtime-at-Ennerdale-0fe7146f-4bae-4a0b-9a51-1471c3bdb61d-ds.

Wiscombe, C. (2017). Events management – Agricultural shows. https://agriculturalevents management.wordpress.com/.

Part II

Cultural and political events

6 "House and techno broke them barriers down"

Exploring exclusion through diversity in Berlin's electronic dance music nightclubs

Naomi Alice Rodgers

Introduction

Berlin is celebrated worldwide as being a city that is open, tolerant, and diverse: a true multicultural metropolis and music plays a central role in the city's claim to this title. Go to any one of Berlin's many notorious alternative nightclubs and you will hear techno, house, and electronic dance music blasting out to hoards of enthusiastic partygoers from all over the world. Electronic dance music (EDM) scholarship often looks to Berlin for examples of how EDM – as both a genre of music as well as a 'movement' has developed, with the fall of the Berlin Wall often being cited as a deeply influential historical moment in this. Within the literature it is often proclaimed that Berlin's EDM nightclubs offer safe spaces for people of 'diverse' backgrounds who are welcome to attend and treated equally once inside. It is as though these nightclubs have managed to temporarily suspend social hierarchies and unite all people under one roof. In this chapter, this 'diversity discourse', as it shall be named, will be deconstructed using an intersectional lens and situated within a wider political context, with a specific focus on perceptions of race, ethnicity, sexuality, and gender. The aim here is not to evaluate the truth or falsity of these claims, but rather to examine the operating logic of this discourse.

Research context

Electronic dance music

Electronic Dance Music (or EDM) is, according to García (2011: 3),

> A field of styles emerging out of the legacy of 1970s disco that includes house, techno, trance, drum 'n' base, jungle, hardcore, ambient, electro, dubstep, garage, two-step, 'minimal' sub-styles, hybrid styles like tech-house, and the rest of an ever-expanding field.

Germany is universally acclaimed as "a creative powerhouse in world techno" and, according to Robb (2002: 131–133), the "birth" of electronic dance music cultures

(EDMCs) in the country occurred after the fall of the Berlin Wall in 1989, which was a moment that he claims to have symbolised "liberation from ideology". The depiction of EDM history as being centred on ideas of unification, acceptance, and diversity is common within the literature in the field. Richard and Kruger (1998: 62), for example, describe techno as a movement that "unit[ed] dancers regardless of race, class, age, gender, or sexuality" (see also Fritsch 1988; Hitzler and Pfadenhauer 2002; Klein 2004). There are, however, scholars who suggest that these EDM 'scenes' may not have been as openly accessible to *everyone, all the time* as many claim them to have been. Most notably, García (2011: 3), in looking at the history of sexuality in dance music, discusses how disco of the 70s became mainstream and "gradually attracted an audience of white, straight, middle class people". This, García (2011) explains, happened despite the fact that dance music culture was born in queer, POC (people of colour) communities; something that few EDMC participants and scholars acknowledge today.

Berlin background

Peter (2014: 1) claims that Berlin is one of the "most vibrant musical cities in Western society," adding that what Berlin has lacked in economic potential, it has made up for in cultural production. During the 2000s, Berlin witnessed the increasing internationalisation of its EDM scenes through the rise of club tourism as well as the development of "a complex network of local and international music producers and promoters, many of whom relocated to Berlin" (Nye 2013: 156). But Berlin's international reputation does not just come from tourism; it comes from its relationship with immigration as well. Peter (2014: 4–5) describes Berlin as having "a diverse pool of international cultural immigrants" but, at the same time, also contends that Berlin is a city with "growing socio-spatial divides". Germany has had a tumultuous relationship with immigration, and there has been much debate about how best to respond to non-Europeans who request citizenship in the country (especially the Turkish *Gastarbeiter* [guest workers] who came to West Germany in the 60s to fill labour shortages). Contemporarily, Germany has received the largest number of asylum applications out of the whole of Europe (360,000 in June 2016); a great deal of those from people coming from war-torn Middle Eastern countries, such as Syria, Afghanistan and Iraq (United Nations High Commissioner for Refugees 2016). As Kil and Silver (2006) recount, immigrants in the city of Berlin face a great deal of social exclusion. In response to this, policymakers have focused on assimilation and integration in an attempt to aid social cohesion (Schönwälder 2010). This socio-political background will inevitably influence the way that my participants comprehend and talk about notions of diversity in EDM nightclubs.

Research methods

This chapter builds on a feminist post-structuralist epistemology, which emphasises the importance of language, textual analysis, and theory-making (Holvino

2010) and critiques discourses that encourage universalising grand narratives. Within a post-structuralist analysis, identity is to be understood as multiple, unstable, and inessential (Holvino 2010), intersecting with various identity categories in different ways. The idea that a researcher can detach themselves from "the world and the objects of study and then form an aloof and elevated position of surveillance" (Lykke 2010: 4–5) and create "objective knowledge" is to be challenged.

Intersectionality, as both a theory and a methodology, also is used here. Intersectionality proclaims that people's experiences are marked not by one, but rather by multiple identities, which intra-act (Barad 2003, cited in Lykke 2010: 50–52) and affect how people experience inequality and privilege. This research pays particular attention to the representations of race, ethnicity, sexuality, and gender, acknowledging that they are categories that interweave with one another and this interweaving contributes to an individual's particular experiences. Also, this research is situated within a post-colonial theoretical framework. Feminist post-colonial theory especially is employed, with Puar's (2007) work on *homonationalism* being called upon extensively in the analysis.

Interviews and auto-ethnographic analysis serve as the two methods used for this research. All of the interview participants were frequent partygoers, cisgendered, and aged between 23 and 34. Participant 'A' identified as female, heterosexual, and "caucasian German" [*sic*]. Participant 'B' shared that he was gay and "white German". Participant 'C' described himself as male, straight, and "white British". The fourth participant 'D' said he was male, straight, and "mixed race". The final participant 'E' identified as male, gay, and "Turkish German". The interviews were carried out as informal, "structured conversations" (Aronson 2003: 909) in an attempt to allow the participants to feel more comfortable about talking about issues which may be highly sensitive, secretive, or even illegal (such as the buying and selling of illicit substances or public sexual activity). Crucially, they were carried out outside of the club environment, usually in a more comfortable (and sober!) location, such as a coffee shop or in a park.

The clubs to be discussed and thereafter analysed were not chosen by the researcher, but rather came up organically in the interviews. The clubs chosen were KitKat Club (specifically the Gegen monthly night), Bassy Club (specifically the Chantal's House of Shame weekly night), About Blank (specifically, for two interviewees, the – now defunct – Homopatik monthly night) and Berghain/Panorama Bar (which was chosen by all five participants); the research therefore focuses on these specific clubs.

Auto-ethnographic material is included here in order to challenge the notion that researchers can somehow distance themselves from "cultural shifts, personal tides and personal feelings" (Ettore 2010: 296) and to acknowledge that knowledge is never value-free. As Lykke (2010: 5) explains, "a researcher is always a participant in the world they analyse and they cannot avoid being co-responsible for the 'knowledge' they produce." The following extract is taken from the author's research diary and describes personal observations and personal experiences at a 'typical' night out in Berlin.

'A night out in Berlin': field notes

Entering the club

It is two in the afternoon and a sunny winter's day in Berlin. I am with a good friend and we are heading to the club. We are still quite a distance from the entrance, but already we can hear the loud music coming from inside. As soon as we have the club in sight, I sense a slight shift between the two of us. I am suddenly more aware of myself, of the way I am walking, what I am wearing, even the manner in which I express myself. The walk up to the bouncers is both exhilarating and frightening. Bouncers in Berlin are notorious for being ruthless when it comes to deciding who is 'cool' enough to enter a club and turning those away who do not fit in.

The two bouncers at the door look us up and down, and after checking that we are aware that we have come to a 'gay' night, for whatever reasons decide we can enter. My feelings of anxiety about not being let in immediately turn to delight when I contemplate the fact that I am passable, I am acceptable. We are in!

We finally enter the club itself, coming across the main dancehall first. It is extremely dark in here, despite the fact that it is so bright and sunny outside. I can tell from the looks on people's faces that I am one of the few sober people in here. One thing that is incredibly striking is the fact that it is so dominated by cis men (the majority of whom are white). Having contemplated this, I suddenly feel even more out of place than before.

It is fascinating how one glass of Sekt [sparkling wine] can transform my experience of the space. I have gone from feeling out of place and self-conscious, to starting to enjoy myself, as I chat and dance with my friends. I like being on this dance floor. Despite it being no more than three degrees outside, the room is warm, thanks to the huge ventilator as well as the human body heat. It is warm enough to take some layers off and be able to move freely as I dance. I am joined by others who have done the same, including quite a few men who are dancing in their underwear, some totally naked.

Right now, I do not have a care in the world. I do not care what time it is, as I have nothing to do today but this. I feel warm and safe and surrounded by people who I trust.

Leaving the club

I step out of the club and the bright sunlight shines at me aggressively, as if to say, 'Welcome back to reality!' What a contrast to the space I have spent the last 18 hours in. I walk arm-in-arm with my friend towards the subway station, both of us dragging our feet along as we go. I am aware of my surroundings so much more than I would normally be. I feel totally detached from the immediate world around me, like I am stumbling through a dream.

Finally on the train, I am fascinated by the people around me, going about their everyday lives. We are sharing the same journey; yet, we are so disconnected. I feel everyone's eyes on me (although perhaps that is just sleep deprivation-induced paranoia speaking). Can they tell what I have been doing all night? The large sunglasses that are covering my face (despite the lack of sunlight on this dimly lit train) are probably a giveaway.

I look over at my friend sitting next to me, who giggles at the ridiculousness of it all. His sunglasses have broken, and they droop under his right eye, providing privacy only for the left one. We look utterly ridiculous. But hey, it is our little (badly kept) secret.

Analysis

Club spaces as sites of identity building

The clubs that were brought forward for discussion were ones that interviewees would attend on a regular basis and that their social group occupied. One significant thing that most of these clubs have in common is their target audience. All of the clubs or club nights that were discussed in the interviews can be found classified online as being either "gay friendly", "gay," or "queer" (Martet 2017; Resident Advisor 2017; Çakır and Bayramoğlu n.d.; Visit Berlin n. d.). With this in mind, it would be imprudent to overlook the role that these labels might play in aiding participants to express or perform certain (sexual) identities. As McVeigh (1997) explains in *Screening for Straights: Aspects of Entrance Policy at a Gay Disco*, clubs that offer "the homosexual community" a place to express themselves freely play an extremely important role in society. Within this context, these clubs can be viewed as spaces that offer certain people (that is, sexual minorities) temporary relief from the constraints of societal surveillance and judgement.

Indeed, many of the participants for this research shared personal stories about how important these clubs had been in providing them with something of a 'shelter' from the outside homophobic world. They felt that within these queer or queer-friendly clubs, they no longer had to worry about homophobic aggression or violence. This is significant, considering that fear of violence and discrimination is a daily concern for much of the LGBTQI community in Germany (Senate Department for Labour, Integration and Women's Issues 2016), as indeed it is elsewhere in the world. The idea that nightclubs can be sites from which participants are able to perform different identities was a common theme through-out all of the interviews. As someone who works at Berghain/Panorama Bar, 'A' said she gets to "see everybody who comes and goes" from the club and feels she has a particularly good idea about the "kinds of people" who attend. She said:

If you saw them on the streets during the day, you would never think 'this guy is into this kind of fetish stuff'... but they really need the space to escape, to get out of their suits and put on... Nothing!

According to 'A', these men must conform to societal expectations whilst outside of the club (such as going to work, wearing a suit, or expressing normative sexual desires), but within the club they are given the freedom to explore different parts of their identities.

As is evident from the auto-ethnographic account above, the author also found these clubs to be important spaces within which personal expression can be made. With this extract, a rather typical night out and return home from a club is presented. The personal experience of clubbing is described as (for the most part) an incredibly enjoyable one. Despite the nerve-wracking experience of being scrutinised by the club bouncers and a brief sense of feeling out of place as a woman within the club, with some time, the personal experience began to feel relaxed. This space is described as a comforting one, as somewhere to feel safe and able to "move freely" and enjoy time with trusted people. This extract also describes sharing a "badly kept secret" with a good friend, and this shared clubbing experience creates a sense of solidarity between them.

Defining the diversity discourse

When looking into the way in which the participant-chosen clubs advertise themselves, there appears to be a common claim that all of them make. That is, within each club space, one can find a true mix of people, a diverse array of participants who are able to socialise together, regardless of social and economic divisions. To take one example, Resident Advisor boldly asserts that Berghain/ Panorama Bar is "famous for its wildly mixed crowd, leaving class and gender divisions far behind" (Resident Advisor 2007). As already stated, these claims are present within academic EDMC literature as well. These powerful narratives that depict EDMCs as a force of unproblematic unification have a big impact on how partygoers perceive EDM nightclubs today. During the interviews for this research, the author found this to be most obvious in the persistent use of the word 'diverse' to describe EDM crowds. All of the participants, without exception, enthusiastically boasted that participating in their chosen clubs meant sharing space with a vast array of different people. In describing the Berghain/ Panorama Bar crowd, 'A' explained to me, "It's very mixed. You have old and young people partying together, a lot of gays, transsexuals [*sic*], straight normal people [*sic*], it is a good mixture for sure." All of the other interviewees also consistently produced such a discourse in their interviews. According to their accounts, EDM nightclubs offer people a safe space away from a wide spectrum of discrimination, with particular mention of racism, sexism, trans* and homophobia. The claims being made by EDMC scholars, the research interviewees, and the clubs themselves are far-reaching and have vast implications for the way that social in/equality in this Berlin context can be understood. This discourse shall be hereon referred to as a diversity discourse. This term shall be used to describe the assertion that within EDM nightclubs all crowd members participate on equal terms and do not face discrimination based on traditional societal constraints.

Cracks and contradictions

Emerging tensions

Intersectionality is a useful theoretical tool to help to unpack this discourse and to examine the inclusionary and exclusionary practices that might be taking place within these EDM nightclubs. It points attention to the possibility that some voices and experiences are overlooked or silenced in dominant discourses. Despite the rather favourable picture painted here of clubbing in the field notes excerpt above, the author's personal experiences have not always been positive, especially when in a heavily cis-male-dominated space. During the interviews, 'B' agreed that Berghain/Panorama Bar was largely attended by males and offered an insightful perspective on the apparent gendered segregation of this club, explaining, "When you talk about gay parties it's always about male gay. The women are... Not really represented." The comments made by 'B' here contrast significantly with those discussed in the section above. In a similar vein, 'A' began her interview by saying that Berghain/Panorama Bar was extremely mixed because it was attended by both "straight and gay people". However, when prompted further about what exactly was meant by "gay people", she added, "[I am talking more about] gay men. You actually don't see so many lesbians there." Here, there is a certain amount of contradiction inherent in the previous claim by 'A' that Berghain/Panorama Bar is "very mixed". By looking closely at these statements, it becomes apparent that for 'A' a "very mixed" nightclub space is in fact one that is predominantly dominated by homosexual, cis men.

There also emerged a number of contradictions when it came to the representation of racial and ethnic diversity within these nightclubs. When questioned further on their claims of diversity, all bar one of my participants singled out Arab and Turkish people as not being well represented within the nightclub crowds. The reasons given for this are further analysed below, but what seemed to be expressed during the interviews was that these identities were somehow at odds with EDM queer clubs. There appeared to be an unacknowledged racialised identity that was seen as unwelcome in these spaces.

'Othering' mechanisms

So far, it has been presented that there is the possibility that these clubs are socially exclusive spaces and certain barriers (based on attitude or physical appearance) for certain groups of people seem to exist. To take this further, the way that participants gave meaning to their own descriptions of exclusion is now analysed. As mentioned, the reasons given by many of my participants for the lack of Arab and Turkish representation in the clubs revolved around the idea that these particular identities were incompatible with regular attendees. This incompatibility was often explained in the interviews via racist stereotypes, which claim Arab and Turkish participants are more likely to possess sexist or homophobic attitudes. An example of this is a comment made by 'C' who said about Arab and Turkish men, "They don't know [which DJ] is playing... and they're not gay and they're just coming... to get a girl." Other interviewees claimed that this racialised group of people did not feel comfortable within queer-dominated social environments, adding that they would react with homophobia and aggression towards queer-identifying people. For example, 'D' explained that few Arab and Turkish people attend EDM club nights due to their differing musical interests and that Arab and Turkish people in Berlin "listen to hip-hop," cited as evidence of homophobic attitudes. He explained, "They listen to hip-hop... There's still a gay scene, [Berghain/Panorama Bar] is still a gay club." He made his point clearer by saying, "My entire youth was spent with Turkish kids and Arab kids.... All of my friends were really homophobic, you know?" Here, 'D' justifies the social segregation that he describes.

There is also no discussion of the existence of queer of colour identities in this conversation, leading to, as we have seen in the previous section, the erasure of non-normative identities. This tells us a lot about the way that hegemonic international 'gay rights' narratives often interweave subtly with racist assumptions. Puar's (2007) work on "homonationalism" is useful in helping to understand and to unpack these claims and provide some context to what is being said here. In her seminal book, *Terrorist Assemblages: Homonationalism in Queer Times,* Puar (2007) situates European and United States' efforts to portray themselves as "tolerant" and "civilised" through the use of homosexuality, within a context of Western[1] imperialism and colonisation. She makes the powerful and critical point that the narrative of progress for gay rights in the West is built on the back of racialised Others (Puar 2007). It is within this historical and political context that we must place the interviewees' claims and the assumptions behind them. What is interesting is that within this Berlin EDMC setting, the research participants are able not only to invoke racist stereotypes about Arab and Turkish people, but also, given the pervasiveness of the diversity discourse, they are able to do so under the guise of participating in something that is socially inclusive.

Historian and gay activist, Bérubé (2003), makes the convincing case for viewing homosexuality as always being shaped by race and gender. He explores the way that the category "gay man" has become *white* within popular discourses in the United States and how unquestioned beliefs about white privilege are dominant within many activist circles (Bérubé 2003). He explains, "In this zero-sum racialised world... gay men are white; gay, lesbian, and bisexual people of colour, along with poor, working-class gay men, bisexuals and lesbians, simply do not exist" (Bérubé 2003: 257–258). This idea that gay equals white seems to be what both 'C' and 'D' are also expressing in their assertions (or, at the very least, stating that gay does not equal Arab or Turkish). Their comments show a binary understanding of identity; what Puar (2007: 13) succinctly describes as, a "binary between queer and something else". The result of these conceptualisations is the construction of a narrative that erases a great number of people's experiences.

Adding to his comments about why he thought Arab and Turkish people are not well-represented within EDMCs, 'C' said he thought it was because, "they're not really into the music" and that, "they've got their own thing". 'C' explained that the responsibility for social segregation in this context is ascribed to a specific group of people:

> In the party... If there were a Turkish guy standing next to me, you know like raving, then I'd be like, 'hey!' You know what I mean? I would. But I think that's the environment it creates. But they don't go there... I think they're just not interested in going to these places.

Here, 'C' talks of a monolithic Turkish identity, which he juxtaposes with that of an EDM participant. This troubling delineation between an 'us' and a 'them' can be considered as an 'Othering' practice. The practice of 'Othering' is a concept that has constituted the focus of a great deal of post-colonial scholarship (see Spivak 1985; Hall 1997; Said 2013/1979) and the comments made by 'C' seem to be very much informed by these types of knowledges. With this quote, 'C' is describing what he sees as mutually exclusive differences between two clashing identities. Importantly, these differences cannot be said to be the fault of the so-called "diverse" EDM nightclub participant (who would happily approach a Turkish person in a club for conversation), but rather he sees the responsibility as lying with the non-conforming Other. As 'C' understands it, racial and ethnic segregation *does* exist within these "scenes" (a fact that of course stands in sharp contrast to the bold claims seen previously), but it is the Turkish Other's own self-exclusion that is to blame. 'C' seems to conjure the "irreconcilably stubborn natures of unassimilating and unassimilatable... Muslims" trope that Puar (2007: 21) discusses in *Terrorist Assemblages*.

Considering that many of the research participants felt that the safety of these nightclubs was an important aspect of their enjoyment of them, it is interesting to examine the extent to which this desire for safety clashed with a desire for a 'diverse' crowd (and whether these two desires were indeed compatible at all). 'A' explained that she thought the Berghain/Panorama Bar bouncers generally made justified decisions about who can and cannot enter the club. She did, however, acknowledge that their decisions over who to let in and who not to let in were often based on "prejudices about Turkish and Arab guys". She explained that often bouncers saw them as "criminals [who] have bad intentions and want to rob you". In the story that 'A' paints here, the safety of those who could be victims of such criminality and "bad intentions" is given priority and the desire for "diversity" within these EDM crowds is suddenly devoid of importance.

Conclusions

It is important to consider the social effects of this diversity discourse and its inherent contradictions. For some, the EDM clubs in this research *are* places of liberation, and it is important to resist the urge to label these clubs as either good or bad spaces. For the interviewees and, indeed, for the author, these EDM nightclubs afford collective acceptance, especially for certain queer identities. They are seen as safe spaces that provide shelter from homophobic harassment and violence, as well as places where one is able to express otherwise socially unacceptable aspects of their identities. However, those very people who describe this experience of freedom are the same people who describe them as sites of exclusion for a significant section of society. There seems to be a huge gap between the principle of this diversity discourse and its practice.

It can be argued that this diversity discourse first of all functions to bond the acceptable/accepted participants together. It works to embolden a sense of unity and solidarity amongst the participants in these clubs as well as to give this social interaction meaning and purpose. The claim that these clubs have been able to carve out a space in Berlin society that is free from all forms of discrimination and intolerance gives the participants something to feel proud of, something that justifies their participation. It also allows for the uncomplicated enjoyment of these social spaces. Crucially, however, this diversity discourse acts as a mask to hide the contradictory, dissonant, and inconsistent aspects of these clubs. The diversity discourse and its aspirations of freedom and inclusivity enable participants to avoid acknowledging the fact that these clubs are also spaces of inequity and exclusion. On the one hand, there is the strong desire by the research participants to uphold the tenets of the diversity discourse; on the other, they were unwilling to enact a more nuanced understanding of these social spaces, which included a critical look at the exclusionary practices that take place there.

Thus, this discourse can be seen to excuse participants "from a critique of [their] own power manipulations" (Puar 2007: 31) and results in reinforcing social segregation. Through the diversity discourse, participants are discouraged from discussing their own privilege and their own roles in upholding hegemonic norms. Yet, there is potential for EDM nightclubs in Berlin to be, to some extent, the emancipatory spaces that many seem to so desperately to want them to be.[2] What is required is a challenging of the idea that within these spaces political debate and discussion is irrelevant or inappropriate. This means that responsibility needs to be taken for the role that these clubs might play in upholding social segregation within society. The onus needs to be on the club managers and owners, bouncers, club night organisers, DJs, and participants in challenging this. Let us not forget that EDM was born out of marginalised communities (García 2014); its history is seeped in political struggle, so it is vital not to see politics and music as mutually exclusive of one another.

Questions for discussion

1. Could it be possible to reclaim the nightclub space as a political one?
2. Can clubbing ever be a form of political resistance? To what extent?
3. Do nightclubs have a role to play in fighting against societal discrimination? Or will it always remain an exclusionary entity?
4. What are the possibilities and limitations of using auto-ethnographic inquiry in academic research?

Notes

1 The term 'Western' refers to Said's (2013/1979) work on Orientalism, which described the historical construction of Europe (and later the United States) as inherently superior to 'The East'.
2 Indeed, it should be noted that there are already a number of artists and activists, in both Berlin and internationally, who are working hard to bring visibility to typically underrepresented groups within EDM scenes, as well as organising EDM events that are political at their core (see, for example, the work of Female:Pressure, Reclaim the Beats; and Room 4 Resistance).

References

Aronson, P. (2003). Feminists or "postfeminists"?: Young women's attitudes toward feminism and gender relations. *Gender & Society*, 17(6), 903–922.

Bérubé, A. (2003). How gay stays white and what kind of white it stays. In M. S. Kimmel and A. L. Ferber (eds.) *Privilege: A reader*. Boulder, Colorado: Westview Press, 253–283.

Çakır, B. and Bayramoğlu, Y. (n.d.). *The politics of partying: Berlin's queer nightlife*. Bantmag. www.bantmag.com/english/issue/post/33/120.

Ettore, E. (2010). Nuns, dykes, drugs and gendered bodies: An autoethnography of a lesbian feminist's journey through "good time" sociology. *Sexualities*, 13(3), 295–315.

Fritsch, U. (1988). *Tanz, Bewegungskultur, Gesellschaft: Verluste Und Chancen symbolisch-expressiven Bewegens* [Dance, movement, culture, society: Losses and opportunities of symbolic-expressive movement]. Frankfurt am Main: AFRA.

García, L. M. (2011). *"Can you feel it, too?": Intimacy and affect at electronic dance music events in Paris, Chicago, and Berlin*. PhD, The University of Chicago.

García, L. M. (2014). *An alternate history of sexuality in club culture*. Resident Advisor. www.residentadvisor.net/feature.aspx?1927.

Hall, S. (1997). *Representation: Cultural representations and signifying practices*. New York: Sage Publications.

Hitzler, R. and Pfadenhauer, M. (2002). Existential strategies: The making of community and politics in the techno/rave scene. In J. Kotarba, et al. (eds.) *Postmodern existential sociology*. Walnut Creek: Altamira Press, 87–101.

Holvino, E. (2010). Intersections: The simultaneity of race, gender and class in organization studies. *Gender, Work and Organization*, 17(3), 248–277.

Kil, W. and Silver, H. (2006). From Kreuzberg to Marzahn. *German Politics and Society*, 24(81), 95–121.

Klein, G. (2004). *Electronic Vibration: Pop Kultur Theorie* [Electronic vibration: Pop culture theory]. Wiesbaden: Springer.

Lykke, N. (2010). *Feminist studies: A guide to intersectional theory, methodology and writing*. London: Routledge.

Martet, C. (2017). *Will Berghain remain the world's filthiest queer club after opening a new floor in March?* https://hornetapp.com/stories/berghain-worlds-filthiest-queer-club/.

McVeigh, A. (1997). Screening for straights: Aspects of entrance policy at a gay disco. *Irish Journal of Sociology*, 7(1), 77–98.

Nye, A. (2013). *Feminist theory and the philosophies of man*. London: Routledge.

Peter, B. (2014). Breaching the divide: Techno city Berlin. In G. Stahl (ed.) *Poor, but sexy: Reflections on Berlin scenes*. Heidelberg: Peter Lang AG, 173–190.

Puar, J. (2007). *Terrorist assemblages: Homonationalism in queer times*. Durham: Duke University Press.

Resident Advisor. (2007). *Panorama Bar/Berghain residents night Nyc at Cielo, New York*. www.residentadvisor.net/event.aspx?29879.

Resident Advisor. (2017). *Clubs: About blank*. www.residentadvisor.net/club.aspx?id=28354.

Richard, B. and Kruger, H. H. (1998). Ravers' laradise? German youth cultures in the 1990s. In T. Skelton and G. Valentine (eds.) *Cool places: Geographies of youth culture*. London: Routledge, Chapter 10.

Robb, D. (2002). Techno in Germany: Its musical origins and cultural relevance. *German as a Foreign Language*, 2(3), 29–49.

Said, E. (2013/1979). *Orientalism: Western conceptions of the Orient*. London: Routledge.

Schönwälder, K. (2010). Germany: Integration policy and pluralism in a self-conscious country of immigration. In S. Wessendorf and S. Vertovec (eds.) *The multicultural backlash: European discourses, policies and practices*. London: Routledge, 152–169.

Senate Department for Labour, Integration and Women's Issues. (2016). *Violence and discrimination against the LGBTI community*. www.berlin.de/sen/lads/_assets/ueber-uns/materialien/factsheets/factsheet_10e_violence_and_discrimination_against_lgbti.pdf.

Spivak, G. C. (1985). The Rani of Sirmur: An essay in reading the archives. *History and Theory*, 24(3), 247–272.

United Nations High Commissioner for Refugees. (2016). *2016 UNHCR Northern, Western and Southern Europe subregional operations profile*. http://reporting.unhcr.org/node/3414?y=2016.

Visit Berlin. (n.d.). *Chantals house of shame: Gay cult party*. www.visitberlin.de/en/spot/house-of-shame.

7 Occupying unapologetically

Friday Late: gal-dem – radical trust and co-production at the Victoria and Albert Museum, London

Keisha Williams

Introduction

In 2003, the Victoria and Albert Museum (V&A) in London created a formal *Strategy for Access, Inclusion, and Diversity*. Spanning all areas of the museum, the document openly acknowledged the V&A as an institution with a complex history, which presents multiple barriers to access[1] (Victoria and Albert Museum 2003). It is increasingly acknowledged that the V&A and institutions like it, their collections, and the activities they produce often fail to represent the diversity of their surrounding communities (Helen Denniston Associates 2003). For many arts and cultural organisations, one of the most difficult challenges is to become recognised as an "inclusive organisation" for certain portions of the population, who perceive museum spaces as not for or representing them. To rectify deeply institutionalised issues of exclusion, many argue positive changes may require re-thinking the museum as a whole, leading the V&A and others to seek methods of engagement beyond strategic policy, allowing event programming, and working with their surrounding communities to emerge (Sandell 2003).

With several recently commissioned reports, including the Department for Culture, Media and Sport *Taking Part* survey (2017), revealing an alarming gap in participation among ethnically diverse audiences, and many institutions experiencing low BAME (Black, Asian and minority ethnic) visitor numbers, museums now face the challenge of ensuring the museum is for and represents all.[2] For many under-represented by the traditional museum narrative, feelings of alienation and exclusion are not being addressed, resulting in a lower engagement within the arts and cultural sector (Arts Council England 2015). It is, therefore, perhaps not only that museums are struggling to be inclusive, but also, in the wider sense, struggling for relevancy (Helen Denniston Associates 2003).

With increased efforts to re-think strategies of engagement in museums, many successful diversity initiatives have produced projects that actively engage under-represented audiences through methods such as consulting with communities and allowing traditional museum practices to be challenged (Helen Denniston Associates 2003). Programming with third parties from diverse, and in particular BAME, communities has become ever more present in museum efforts to create more representative institutions (Gorier 2009). While several definitions exist to describe these concepts, Nina Simon, leading authority on participation in museums, believes these types of partnerships can be broken down into collaborative and co- creative participation (referred to here as co-production) (Simon 2010).

Within *The Participatory Museum*, Simon (2010: 187) defines collaboration as projects in which "visitors are invited to serve as active partners in the creation of institutional projects that are originated and ultimately controlled by the institution". In contrast, co-produced projects offer more power to participants and are defined as projects in which "community members work together with institutional staff members from the beginning to define the project's goals and to generate the program [*sic*] or exhibit based on community interests" (ibid.). However, Alberti and Lynch (2010: m30) argue in order for co-production to truly flourish, radical new levels of trust and cooperation need to be given; a radical trust "based on the idea that shared authority is more effective at creating and guiding culture than institutional control". If radical trust is given, collabora- tion and co-production have the potential to not only diversify the dialogue within institutions, but also enable museums to acknowledge their legacy of prejudice, correct historical disparities in representation, and begin a more honest approach to acknowledging power (ibid.).

In recent years, several London institutions have taken these suggestions to heart, showcasing more diverse narratives through event programming. Perhaps by hosting these events, museums are allowing themselves to be more challen- ging and experimental, for while it is easy to call for radical change, it is undoubtedly more difficult to implement it. Further, while most museums are perhaps unable or unwilling to completely alter their purpose and goals as radically as some have called for, the use of co-production, collaboration and radical trust in programming has the ability to allow more diverse audiences and narratives to emerge (Arts Council England 2015).

Despite challenges of representing more diverse audiences, execution of high- quality and successful programmes are believed to have the ability to overcome scepticism and with time, build trust and loyalty (National Museum Directors 2006). Working to re-evaluate the role of visitor experience, many western museums have seen the emergence of special programming such as 'After Hours', 'Lates' and co- produced events as important elements to wider representation of their audience's interests, and based on recent initiatives, is precisely the strategy the V&A has used to create a more inclusive environment for ethnically diverse audiences (Cretaro 2009). For the V&A, their *Friday Late* programme provides an opportunity to implement strategies of co-production and collaboration, inviting collectives and organisations to create a night of unique one-off programming. A monthly late night opening revolving around changing themes, the V&A describe their 'Lates' as:

> The original contemporary late night event. *Friday Late* celebrates all aspects of contemporary visual culture and design in society, bringing audiences face- to-face with leading and emerging artists and designers through live perfor- mance, film, installation, debate, DJs, and late-night exhibition openings.
>
> (Victoria and Albert Museum 2018)

This type of programming allows for the flexibility and shared authority needed for marginalised voices to flourish.[3]

Although co-produced and take-over type events are not are not necessarily a new topic, the *Friday Late: gal-dem* in October 2016 at the V&A was viewed by many attendants to mark a shift in representation by one of the most prominent institutions in the UK. Despite the V&A having used ideas of collaboration and co-production before, this is arguably one of the most radical and significant examples, attracting an estimated 4,000–6,000 attendees, many of whom were from BAME backgrounds (Brinkhurst-Cuff 2016; Okolosie 2016). Through the use of co-production, collaboration, and radical trust, a self-identifying collective of women of colour, non-binary people of colour and their surrounding communities were able to take ownership of one of the most significant art and cultural spaces in London. Qualitative evaluations, including conversations during the night amongst fellow attendees and programmers, interviews leading up to and immediately following the event, social media response, and levels of attendance all suggest the evening marked a significant moment for people of colour, communities often marginalised by the traditional museum space, and their allies, making it a particularly significant case study.

Case study: *Friday Late: gal-dem* at the V&A Museum

One of the most recent iterations of the V&A's efforts to represent a more ethnically and culturally diverse audience – and argued here as the most significant enactment to date of co-production and radical trust at the V&A in special event programming – was the *Friday Late: gal-dem* on Friday 28 October, 2016.[4] Taking the form of event-based programming, as described by the V&A:

> This October, the V&A teams up with online magazine and collective gal-dem. Made up of almost 50 women of colour, gal-dem offers their take on the world. Come to the Museum for an all-female line up, as we invite you to twerk to empowerment, share a soul food recipe and hear London's best MCs.
>
> (Victoria and Albert Museum 2016)

Events were held across the building during a special late night opening that included Black history tours, a female MC corner, *Black in the Day* (an audio-visual photo display of personal photographs documenting the everyday lives of black people in Britain), and much more. Themes of occupation and social activism were rife throughout the evening of programmed events as the traditional and most recognisable spaces within the V&A became stages for the art, lifestyle, and culture of marginalised people.

Although the *Friday Late: gal-dem* for many in attendance marked a significant moment of programming, the V&A has dedicated years to creating a more inclusive and welcoming environment, some more successful than others. A notable example which tested ideas of collaboration and representation of BAME narratives at the V&A was the 2007 *Uncomfortable Truths: the Shadow of Slave Trading on Contemporary Art*. Installed across the museum as a means of 'intervention', *Uncomfortable Truths* displayed throughout the museum the work of 11 contemporary artists, including the *Gates of Return* by Julien Sinzogan, *Sir Foster Cunliffe Playing* by Yinka Shonibare MBE, and *Regina Atra* by Fred Wilson.

Uncomfortable Truths, like many exhibitions that deal with the harsh realities of the legacy of slavery, racism, prejudice, and exclusion, was met with mixed reviews. Some visitors expressed their enjoyment by requesting more such programmes, and to not to wait for another anniversary to address such important subject matter; others viewed the spread-out placement of the artworks to be a tokenistic missed opportunity (Nightingale 2011). In hindsight, perhaps the scattered nature of the exhibition throughout the V&A should have been re-thought; for example, instead of placing temporary works in spaces that fit around the more permanent displays, better communication could have been provided to link the narrative of intervention and spatial politics the exhibition sought to address. Further, several visitor feedback comments suggested the V&A should have consulted with black people and communities (ibid.). While it is perhaps unfair and unrealistic to assume there were no people of colour involved in the planning of the exhibition (outside of the artists themselves), what these comments seem to highlight is the need for consultation, collaboration, co-production, and the presence of people of colour within these spaces.

Critical comments about the exhibition seemed to call for a more radical form of trust, which would have allowed people who see the history and legacy of slavery as an important aspect of their own heritage to represent themselves, perhaps creating a more accurate self-portrait. A radical trust that it seems the V&A was unwilling or unable to give at that moment in time. As Simon (2010) stresses, a significant amount of trust needs to be allowed for successful collaboration and co-production.

> More than any other type of visitor participation, co-creative projects challenge institutional perceptions of ownership and control of content... To execute a successful co-creation project, staff members must not only trust the competencies and motivations of participants but deeply desire their input and leadership.
>
> (Simon 2010: 274)

Despite criticism, this exhibition appears to have been an important step for the V&A towards a more culturally diverse and radical form of trust that would later evolve, bearing traces learned from the *Uncomfortable Truths* exhibition and other cultural diversity initiatives of the time. It is arguably somewhat 'natural' for a museum to dedicate a temporary exhibition to examining more diverse topics, as the ultimate control remains within the realm of the institution (a collaborative effort more than co-produced, as defined by Simon (2010). Allowing for the takeover of a space as done through the *Friday Late: gal-dem* was, in contrast, quite unique, perhaps truly engaging in the "radical" trust and change called for (Alberti and Lynch 2010).

The thousands of attendees of the *Friday Late: gal-dem* saw their involvement not only as a way to celebrate their diverse experiences, but also as an act of resistance and social activism, creating their own visibility so often denied[5] (Okolosie 2016). For many attendees, and specifically people of colour, the event was not simply a special late night event at the V&A; it was about people of colour taking up space, unapologetically. Many public spaces within the museum were claimed on that October night to showcase and share the experiences of women, people of colour, non-binary people, and those who felt marginalised by wider society. In many ways, this event offered a second chance to address the issues that emerged from *Uncomfortable Truths*, and the conclusions reached in the 2003 *Strategy for Access, Inclusion and Diversity* present a case for creating more representative programming and institutional change, stating:

> The lessons for the future are apparent... Care needs to be taken to ensure events are not perceived as tokenistic and take account of sensitivities of communities who have previously felt marginalised... It is only by a more sustained audience development approach that does not rely on one-off programmes, or ignore the diverse interests and aspirations of black and other audiences, that the V&A will be able to have a significant impact on overall visitor figures.
>
> (Nightingale 2011: 56–57)

The takeover allowed many of these objectives to be met. Although it may not have, as of yet, publicly had a wider impact on more permanent areas of the V&A such as collections, publications, galleries (at least at this moment of writing), it had a profound effect on programming and creating more diverse representation. In this instance, the V&A gave a significant amount of power to not only gal-dem, but to the other organisations and artists they chose to collaborate with, perhaps providing an opportunity to take the 'institution' out of the V&A and allowing differing voices and perspectives to determine their own representation.

In contrast to previous collaborative efforts by the V&A, the 2016 *Friday Late: gal-dem* allowed the traditional front-facing spaces of the V&A to be transformed into venues where participants could carve out their own representation with less focus on the museum displays themselves and instead on how the space could be transformed to fit the life and narratives of the participants and attendees. The Raphael Room – a hall dedicated to masters of painting and design – became a speaker's corner where women of colour aimed to discuss and unpack their roles across arts, music, and politics. In these discussions, themes of occupation, social activism, and resistance were prevalent with one speaker stating: "If you feel there is something missing from the representation slot, you represent it... We need to address the multiplicity of our identities" (Speak Up 2016). The Daylight Gallery featured the pop-up exhibition *Unmasked Women: Identity* where the idea of occupying space could be seen at perhaps one of its most physical interventions, draping images of women of colour highlighting the female black British experience over the permanent displays within the gallery. BBZ, a collective to celebrate women of colour from all spectrums, brought their monthly exhibition and club night to the Fashion Room, where the opulent clothing took a backseat to the art/video installation and dance party. The Lecture Theatre was taken over for a 'Twerkshop', tracing the origins of the dance move from Africa to its current mainstream popularity; this is something it is likely safe to say has never, if rarely, been done on that scale at a museum (Victoria and Albert Museum Friday Late 2016).

Fifteen of the public-facing areas of the museum were taken over with music, politics, art, discussions, food and dance to support the narratives and visibility of the communities gal-dem and their partners represent. As a public gallery, the programming of these spaces is not unique. However, programming viewed by their attendees as a historic moment in claiming their own representation within the museum is. Opinions Editor for gal-dem, Brinkhurst-Cuff, echoed this sentiment following the event:

> It felt as though there was a new kind of electricity lighting up the stale air. We were taking up space in a place that wasn't meant to be for us, filled with the busts of long dead white men and the marble-stone curves of the women they dreamed up. It was magical.
>
> (Brinkhurst-Cuff 2016)

What separated the *Friday Late: gal-dem* from other programming was not only occupying a space, but also in occupying this particular space with these particular people; of having an opportunity to take over an important fixture of the museum sector with a complex history often unrepresentative of diverse narratives (Victoria and Albert Museum 2003).

While the academic sphere was slow to acknowledge the significance of the event, the immediate aftermath saw praise from many attendees on social media and popular culture media outlets. For those in attendance this event was not simply a night of talks, workshops, music and dancing, but an important moment in the social activism of the arts and cultural sector. It was an opportunity to take ownership over those cultural spaces that had traditionally and consistently ignored their experiences and existence. As a woman of colour, the experience of the event was profound for Okolosie (2016), contributor to *The Guardian*, as it was for many others, as she stated, "For once, we could gather in such a space and view it not as a diminishment of our value, but rather a celebration of our worth." Another attendee declared the event "a striking clash of fossilised artefacts with active, energetic voices; of a hegemonic establishment with non-normative, progressive feminism" (Kay 2016). The event was even paralleled to the Occupy Movement of 2011, an opportunity for the disenfranchised to occupy public and civic spaces giving themselves the voice they often felt was denied (ibid.).

Liv Little, founder of gal-dem, clarifies that this was a joint effort, an act of co-production in practice: "[The V&A] are definitely conscious of the fact that they need to do more to reach our audiences, so it's a great opportunity for them as well as us" (Kane 2016). For both gal-dem and the V&A, this event marked an important moment. Much of the theory of co-creation/co-production can be seen at the heart of this event. As Simon (2010) stresses in *The Participatory Museum*, producers of collaborative and co-produced projects must understand their institutions as community-based organisations, ones which place visitor experience above traditional services of the institution; as co-produced projects are "demand-driven", they often require community goals to supersede those of the institution. Developing a platform for audience-centred participation creates the ability to reconnect museums with their public, retain their relevance in contemporary life and transform visitors from "passive consumers" to actively engaged participants (ibid.). Further, for audiences who view the museum as irrelevant or unrepresentative of their lives, providing a stake in the museum and specific projects is key to engagement, and in some cases may be the only way (Sandell 2003).

In order for the event to succeed, the mission of the partner superseded, or became, the focus of the event. A collective of women and non-binary people of colour who work to carve out the representation that they feel is often denied to people of colour, gal-dem defines their mission is to:

> open up our take on the world to a wider audience. We want people of different shapes, sizes, sexes, and ethnic backgrounds to engage with the work we are doing. It is no secret that the mainstream media doesn't represent or reflect us, so we are doing it for ourselves.
>
> (Kane 2016)

By allowing the mission of gal-dem to become the focus that drove programming, institutional perceptions were allowed to be challenged, content that attracted a diverse group of people was programmed and an outside third-party organisation had a chance to contribute and lead, showcasing the potential not only for co-production, radical trust, and collaboration creating a more inclusive space, but also the potential for events within museums to be a form of activism within themselves.

The participants themselves reflect these ideas. For Little, partnerships are vital to reaching more diverse groups of people. As she stated in an interview preceding the event, "I think it's [the V&A's] duty to work with young people and smaller publications – we exist within society and so should definitely take up space within them! ... I feel like something really special is happening at the moment" (Kane 2016). Taking up space became arguably the most vital part of this co-produced event, as Little stated,

> Women of colour are rarely given the chance to take up space in institutions like the V&A, so we took the task very seriously – we thought about representing a spread of interests and identities and the fact that we wanted to build upon our pre-existing relationships with people.
>
> (ibid.)

There was a desire to bring creativity, politics and innovation to the spaces they were invited to programme, creating an important moment for those represented. Although statistical demographics of attendees is not available, the co-produced partnership was able to attract a significant number of people of colour, women, non-binary, and people from a wide range of other diverse demographics; indeed, far more than would normally visit the V&A at one time based on visitor statistics (20–21% of UK adult visitors from ethnic minority backgrounds in 2015/16 and 2016/17) (Victoria and Albert Museum 2017). Accounts from social media posts, photographs from the night, and observations by the author validate this.

Despite the significant triumphs of the event, it is important to acknowledge gal-dem is not the be-all and end-all organisation that represents all people of colour within London, and, indeed, they do not claim to be. This group is composed of women of colour, who are well educated, liberal, and have a significant amount of cultural capital; therefore, this does not represent all those marginalised by the museum. While nowhere is it ever stated that the V&A or gal-dem themselves hope to be the voice for all people of colour, it is important to acknowledge this fact. There are many different cultural communities within the makeup of London, and it would be impossible and highly prejudicial to expect any one group to represent all, an important lesson for practitioners to learn if they wish to make positive change through co-production. Indeed, the *Friday Late: gal-dem* itself is evidence of this. The event was not solely programmed or run by gal-dem; the collective collaborated with several other organisations and partners to have a more representative and wide range of activities and voices.

As a collective dedicated to research and writing of representative and thought-provoking stories, and creating space within the wider cultural map of London, was it truly radical for the V&A to choose gal-dem? Some would likely argue that putting trust in this type of partnership would be far easier than others who would seek more aggressive actions. However, based on conversations during the night, and discussions led by gal-dem at other co-produced and collaborative events, their willingness to participate is not, in their opinion, a willingness to placate. During a discussion at Tate Britain in November of 2016, an event addressing the shift in identity politics, race, and gender which shared many parallels with the takeover at the V&A and of whom gal-dem was invited to lead a discussion on the representation of women of colour in music and the arts, a member of gal-dem explained, "It's about creating our own spaces; that's why we're here" (Tate Britain 2016).

These sentiments were further echoed by a woman within the audience, identifying herself as an artist and woman of colour, who stated, "push your way in, get in there and have your way... it's a revolution out there" (Tate Britain 2016). The conversation during this event was not censored because of its location, and *gal-dem*, Tate Collective, and members of the audience did not shy away from expressing their frustrations with traditional museum spaces and their lack of appropriate collections, materials, and interpretations that represent people of colour. If museums provide a space where discussion can be open and serve the mission of the event and its participants, conversations can be more open and inclusive, allowing activism and more diverse representation to occur beyond the traditional constraints of the museum setting.

One audience member drove the importance of representation not only in the events that are hosted, but also in the visible front-facing areas of museums themselves when she said in reference to paintings in the 1840s room of Tate Britain, "Looking around the room and not seeing myself [represented in the paintings] made me want to cry" (Tate Britain 2016). She explained she rarely visits places such as Tate Britain because she believes they do not properly acknowledge or represent her background. However, she did attend this event, perhaps serving as evidence to further support the belief that quality programming and partnerships through collaboration and co-production, can begin to open the museum to more diverse narratives, becoming more inclusive for all.

While making a firm stance in favour of the argument of representation, the *Friday Late: gal-dem* at the V&A was also a moment of celebration and enjoyment. This is vital to acknowledge. While gal-dem and the organisations and artists who support them undoubtedly take a political and social stance within the wider arts and cultural sector, they also have the right to enjoyment and celebration without the confines of constant activism. Indeed, true representation would not mean a constant David and Goliath type battle between the under-represented and the institution (Copland 2010). The question that arises then is, can groups like gal-dem, who represent marginalised audiences programme and co-produce events within such spaces without the constant struggle for recognition and representation? If so, it will require both partners in co-production to understand and share the same intentions for the event, allowing radical trust to influence positive change and shape the way traditional institutions work with outside partners.

The co-produced case for diversity

Responses after the *Friday Late: gal-dem* at the V&A suggest that although the event was for one night, the impact was profound and even historic for attendees. Not only did the audience encounter others with similar shared experiences, hundreds took to social media to share their feelings of being far more represented than ever in a museum. As one visitor later shared on social media (2016):

Let me tell you, for one of the few moments of my life, I felt completely comfortable and at ease with myself. I was so blessed to be in a space with people who don't see me as some "angry black girl" or "dramatic". I was not gaslit; I was in a safe environment to express myself amongst people who share the same lived experiences as me and that NEVER happens.

Perhaps this is the true legacy of this event: allowing, even for one night, to see people of colour's experiences showcased. Perhaps that is enough, at least for this moment in time? In an institution such as the V&A, it would be impossible and inappropriate to completely shift the entire narrative of the institution to represent one group. The key is finding the balance, an ambitious and complex task, to say the least.

The high turnout for this event not only seems to counter the statistics about BAME participation (or lack thereof) in the sector, but also provides evidence that London already has large numbers of BAME people interested in participating in events within the arts and cultural sector. From the responses of attendees on social media following the event, the message from the night seems to be: we are here; we want to participate; and we want representation. Perhaps, then, one of the strongest messages that can be learned is that the conversations surrounding BAME engagement need to change and initiatives re-evaluated.

As this event was but for a single night, the impact and significance is likely not to have the lasting effect or legacy compared to more long-term institutional efforts, unless used as a model to evaluate and reconstruct their strategic policies. However, perhaps in some way, the act of academically writing about these types of events and analysing their significance will help widen the impact (a sort of academic activism, if you will). It is, therefore, important to stress here that it would be unrealistic, if not completely reckless, to expect one event and one iteration of radical trust and co-production with a group composed of people of colour to solve the problems that a large and well-funded institution with all its highly trained staff, consultants, and departments have been unable to do. This line of thinking could bring forth instances of pressurised institutional tokenism. Overall, it is important for this to be remembered. It is not the responsibility of people of colour to solve the institutional exclusion that has so often marginalised them (Copland 2010). However, this event was an important step to further the efforts the V&A, through their 2003 Strategy, seemed committed to making, adding another milestone to the timeline towards their goal for true access, inclusion, and diversity.

What the *Friday Late: gal-dem* was able to reveal is the large amount of people of colour and their allies who are willing and interested in participating in the arts and cultural sector of London. Simon (2010: 261) supports this idea stating:

> When collaborative processes produce outcomes that are different from the norm... the impact is often quite significant. Like contributory projects, collaborative [and co-produced] projects can incorporate new voices that can make exhibitions authentic, personal and relevant ... collaborating participants are also more likely to take ownership of the projects they work on and to share their enthusiasm.

The *Friday Late: gal-dem* was in some ways able to reveal the faces behind the statistics of diversity reports and audience demographics, filling a space with those not often represented or present in the museum.

Conclusions and lessons for the future

Despite triumphs of the night, it is important to ensure that museums do not become complacent in shifts towards institutional change simply because they are able to contract outsiders to 'tick strategic boxes' toward inclusion. Engaging with potential partners will require staff and institutions as a whole to reinterpret and re-evaluate their mission, roles and responsibilities (Simon 2010). Unfortunately, in some instances it is possible to see co-production, collaboration, and radical trust as a plaster to a broken system, not the revolutionary change needed to challenge museums to practise what they so often preach in their mission statements (Copland 2010). Evidence of potential for complacency of many institutions can perhaps best be seen through the 2007 commemoration for the *Bicentenary of the Parliamentary Abolition of the Transatlantic Slave Trade*. Arguably one of the most significant moments for museums in the UK to collaborate and increase the stories of people of colour, and in particular the black British experience, this year of commemorations could have marked a turning point for the sector (Hall 2010). However, ten years later, many of the same problems still exist, and, while not suggesting these events and programmes were in any way wasted time, unsuccessful, or insignificant, it does suggest collaboration, co-production, and radical trust can only be a part of the solution to create a more inclusive museum.

Co-production, collaboration, and radical trust can make positive change, but only when it is used as a catalyst for changing the museum institution as a whole into a more inclusive space.[6] Although it is doubtful that the consequence of complacency can be linked to all diversity initiatives, the argument does need to be understood when evaluating programmes created and legacies they leave behind. It should be understood that bringing a more diverse dialogue into the museum does not mean placing BAME audiences into a system that has both historically and more recently excluded them, but to invite diverse audiences to become part of a changing system through the true definitions of co-production, collaboration, and radical trust.

As evidenced through the takeover, working with diverse communities and groups is a key method for museums to provide more ethnically and culturally diverse representation. Through inviting voices that represent more diverse communities, the V&A in partnership with Gal-dem was able to create a significant moment of inclusion within the sector. gal-dem have since gone on to work with other museums and arts organisations as well as continuing to develop their own unique content, carving their own space in the cultural sector of London. Perhaps what they prove is that it is not lack of interest in arts and culture that prevent people of colour from engaging with institutions, but that institutions need to make a conscious effort to support the voices, identities and interests of the audiences they wish to engage. Only time will tell if institutions are prepared to allow these partnerships to truly impact their internal structures and become the agents of change they wish to be. However, judging by the response to the takeover by those in attendance, it seems that the time is now to listen to the voices of those who call for more inclusive representation and wider change to the arts and cultural sector.

Questions for discussion

1. Can collaborating and co-producing with outside organisations associated/connected to target communities create a more welcoming, inclusive, and representative space?
2. Can event-programming play a significant role in increasing representation and engagement with BAME audiences?
3. Does event programming have the power to influence wider institutional change?
4. Is it possible for the arts and cultural sector to co-produce events with groups of people who have been historically marginalised without a consistent struggle for recognition and representation? Can radical trust and co-production be used to create genuine partnerships that address issues of inclusion without placing institutional pressure on third-party partners?

Notes

1 Despite the now formal strategy, the V&A stresses that their work on cultural diversity long predates the formal 2003 strategy by at least 20 years (Nightingale 2011).
2 Statistical analysis has found no statistically significant increase in participation among BAME audiences within an eight-year gap from 2005/06 to 2012/13 (33.6% to 44.2%) (Department for Culture, Media and Sport 2017). Further, when compared to the increased participation among white audiences during the same time, the gap in participation amongst BAME and white audiences has actually increased (Arts Council England 2015).
3 The use of multiple terms, including BAME and people of colour, in this chapter are based on language preferences surrounding academic literature and self-identifying terms used by the groups and people discussed.
4 The co-produced partnership with the V&A and gal-dem consisted of two events; however, the second did not occur on-site at the V&A, so will not be discussed in this chapter. For more information on the second event which took place in February 2017, see: www.dazeddigital.com/artsandculture/article/34880/1/whats-happening-at-the-next-gal-dem-va-takeover.
5 Visitor statists were not provided following the event, so it is difficult to factually say the percentage of BAME audience; however, many accounts, and the author's personal experience at the event, suggest that a large number, if not majority, of the audience were of diverse ethnic backgrounds.
6 One cannot help compare criticism of Fred Wilson's prolific *Mining the Museum* exhibition iwhich aimed to create new and more diverse dialogues within the traditional museum space with the current efforts museums are using to further represent BAME audiences. As Huey Copland (2010: 55), addressing the efforts of Mining to create a more representative dialogue argues, "The institutional attempts at racial inclusiveness fit within a mode of redress aimed at conditioning black subjects to their lot within a white hegemonic order that remains structurally inviolable to revolutionary change".

References

Alberti, S. and Lynch, B. (2010). Legacies of Prejudice: Racism, Co-Production and Radical Trust in the Museum. *Museum Management and Curatorship*, 25 (1), 13–35.

Arts Council England. (2015). *Equality, Diversity and the Creative Case 2012–2015*. Manchester: Arts Council England. www.artscouncil.org.uk/sites/default/files/download-file/Equality_and_diversity_within_the_arts_and_cultural_sector_in_England_0.pdf.

Brinkhurst-Cuff, C. (2016). Perspective: Gal-Dem and the Elevation of Unheard Voices. *Crack Magazine*. https://crackmagazine.net/article/opinion/perspective-gal-dem-eleva tion-unheard-voices/.

Copland, H. (2010). *Bound to Appear: Art, Slavery, and the Site of Blackness in Multi-cultural America*. Chicago: University of Chicago Press.

Cretaro, A. S. (2009). The Effectiveness of Museums Making Late Night Programming to the Twenty-Five to Forty Age Group. MS diss., Drexel University.

Department for Culture, Media and Sport. (2017). *Taking Part 2016/17 Quarter 2 Statistical Release: Museums And Galleries. Taking Part: Statistical Releases*. Department for Culture, Media and Sport.

Gal-Dem. (2015). *About Gal-Dem*. www.gal-dem.com/about/.

Gorier, L. (2009). Leaders in Co-Creation? Why and How Museums Could Develop their Co-Creative Practice with the Public, Building on Ideas from the Performing Arts and other Non-Museum Organisations. MLA Museums Clore Leadership Fellow, University of Leicester, www2.le.ac.uk/departments/museumstudies/rcmg/projects/leaders-in-co-creation/Louise%20Govier%20-%20Clore%20Research%20-%20Leaders%20in%20Co-Creation.pdf.

Group for Large Local Authority Museums. (2000). *Museums and Social Inclusion the GLLAM Report*. Leicester Research Centre for Museums and Galleries, Department of Museum Studies, University of Leicester.

Hall, C. (2010). Afterward: Britain 2007, Problematizing Histories. In C. Kaplan and J. Oldfield (eds.) *Imagining Transatlantic Slavery*. London: Palgrave Macmillan, 191–201.

Helen Denniston Associates. (2003). *Holding up the Mirror Addressing Cultural Diversity in London's Museums*. London: London Museums Agency.

Kane, A. (2016). *Gal-Dem Take Over V&A with London's most Inspiring Women*. Azed Digital. www.dazeddigital.com/artsandculture/article/33498/1/gal-dem-take-over-va-with-londons-most-inspiring-women.

Kay, T. (2016). *Occupying Space: V&A Gal-Dem Takeover*. Thandie Kay. Webblog, http://thandiekay.com/2016/11/02/occupying-space-gal-dem-va-takeover/.

National Museum Directors. (2006). *Cultural Diversity Final Report and Recommenda-tions*. National Museum Directors' Conference, March. www.nationalmuseums.org.uk/media/documents/publications/cultural_diversity_final_report.pdf.

Nightingale, E. (2011). From the Margins to the Core? Working with Culturally Diverse Communities at the V&A Museum. *The International Journal of the Inclusive Museum*, 3, 49–63.

Okolosie, L. (2016). People of Colour are Painfully Absent from our Museums, Let's Change that. *The Guardian*. www.theguardian.com/commentisfree/2016/nov/04/people-of-colour-absent-museums.

Sandell, R. (2003). Social Inclusion, the Museum and the Dynamics of Sectoral Change. *Museum and Society*, 1 (1), 45–62.

Simon, N. (2010). *The Participatory Museum*. Santa Cruz: Museum 2.0.

Speak Up. (2016). *Interview by Zahra Swanzy*. London: Victoria and Albert Museum, 28 October.

Tate. (2016). *BP Loud Tate: Shift*. Tate. www.tate.org.uk/whats-on/tate-britain/festival/bp-loud-tate-shift.

Tate Britain. (2016). *BP Loud Tate: Shift*. London: Tate Britain, 12 November.

Victoria and Albert Museum. (2003). *Strategy for Access, Inclusion, and Diversity*. London: Victoria and Albert Museum.

Victoria and Albert Museum. (2016). *Friday Late: Gal-Dem. V&A Presents, Event Programme*. London.

Victoria and Albert Museum. (2017). *Annual Report and Accounts 2016–2017*. Victoria and Albert Museum. https://vanda-production-assets.s3.amazonaws.com/2017/07/14/10/40/11/325d184c-c4f2-4ad7-81ee-1fcd1dd35dff/VAAR-Report-0707-Final-HR.PDF.

Victoria and Albert Museum. (2018). *Friday Late*. https://www.vam.ac.uk/info/friday-late.

Victoria and Albert Museum Friday Late. (2016). *Friday Late: Gal-Dem*. London: Victoria and Albert Museum, 28 October.

Warwick Commission on the Future of Cultural Value. (2015). *Enriching Britain: Culture, Creativity and Growth*. University of Warwick. https://warwick.ac.uk/research/warwick commission/futureculture/finalreport/warwick_commission_report_2015.pdf.

8 In our own words

Organising and experiencing exhibitions as Black women and women of colour in Scotland

Layla-Roxanne Hill and Francesca Sobande

Introduction

This chapter is based on the authors' reflections on co-ordinating creative work, associated zine workshops, and launch as part of *The House that Heals the Soul*, a 2017 exhibition at the Centre for Contemporary Arts (CCA) in Glasgow. It focuses on personal experiences of co-organising *Yon Afro Collective: In Our Own Words*, as co-founders of a Black women-led collective of women of colour in Scotland (Yon Afro Collective). The authors reflexively draw upon this case study to examine issues regarding the encounters of Black women and women of colour in relation to arts and cultural spaces in Scotland and to emphasise the need for their narratives to be archived, creatively expressed, and publicly acknowledged. There is also discussion of preparing to participate in Glasgow International 2018, a biennial contemporary visual arts festival.

Although this chapter is written as co-founders of Yon Afro Collective (YAC), the authors do so with a focus on individual and shared experiences as cisgender, middle-class, and light-skinned women who are both Black and mixed-race. The authors are aware of the privileges and social capital (Isoke 2013) attached to these personal experiences, which is why, in writing this chapter, the authors do not attempt to speak on behalf of all Black women and women of colour in Scotland. Instead, the aim is to shed light on aspects of the under-representation and (mis)representation of such individuals within the Scottish arts scene. We have lived in the words and worlds of others, rarely reading about experiences similar to our own, written by women similar to ourselves. This chapter builds upon work on those who are societally 'Othered', particularly Black women and women of colour, and their engagement with media and the arts (Hill 2017, 2018; Sobande 2017, 2018). It is intended to catalyse and address questions pertaining to the necessity for Black women and women of colour in Scotland to locate their experiences within the context of what is happening to Black people within the United Kingdom. It is intended for this chapter to serve as stimulus for further critique of the extent to which Black women and women of colour are included in the creative arts scene in Scotland. as curators, creators, and audience members.

Intersectional insights and diversity discourse in Scotland

Black women and women of colour are often made invisible amidst data and discourse related to gender, race, and diversity in Scotland. It is all too common that discussion of gender and women in Scotland is synonymous with the perspectives of white women, and that conversations to do with race do not explore the entanglements of racism and sexism. Even when participating in spaces intended to foreground intersectionality and marginalised voices, there can be a lack of dialogue about, and between, Black women and women of colour. As O'Brien and Oakley (2015: 4) note, "inequality is bound up with how society is stratified and structured." When situating the lives of Black women and women of colour in Scotland, an intersectional approach enables understanding of how systemic oppression functions in interdependent ways.

This research is approached from a Black feminist and intersectional perspective of the structural subjugation of Black women and women of colour (Crenshaw 2017; Emejulu 2015; Essed 1991; Hull, et al. 1982). The starting point of this writing is acknowledgement of how such women are negatively affected by the interlocking nature of racism and sexism in addition to other societally embedded forms of oppression, such as those related to sexuality, class, dis/ability, non-binary identity, and migrant status. Intersectionality is about observing issues of power and ideology, not just those to do with identity. Embarking from this position, the focus is on the authors' organisation of *Yon Afro Collective: In Our Own Words*. Bolstered by Black feminist principles of recognising the knowledge that is inherent to the lived experiences of Black women (Hill-Collins 2016), the authors place personal perspectives firmly at the centre of this work.

Questions regarding inclusion, inequality, and exclusion circulate amidst the British creative and cultural industries (Allen, et al. 2013; Finkel, et al. 2017; O'Brien, et al. 2017). However, discussions related to race rarely take priority (Hesmondhalgh and Saha 2013; Saha 2017), let alone those regarding the intersections of racism and sexism (Thompson 2017). Further still, there is a dearth of creative and cultural policy research that specifically concerns Black women and women of colour in Scotland and the UK more widely. Black women are part of an under-represented demographic in the creative and cultural industries in Scotland and the UK, as is highlighted in Thompson's (2017) online article, *Excerpts from the diary of a Black Woman at the Edinburgh Fringe*. Thompson's (2017) account of participating in this festival illustrates the difficulties that such women encounter when pursuing creative work, including the discomfort involved in facing a solely white audience. Anticipation of the introspective and isolating dynamics involved in presenting creative work as Black women and women of colour to predominantly white audiences is a potential barrier to their inclusion in creative spaces, which sweeping statistical data alone cannot articulate.

It is not enough for conversations about accessibility and diversity to merely occur. Such discussions need to include and be led by those least represented in these sectors. In the spirit of Black feminist foundations, the authors seek to record the lives of such women, whose presence and history in Scotland is not often the focus of public commentary or media (Hill 2017, 2018). Whilst this work relates to issues of representation, it is also focused on power and politics, because without transformational and structural changes, increased surface level representation is meaningless. We echo the words of Finkel, et al. (2017: 281), who affirm that "the call to 'diversify the creative' invokes critical engagements with both the concept of 'diversity' and that of 'the creative'." Broad use of the language of 'diversity' and 'creativity', without clear reference to particularly marginalised identities, results in their specific experiences remaining unexplored, or misrepresented.

(Dis)locating race in Scotland and beyond BAME

Unspoken issues related to race, access, acceptance, authority, and the arts in Scotland, which negatively affect Black people and people of colour, regardless of their gender identity, can often present themselves in circumstances which are unprovocative. Amongst these was online backlash faced by Mercury Prize-winning Scottish band, Young Fathers. In 2017, band members, Kayus Bankole and Alloysius Massaquoi, featured in a video commissioned by National Galleries of Scotland and the National Portrait Gallery, London. The video, which was a creative meditation on issues of inclusion, exclusion, race, Scotland's art scene and history, resulted in much reactionary and vitriolic racist online commentary. This is indicative of the need to unsettle ideas regarding who, and what perspectives, pictures, and politics, have a place in creative contexts in Scotland. Racist and racially-coded rhetoric related to the afore-mentioned video also raises important questions concerning who is (dis)located or (mis)placed in Scottish creative and arts locations. Not only are arts events and exhibitions located (situated somewhere, rooted in a specific and tangible space), they can also involve people – like artefacts – becoming (dis)located (moving in and out of the space in ways influenced by their access to it). Locations can be used liberally in relation to fixed physical spaces and more ephemeral social positions that people are able to access by virtue of their socio-cultural capital (Milestone 2016).

O'Brien and Oakley (2015: 7) assert that "the fine grained understandings of minority ethnic cultural consumption and its relationship to cultural value requires a research approach that is not possible with the current survey data", which "brings a range of diverse and different communities together under the Black Asian Minority Ethnic (BAME) category". Without an interpretive inspection of challenges faced by Black women and women of colour traversing Scottish arts and cultural terrain, the intricacies of their experiences remain unconsidered by those actioning policy and practice change. Creative Scotland's (2015: 3) report on equalities, diversities, and inclusions recognises that:

Scotland is a country where art and culture are highly valued as an integral part of our social, emotional, intellectual, and economic lives. But Scotland is changing. It is increasingly diverse. Our cities are home to a significant and growing BAME population.

The term, 'Black Asian and Minority Ethnic (BAME)', has often placed much-needed attention on the experiences of individuals who are not racialised as white. However, this acronym is also used to homogenise the experience of people of colour by reducing their differences to such an extent that any meaningful understanding of their lives is completely compromised. Recent articles such as, *Why It's Time To Ditch The Term 'BAME'* (Barett 2018), highlight how this language rarely captures how people self-identify, and instead, serves as a rhetorical device used by politicians, policymakers, and media professionals. To more precisely name the experiences of Black women and women of colour, whilst also affirming that these two terms are not interchangeable, it is time to move away from this acronym.

Encourage(d), engage(d) or involve(d)?

In 2016, Black, trans, gender non-conforming artist, Travis Alabanza, was invited to take part in an arts festival in Glasgow, Scotland. As part of an article for gal-dem, Travis commented on being one of very few "visible black faces contributing" and questioned why the only artist involved was not from Glasgow (No 2017). Despite

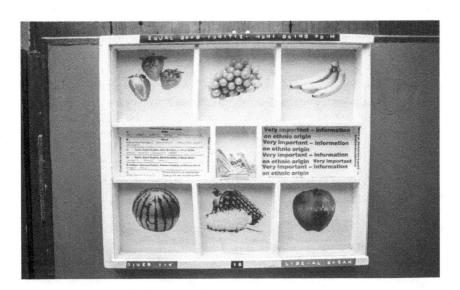

Figure 8.1 Equal Opportunities Monitoring Form from *Mullata Manifesto: Tragic Retelt* (Hill 2018).

Source: private collection of Layla-Roxanne Hill.

a number of Black and people of colour artists/creators in Glasgow, Yon Afro Collective consists of several creative practitioners; and, around Scotland, the invitation extended to Alabanza was in response to the lack of diversity reflected in the festival programme. The opportunity for funded bodies and key partners to apply the Race Equality Framework to encourage visibility of Black people and people of colour within the arts in Scotland was not implemented and a familiar short-sighted approach of looking elsewhere was adopted; looking for 'AnOther Othered' artist. Alabanza vocalised this missed opportunity and, upon receiving a second invite to Scotland, undertook a curatorial role and gave voice to Black Scottish artists who had been overlooked (Alabanza 2017). The *Other'd Artist* (May–June 2017), an exhibition with over 20 Black artists, responding to how they felt within institutions was held at Transmission Gallery, Glasgow. The event further signalled the need for increased representation of Black people and people of colour in Scottish creative contexts, which spurred plans for a Yon Afro Collective event.

The arts festival referred to by Alabanza was Glasgow International Festival. Funded by Creative Scotland and Glasgow Life (amongst others), the acclaimed biennial festival includes aims to show "work in non-traditional spaces as well as museums and galleries" (Glasgow International 2017). Glasgow International 2016's programme vision was to be one which looked at the industrial heritage of Glasgow and the city's status as a cultural centre in present day (Glasgow International Festival 2016). Sarah McCrory (2016), Director of Glasgow International 2014 and 2016, described Glasgow as being "very culturally vibrant – an exciting place to live. North, south, east and west are such diverse neighbourhoods... and because it's a small city, you get to know it really well." The Glasgow International 2016 programme exhibited work by more than 228 local and international artists – of which, none were identifiable as Black and Scottish. Eleven years on from the first Glasgow International art festival, the seventh edition excluded the Black Scottish voice from Glasgow's post-industrial narrative, mirroring the erasure of our vital role in Scotland's industry triumphs (Heuchan 2016).

The arts and creative industries can (and should) be spheres where barriers to expression do not exist and where oppressions and disparities are communicated in a universal language; however, when these arenas fail to adopt an intersectional approach, programmes such as the one in the Glasgow International Festival can become as homogeneous as the art galleries, museums, and institutional cultural spaces they often claim to be resisting against. If Black and women of colour were involved in the arts and creative sphere, would this exclusion have occurred? Spring 2017, and applications to Glasgow International Festival 2018 opened. Following McCrory's departure to Goldsmiths, the 2018 programme had no theme and would be under new direction. Encouragement from the CCA for *Yon Afro Collective: In Our Own Words*, as well as our efforts to build Yon Afro Collective itself, had increased the confidence of members, and a group show, *(Re)imagining Self and Raising Consciousness of Existence Through Alternative Space and (Re)imagined Place* was pitched to Glasgow International Festival 2018.

Though most Yon Afro members involved with the Glasgow International project are creative practitioners, attempting to give voice to Black and women of colour within the Glasgow International framework is one which is unfamiliar and mystifying to all. The authors' research notes from early in the process highlight:

> Application in... hear back soon. Delays. Rejected... encouraged (expected?) to apply to Across The City strand. Was endorsement not enough? Proposal/ budget not clear enough? Ask for too much/little? Not from a taught art perspective... All not enough/too much? Requested feedback.

> Going for ATC strand.. UPDATE: Accepted. Wonder if alternative ways to match figures put in budget can be found? SELF-RELIANCE. Still no feedback. Maybe shouldn't have gone for this.

> Struggling to find spaces for exhibition. REASONS: too political/radical/ doesn't fit with 'values'. Venues already promised to prospective GI partici- pants – long before anyone has been told of application outcome (!). UPDATE: Secured Govanhill Baths!!! Wonder if been able to use this space if it wasn't community owned? One of the GI Director's artist(s) is also using the Baths – inadvertently increasing our footfall. UPDATE: GI not using the space after all. Why?

> Is YAC ready/strong enough for this? What if it doesn't work out?

As Yon Afro Collective undertook its most public effort to centre voices of Black and women of colour in Scotland, an extract of an email from Richard Parry, Director, Glasgow International Festival 2018, reminds us of where we began and why we cannot end:

> I did want to share one thing with you, which I think might be of interest. When Lubaina Himid visited last year to do a site visit, I also took her around the 'House that heals the soul' show at the CCA. There were a couple of things that especially caught her eye. The first was a book with a painting of hers on the front cover, which she revealed had been entirely paid for by Maud Sulter back at the time in the early 1970s. The second was your shelf of books. She looked at what it was and exclaimed 'There we go – it was all worth it, that struggle that we went through in the '70s and '80s'. It struck me quite powerfully in any case.

With such words in mind, Yon Afro Collective continue to co-ordinate creative activities which provide a platform for the talent and thoughts of Black women and women of colour in Scotland and beyond, and are particularly motivated to do so given what was learned when putting together a small showcase at the Centre for Contemporary Arts in Glasgow.

Case study: Yon Afro – in our own words

Yon Afro Collective (YAC) is a Black-led collective for women of colour in Scotland which was conceptualised early in 2016. Following the energy mobilised by the first *Black Feminism, Womanism, and the Politics of Women of Colour in Europe Conference* (University of Edinburgh, September 2016), in addition to *Women of Colour, the Media & (Mis)Representation* (National Union of Journalists Scotland, October 2016) events, YAC was established later in 2016. As well as the referendum of 2014 (Scottish Independence Referendum, September 2014) and 2016 (United Kingdom European Union Membership Referendum, June 2016), which would shift understandings of Scottish, British, and Black identities, it felt instinctive to organise and bring Black and women of colour together and, partly as a result of subsequent conversations that took place at the CCA in Glasgow, YAC was formed.

Since first meeting at *Gender and Poverty: Understanding the Connections* (The Poverty Alliance, March 2016), where Prof. Akwugo Emejulu put us in contact with each other, YAC has collaborated on activities related to addressing the marginalisation of Black women and women of colour in Scotland and beyond. Whilst we use the terms, 'Black women' and 'women of colour', the distinct differences that exist between both are recognised. This includes those related to the anti-blackness that can be perpetuated by women of colour and which can constrain the scope for interracial solidarity in certain contexts. When referring to Black women, YAC specifically does so with reference to individuals of Black African and/or Caribbean descent. YAC is predominantly led by Black women, including individuals who were born in Scotland and those who arrived there at different points in their lives.

YAC remains an evolving project that is not free from challenges, as is often the case with collective organising and consciousness-raising around issues of race, gender, inequality, and social justice (The Combahee River Collective 2009; Cooper, et al. 2017; Emejelu 2015; Henderson and Mackay 1990). As Amos and Parmar (1984: 4) note, "The power of sisterhood stops at the point at which hard political decisions need to be made and political priorities decided." The longevity of collectives involves overcoming differing political positions, personalities, in addition to personal and professional commitments, which can disrupt solidarity forming. There is also a need to (self)examine the privileges of those who are marginalised as Black women and women of colour, yet do not face the same plights as other such women who deal with the sharpest edges of intersectional oppression. Such (self)examination can prove too uncomfortable for some, who may stop short of a radical politics that requires scrutinising their simultaneous social capital and oppression. The neoliberal logics of diversity can consume the radical potential of collectives, who may become 'flavour of the month' when funding opportunities arise, and can quickly become caught up in the very 'tick box' activity that they intended to dismantle in the first place. As YAC co-founders, one of the authors' aims was to improve the visibility of Black women and women of colour in Scotland, and whilst it is not possible to predict or shape the future of YAC, its (hi)story needs to be publicly documented.

The Scottish Government's *Race Equality Framework for Scotland 2016–2030* (2016: 44) aims to "promote inclusiveness and participation by making better connections between minority ethnic communities, organisations and institutions involved in heritage, culture, sports and media", and will achieve this through encouragement directed at funded bodies and key partners, and engagement with minority ethnic communities. Striving to engage, but yet not involve minority ethnic communities, reflects a disconnect between policy-makers and the creative needs of Black women and women of colour in Scotland, as is echoed by Rowena Arshad of the Scottish Black Women's Group, a group of Black women who began meeting in 1985. Arshad recalls the demands made on the group to engage, "comment on this, what about that, help us to get more Black women to come to our event". When in fact the Scottish Black Women's Group "wanted a stake in making the rules of the game of life, and when we did, the doors began to close or seemed incredibly stiff to open" (Arshad, 1990: 119). Organising as Black and women of colour in Scotland, over 25 years later, it would be difficult not to see personal experiences mirrored in those words. Though relatively little is known about Yon Afro Collective (who are we, why are we here), movement on social media has lent itself to requests to "speak at, contribute to, 'meet to discuss your organising?' and attend this". All too often, YAC is brought in after something has already been created, an afterthought as a result of a mistake and rarely the first thought. Such experiences are consistent with how diversity and multiculturalism has been marketised in ways that incentivise institutions to indicate their connection to "diverse" groups and communities (Taylor 2012), yet without necessarily including them in substantive and long-term ways.

In the summer of 2017, the authors organised *Yon Afro Collective: In Our Own Words* as part of *The House that Heals the Soul* (22 July–3 September 2017) at the Centre for Contemporary Arts (CCA) in Glasgow. The exhibition focused on the radical and political status of libraries and curating the event entailed exhibiting selected books, creating a short video, producing written material, hosting zine-making workshops, and a launch event; all of which related to the lives and narratives of Black women and women of colour. Obstacles to entry and participation in the arts are not always obvious or measurable (Allen, et al. 2013). It is for this reason that strategies, to foster inclusivity, must be based on a nuanced understanding of the concept of 'barriers' and their intersectional nature. When embarking upon the project which would ultimately involve being on display and taking up (white) space, the authors were filled with a mixture of excitement and trepidation, unsure of what we had to offer, and who for. Such unsureness seems symptomatic of the experiences of individuals who rarely see people who are similar to themselves represented in exhibition and arts environments. Whilst assured of the value of YAC's participation in the overarching exhibition by our contacts at the CCA, at various stages in the preparation process, the authors experienced bouts of unease:

Who will attend?
Will they get it?
Who is this for?
What are we trying to say?
Do we need to say something specific, or is saying anything enough?
Where and who are the Scottish, Black/woc artists and writers?
Who is this for?
Do we need to explain it?
Will they get it?
Who is this for?

When YAC first began speaking about the idea of coordinating, *Yon Afro Collective: In Our Own Words*, the organisers struggled to think of (m)any examples of national exhibitions attended which primarily exhibited the work and words of Black women and women of colour of Scotland, beyond a refugee, slave, or colonial narrative. Whilst the goal was to engage people from a broad demographic with the creative space, it was important to attempt to prioritise and attract Black women and women of colour, who are frequently absent from arts venues and vocations (Thompson 2017). Questions that were raised when discussing curating *Yon Afro Collective: In Our Own Words* included: What does it mean to feel (un)comfortable in creative spaces? Whose comfort is prioritised as part of the construction of such settings? Who is involved in organising these activities, and with what audience in mind?

There were no clear plans to measure levels of engagement other than to include a comments book onsite at the exhibition space within the CCA and make contact information for Yon Afro Collective available (see Figure 8.2 below). In hindsight, a more strategic approach to collating data in response to *Yon Afro Collective: In Our Own Words* may have yielded more information to draw upon for this chapter. However, the quantitative ways that arts and public engagement activity is often measured can be perceived as being problematic; this is particularly the case when accounting for *Yon Afro Collective: In Our Own Words* having less mass appeal due to its focus on a 'minority' group. Choosing to not record the experience through conventional audience data capture techniques, such as questionnaires and footfall tracking, seemed appropriate given the aim to challenge existing approaches to the public display of creative practice.

This is a story situated in Scotland; yet, the issues that Black women and women of colour encounter in such a setting, including the intersections of racism and sexism, are ones that can play a part in the lives of such individuals elsewhere in the world. Amongst the writing left in the comments book was the following statement which signals how work such as *Yon Afro Collective: In Our Own Words* can cultivate connections between the narratives of Black women and women of colour in Scotland and other parts of Europe: "Thank you for being here – representing a minority in literature. As a mulatto Franco-African-American, it is pleasing and reassuring to see the 'black' culture everywhere, even in Glasgow. This inspires me to see and do the same." Other comments we received which

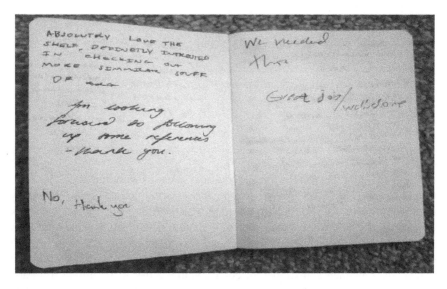

Figure 8.2 Yon Afro Collective: In Our Own Words comments book content.
Source: Photograph by the Author.

signalled a positive response, included: "Fantastic. Needed. Stay strong! Resist! Solidarity!", as well as the words "We needed this", and encouragement from Turner prize-winning artist, Lubaina Himid. Additionally, someone wrote about being "really glad to hear that a Black/POC women's radical voice is being heard at last in Glasgow". The "at last" sentiment is further testament that we are not alone in wanting to see Black women and women of colour in Scotland better represented and undiluted in creative and cultural contexts.

Whilst the comments left as a result of *Yon Afro Collective: In Our Own Words* may seem inconsequential in the grand scheme of audience engagement big data and analytics, the pages which were filled are indication of demand for creative activities which foreground the voices and visions of Black women and women of colour in Scotland. Moreover, the zine launch event brought together a varied cohort of approximately 30 people to the CCA (see Figure 8.3 below). These were people perhaps curious to know who and what was Yon Afro, people keen to connect to the 'Other' through discussion of literature, or merely there to support the presentation of creative work by Black women and women of colour in Scotland. There is a need to make visible the trauma that can play a part in the lives of Black women and women of colour in Scotland, who are commonly on the receiving end of pervasive and interwoven racism and sexism. However, the importance for Black women and women of colour in Scotland to express themselves in creative ways that extend beyond expectations and/or fetishisation of work defined by pain, internal turmoil, and (dis)location also must be asserted. Black art does not always need to be about Africa and the Caribbean, or the

Figure 8.3 Yon Afro Collective: In Our Own Words display of selected books.
Source: Photograph by the Author.

notion of 'home' being elsewhere. Black women and women of colour in Scotland are not a monolithic group. Their experiences are complex and varied. They are deserving of understanding and an outlet in Scotland's creative arts scene, whereby people may learn to embrace difference, including when it does not look and sound as is expected.

Conclusion and call to action

The rising success of creative content, publication collectives, and outlets led by Black women and women of colour in Britain, such as gal-dem and Black Ballad, speaks to the appeal of their expressive work and marks a documentation of the lives of Black women and women of colour. Additionally, Digital Desperados, a DIY grassroots organisation by Nosheen Khwaja and Cloudberry MacLean, offers free filmmaking courses and workshops for women of colour and also a programme, *GLITCH Film Festival*, providing Scotland with a much-needed international platform for film and art created by LGBTQ+ and people of colour. Other creative collectives include Sister Collective, a duo (Cass Ezeji and Siobhain Ma), who explore the experiences and challenges facing mixed race Scottish women through performance, soundscapes, and text. OH141 and Grassroots Glasgow, led by Sarra Wild, aims to create safe club environments and improve representation in electronic music by providing support to women, people of colour, and members of the LGBTQ+ community. Transmission Gallery in Glasgow is currently led by a people of colour (POC) committee, and other activities intended to challenge the under-representation and mis-representation of people of colour in Scottish arts spaces include those organised by the Glasgow School of Art POC Society, Split Collective, Zanana Project, and Glasgow Women's Library's Collect:if. There is a rich history of Black and POC artistic expression in Britain (Chambers 2014; Hall 2006; Tawadros 1989); yet, cultural institutions often treat demand for the creative work of Black women and women of colour as more of a question than an observation.

Perceptions of the narrow appeal of the creative output of Black women and women of colour, as well as their alleged reluctance to participate in arts activity, is often cited as an excuse for their scarce representation in cultural industries. We have attended numerous events where people have professed that Black communities in Scotland are "too difficult" to engage with, or that researchers are not equipped to reach out to them. These unfounded claims obscure the lived realities of Black women and women of colour in Scotland, including those who do not live within clear communities of other Black people or people of colour. If it is not the alleged indifference of Black women and women of colour that is dubiously cited as the reason for their absence in creative contexts, alternatively, the phrase "statistically insignificant" frequently takes its place. More research is needed that is qualitative and methodologically innovative to provide an outlet for the words and worldview of Black women and women of colour in Scotland.

As part of how organisations "respond better to Black, Asian and minority ethnic communities in Scotland, and support the development of BAME leadership, employment and representation in the arts" (Creative Scotland 2015: 3), the authors urge them to identify and action ways to support the co-ordination of events and activities which offer Black women and women of colour in Scotland a public platform. Sometimes, this may involve them creatively conveying much about their racialised and gendered identities. Other times, this may involve Black women and women of colour producing and curating art that ostensibly has little to do with race and gender. Regard-less of the content and form of their craft, such women should have the chance to share it and be credited for it. They should have the opportunity to spark dialogue about the difficulties in their lives, or to capture surreal and joyous moments that are far removed from issues of trauma. Whilst *Yon Afro Collective: In Our Own Words* was organised at a low cost and with the support of the CCA, many other Black women and women of colour do not have the unpaid time and financial resources to draw upon as part of such processes. This experience of coordinating *Yon Afro Collective: In Our Own Words* may be but one case study, but, by documenting what it entailed and questions that it stimulated, it makes a contribution to efforts to improve the experiences of Black women and women of colour amidst Scottish creative and cultural industries.

Questions for discussion

1. How can those involved in the creative and arts industry in Scotland ensure that Black women and women of colour are included in these spaces in ways which go beyond demonstrating a commitment to inclusion/multiculturalism and fulfilling diversity quotas?
2. Why can an intersectional understanding of structural oppression play an important part in addressing issues of inclusion/exclusion and inequality amidst the organisation of events and cultural activity?
3. DIY collectives often have an ethos of idealised inclusion and radical politics, but how (in)compatible is this with a goal for oft ignored societal issues to be communicated to a wider audience, including via external institutions?
4. Have you ever felt (un)comfortable at an event, or the prospect of having to attend one? If so, why? What changes to the event might have made you feel differently?

References

Alabanza, T. (2017). *The Other'd Artist/s*. http://travisalabanza.co.uk/the-otherd-artist-exhibition/.

Allen, K., Quinn, K., Hollingworth, S., and Rose, A. (2013). Becoming employable students and 'ideal' creative workers: Exclusion and inequality in higher education work placements. *British Journal of Sociology of Education*, 34(3), 431–452.

Amos, A. and Parmar, P. (1984). Challenging imperial feminism. *Feminist Review*, 17, 3–20.

Arshad, R. (1990). The Scottish Black women's group. In S. Henderson and A. Mackay (eds.) *Grit and Diamonds: Women in Scotland Making History 1980*. Edinburgh: Stramullion Ltd and The Cauldron Collective, 118–120.

Barett, G.M. (2018). Why It's Time To Ditch The Term "BAME". www.refinery29.uk/2018/05/199526/what-does-bame-stand-for.

The Combahee River Collective. (2009). A black feminist statement. In S. M. James, F. S. Foster and B. Guy-Sheftall (eds.) *Still Brave: The Evolution of Black Women's Studies*. New York: Feminist Press, 3–11.

Chambers, E. (2014). *Black Artists in British Art: A History Since the 1950s*. London: I.B. Tauris & Co.

Cooper, B. C., Morris, S. M., and Boylorn, R. M. (2017). *The Crunk Feminist Collection*. New York: Feminist Press.

Creative Scotland. (2015). Equalities, siversities and inclusion report 2015 www.creativescotland.com/__data/assets/pdf_file/0004/31279/Equalities,Diversityand-Inclusion-Report-April-2015.pdf.

Crenshaw, K. (2017). *On Intersectionality: The Essential Writings of Kimberle Crenshaw*. New York: New Press.

Emejulu, A. (2015). From #BlackLivesMatter to anti-austerity: Women of colour and the politics of solidarity. www.versobooks.com/blogs/2303-from-blacklivesmatter-to-anti-austeritywomen-of-colour-and-the-politics-of-solidarity.

Essed, P. (1991). Knowledge and resistance: Black women talk about racism in the Netherlands and the USA. *Feminism & Psychology*, 1(2), 123–143.

Finkel, R., Jones, D., and Sang, K. (2017). Diversifying the creative: Creative work, creative industries, creative identities. *Organization*, 24(3), 281–288.

Glasgow International. (2017). http://glasgowinternational.org.

Glasgow International Festival. (2016) *Glasgow International Festival Announces 2016 programme*. [Online] http://glasgowinternational.org/wp-content/uploads/2015/09/GLAS GOW-INTERNATIONAL-FESTIVAL-OF-VISUAL-ART-2016.pdf.

Glasgow International Festival. (2018) *About Glasgow International*.http://glasgowinterna tional.org/about-2018.

Hall, S. (2006). Black diaspora artists in Britain: Three 'moments' in post-war history. *History Workshop Journal*, 61(1), 1–24.

Henderson, S. and A. Mackay. (1990). *Grit and Diamonds: Women in Scotland Making History 1980*. Edinburgh: Stramullion Ltd and The Cauldron Collective.

Heuchan, C. (2016). *Race, History and Brexit: Black Scottish Identity*. https://sisteroutrider. wordpress.com/2016/10/26/race-history-and-brexit-black-scottish-identity.

Hesmondhalgh, D. and Saha, A. (2013). Race, ethnicity, and cultural production. *The International Journal of Media and Culture*, 11(3), 179–195.

Hill, L. R. (2018). An Other World. *Bella Caledonia*, 8 May.https://bellacaledonia.org.uk/ 2018/05/08/an-other-world/.

Hill, L. R. (2017). News Blackout – Why aren't black British women treated fairly in the media? *National Union of Journalists*, 30 March. https://nujscotland.org.uk/2017/03/30/ news-blackout-why-arent-black-british-women-treated-fairly-in-the-media/.

Hill-Collins, P. (2016). Black feminist thought as oppositional knowledge. *Departures in Critical Qualitative Research*, 5(3), 133–144.

Hull, G. T., Scott, P. B., and Smith, B. (1982). *But Some of Us Are Brave: Black Women's Studies*. New York: The Feminist Press.

Isoke, Z. (2013). *Urban Black Women and the Politics of Resistance*. New York: Palgrave Macmillan.

McCrory, S. (2016). My Glasgow: Curator Sarah McCrory talks culture in the city. *The Independent*, 21 October. www.independent.co.uk/travel/uk/my-glasgowcurator-sarah-mccrory-talks-culture-in-the-city-a7373096.html.

Milestone, K. (2016). 'Northnernness', gender and Manchester's creative industries. *Journal for Cultural Research*, 20(1), 45–59.

No, M. (2017). *Travis Alabanza Reframes the Traditional Gallery with THE OTHER'D ARTIST/S*. www.gal-dem.com/otherd-artists-travis-alabanza/.

O'Brien, D., Allen, K., Friedman, S., and Saha, A. (2017). Producing and consuming inequality: A cultural sociology of the cultural industries. *Cultural Sociology*, 11(3), 271–282.

O'Brien, D. and Oakley, K. (2015). *Cultural Value and Inequality: A Critical Literature Review*. A Report commissioned by the Arts and Humanities Research Council's Cultural Value Project https://ahrc.ukri.org/documents/project-reports-and-reviews/cultural-value-and-inequality-a-critical-literature-review.

Parry, R. (2018). *Hello/GI/2018. [Email]*.

Saha, A. (2017). *Race and the Cultural Industries*. Cambridge: Polity Press.

Scottish Government. (2016). *Race Equality Framework for Scotland 2016 to 2030*. Scottish Government, 21 March. www.gov.scot/Publications/2016/03/4084.

Sobande, F. (2018). Managing media as parental race-work: (Re)mediating children's black identities. In S. N. N. Cross, C. Ruvalcaba, A. Venkatesh, R. W. Belk (eds.). *Consumer Culture Theory*, Volume 19. London: Emerald Publishing.

Sobande, F. (2017). Watching me watching you: Black women in Britain on YouTube. *European Journal of Cultural Studies*, 20(6), 655–671.

Tawadros, G. (1989). Beyond the boundary: The work of three black women artists in Britain. *Third Text*, 3(8–9), 121–150.

Taylor, Y. (2012). *Educational Diversity: The Subject of Difference and Different Subjects*. Basingstoke: Palgrave Macmillan.

Thompson, S. (2017). Excerpts from the diary of a Black Woman at the Edinburgh Fringe. *Exeunt Magazine*, 21 August. exeuntmagazine.com/features/excerpts-diary-black-woman-edinburgh-fringe.

9   Outside the comfort zone

Intercultural events in suspicious times

Roaa Ali

Introduction

With terror-related incidents constituting a sizeable and recurrent portion of the daily serving of UK news coverage, a socio-political discourse attempting to combat radicalisation, and a surge of Islamophobia in the UK, a heightened public anxiety grows concerning speech that could potentially be labelled 'radicalising' or 'Islamophobic'. Academic events and community events which include presentations that touch upon cultural Islam in the UK often require special consideration from the speaker, organiser, and the audience. This chapter explores a network of stakeholders engaged in the making of an event including the speaker, audience, and socio-political context. Within this, it considers the reticence or receptiveness that both presenters and audience members experience in events incorporating the subject of Muslim identity in the UK. As case studies, the chapter focuses on three UK events that included presentations on the role of the Muslim artist in contemporary Britain. As a presenter at two of the events, the author employs auto-ethnography as part of the research methodology for this chapter, complemented with analysis of relevant scholarly resources on the topic, as well as field observation on audience reception.

Two of the events analysed in this chapter are academic, while the third is a community event. Through these events, the chapter investigates the challenges facing the presenter of politically and culturally sensitive topics. These include managing a degree of suspicion that organisers and audiences might have, exercising self-censorship to cater for ideologically polarised audiences, and facilitating audience participation in a way that encourages inclusion and combats marginalisation. This chapter also documents audience reception and their willingness or hesitation to participate in polemic and culturally uncomfortable conversations. In essence, this chapter aims to highlight some of the difficulties and sensitivities that accompany holding events which, in part, negotiate Muslim representation in the UK. The hope is that by acknowledging and addressing these hurdles, special attention will be made when organising or managing such events in order for them to become unencumbered tools in the service of a diverse and integrated society.

Three case studies: the what, when and how

The three events analysed in this chapter all included presentations and/or discussions about Muslims as part of the cultural composition of the UK. Two of the events were academic and the third was community-led. The first of the academic events contextualised in this chapter is the AHRC-sponsored 'Co-Creating Cities and Communities' forum held in Bristol (July 2017) in which the author presented on how British Islamic street art mediates an inclusion of 'Otherness'. The other academic event is the 'Theatre and Performance Research Association (TaPRA)' conference held in Salford (September 2017), where the author presented on the impermissibility of certain British Muslim representations in the UK. While the theme of the two events was not Islam in Britain, both events encouraged topics about diversity and inclusion in the UK. Aimed at general audiences, the 'Hubb Debate' is the third event to be discussed in this chapter, and was organised by a local art organisation called Birmingham Soul City, held in the city of Birmingham (August 2017). In that event, presenters, host, and audiences debated the topic of empathy in the 'age of hatred' with a Muslim focus. In varying degrees, all three events were advancing a vision for a more inclusive environment in academia and society, and can be considered intercultural. These events offered their speakers and audiences a space to debate cultural issues, including the representation of Muslims, in the UK.

A combination of research methods has been employed to explore the mentioned events and interrogate the subject position of both the speaker and audience member. The impetus behind this study stemmed from employing an auto-ethnographical approach to events, which was initially adopted unconsciously, but later turned into a conscious decision when analysing the events. Maréchal (2010: 43) defines auto-ethnography as "a form or method of research that involves self-observation and reflexive investigation in the context of ethnographic field work and writing". Through self-observation, the researcher is able to record his/her understanding of a certain situation or event, and the interactions and emotions generated through this event. When conducting auto-ethnographic research, the researcher seeks to employ an objective assessment of his/her surrounding and subject position, while acknowledging his/her own subjective viewpoint. As a consequence, the researcher creates a narrative of the event that simultaneously offers an accurate observatory account of it, and introspective reflections integral to its analysis.

Events stakeholders

The nature of an event as an organised public spectacle renders it subject to societal and governmental vigilance, and sometimes circumspection. This is particularly true when the topic of discussion at a given event is that which could potentially be socially unacceptable or politically problematic. Ultimately, this governs what gets to be spoken or unspoken and shapes the overall event. Thus, it is important to understand the explicit or implicit roles at play at such events. The three events selected for analysis in this chapter can all be arguably described as multicultural or intercultural. The community-led 'Hubb Debate' was organised to foster a plurality of ethnic and religious representations (Soulcityarts 2018). The academic 'Co-creating Cities and Communities' event was a forum to debate how communities of different denominations can collaborate to advance urban and cultural spheres. The 'TaPRA' conference, albeit being a theatre-specific event, enabled many discussions on the intersection of ethnicity, society and politics as represented on the theatre and world stage. These factors contributed to a multicultural atmosphere in all three events, where speakers and audiences exchanged different cultural iterations and positions.

Multicultural events are complex organisms encompassing "the involvement of a wide variety of different groups and actors – many of whom represent multiple identities and reasons for participation" (Nagle 2016: 4). If one was to borrow from stakeholder theory, these groups and actors represent some of the stakeholders at a given event (Crespi-Vallbona and Richards 2007). Stakeholder theory provides an understanding of the various parties engaged in an organisation, and applying it to the study of events allows an exploration of the different constituents of an event and the interplay of relationships between them. According to Freeman (1984: 46), a stakeholder is "any group or individual who can affect or is affected by the achievement of the organisation's objectives". These stakeholders possess variable degrees of "power", "legitimacy", and "urgency" according to Mitchell et al. (1997). In an event, stakeholders could include the organisers, the speakers, audiences, volunteers, and others. These stakeholders are all governed by the political systems within which they are situated (Hall and Rusher 2004).

The myriad of decisions concerning the engagement with, hosting, and organising of an event "emerge from a political process," according to Hall and Rusher (2004: 220), who explain that: "[t]his process involves the values of actors (individuals, interest groups and public and private organisations) in a struggle for power" (ibid.). Indeed, this political process stems from a political context, which interpolates cultural and social values (such as attitudes toward race, gender, sexuality and religion) to create a framework for social governance and public engagement. As public spectacles, events are affected by their political contexts just as they influence those same contexts in which they are held. As such, one could argue that an event's political context can be identified as one of its stakeholders, equally influencing and being influenced by its occurrence.

It can be suggested that events' stakeholders can be classified in two categories: *visible-corporeal* stakeholders, such as the speakers, audiences, organisers, funders, volunteers; and *invisible-incorporeal* stakeholders, such as the political context, social values, and cultural milieu within which the event takes place. Because of the latter's invisibility, its power and dominance can rarely be measured or quantified. However, it is undoubtedly in operation with a considerable degree of power, legitimacy, and urgency. These *invisible-incorporeal* stakeholders are instrumental in determining who gets in, and what gets said at events, and are thus the gatekeepers of inclusivity and diversity in these public displays.

Governing the speech on Islam

With prejudice and anti-Muslim sentiments increasing in many Western countries (Amnesty International 2012), events that provide a platform for positive discussions on Islam and Muslims in the West have the potential to combat Islamophobia and to advance diversity and inclusivity in the public imagination. Albeit inadequately, the urgency for Muslim representation in UK events is being slowly addressed, particularly by universities and community groups in the hope of encouraging integration and social harmony. However, when it comes to public discourse on Muslims and Islam in the UK, speech is typically framed within the two alarming discourses of radicalisation and Islamophobia.

Apprehensions over radicalisation and the efforts to counter it are real and persistent in the UK public imagination. The need for counter-terrorism measures and policies rightly occupy both the public and governmental consciousness. Since 2011, news of the Prevent Strategy, as one of the UK's counter-terrorism policies, has been parsimoniously reaching the public space. Prevent is "one of four strands of the government's counter-terrorism strategy, known as Contest" (BBC 2017). Prevent's objectives are to "respond to the ideological challenge of terrorism", "prevent people from being drawn into terrorism" and "work with sectors and institutions where there are risks of radicalisation" (Prevent Strategy 2011: 7). The policy has faced criticism from some politicians, academics, freedom of speech non-profits, the National Union of Teachers and the Muslim Council of Britain (BBC 2017; *Independent Voices* 2015; *Graham* 2017). The main points of criticism against Prevent have been that the strategy: 1) alienates the minority groups it is trying to reach or rehabilitate; 2) circumscribes Muslims with suspicion; and, 3) stifles debate and free speech. In a letter signed by more than 280 academics and activists, the signees argue that among others, "Prevent will have a chilling effect on open debate, free speech and political dissent. It will create an environment in which political change can no longer be discussed openly, and will withdraw to unsupervised spaces" (Independent Voices 2015).

Universities have been highlighted by the Prevent Strategy as one of the public institutions where Prevent must be in operation. Reports of emails being read and monitored by a London university (Turner 2017) led many critics to equate Prevent with surveillance at university spaces. Allen (2017: 39) has warned that one of the "insidious impacts of the Prevent duty is the extent to which universities become spaces for covert policing and surveillance". Universities are places of education and ideas exchange for students, academics, external speakers, and audiences. It is also the space where research and academic events take place. Although not directly, the Prevent Strategy influences events held at universities. In some universities, the code of practice for freedom of speech stipulates that an event organiser must submit an 'external speakers' form' through which the content of speech, as well as any risks arising from such event, could be assessed and addressed. Some universities cite the Prevent Strategy directly as a policy they adhere to and implement in their internal policies. With this, it is plausible to assume that Prevent is, in fact, a stakeholder in events which are organised at universities.

Evidently, Prevent governs the speech on radicalisation. Albeit indirectly, this inexorably affects speech about Islam in the UK since Islam is often evoked when discussing radicalisation. Therefore, even if an event aims to hold an open dialogue about the position of British Muslims, the permissibility of that speech is conditioned on what is and is not allowed to be said about Islam. While speech that might be perceived as radicalising should certainly be barred, one wonders how speech about Islam in general is being produced, governed, and even censored in the UK. In 2015, a play entitled *Homegrown* was censored in London because it was unfairly purported to be potentially "radicalising" (Ali 2018). One also questions: to what extent does this political and social environment cultivate suspicion and encourage caution around speech about Islam? And how does this political context, operating as an *invisible-incorporeal* stakeholder, affect other stakeholders in an event? As two of the *visible-corporeal* stakeholders in an event, both presenters and audiences are directly influenced by their political context.

The presenter

Events are a place of public performance for their speakers. The speaker takes centre-stage, and for a specified time becomes the star of the show. Usually cloaked with authority when presenting, the speaker's words are inadvertently interpreted as a reflection of his/her attitudes and belief systems. Moreover, these words are typically recorded or reproduced in some printed or digital form. Academic events in particular are a place where presentations and scholarly papers are often meticulously prepared and rehearsed, and an academic persona or brand is on show. As Barcan (2016: 204) writes, "Academic life has always involved the creation and maintenance of an academic persona – the public performance of oneself as authority or expert." As such, academic events are public spectacles where the presenter is arguably being audited by audience members, colleagues, and experts in the field, who all contribute to the speaker's future career and professional standing.

These factors are applicable to most academic events, and non-academic events with 'expert' guests; and, to some extent, they influence the speaker's topic, tone, and delivery. However, when an event offers a platform for a discussion on British Islam, these factors become instantly more precarious. That is because such an event evokes the *invisible-incorporeal* stakeholder, which stipulates that speech should be constructed carefully in a way that could neither be purported as radicalising or Islamophobic. It also hails the event to comply with the requirements of the Prevent Strategy; whether that entails obtaining previous permission to host speakers or, in extreme circumstances, conducting monitoring and surveillance. It is, thus, not unwarranted for a speaker to harbour anxiety over a public speech on the subject, and for that anxiety to influence his/her speech or censor elements of it for the sake of avoiding any potential controversy.

In the two academic events chosen as case studies here, the author of this chapter was a speaker. At the 'Co-creating Cities and Communities' forum, the author presented on intercultural Muslim street art, and, at the 'TaPRA' conference, the subject was the censorship of a play contextualising British Muslims in London. As mentioned earlier, the general theme of the two events did not directly address Islam in the UK, but called for diversity as a topic. Neither of the authors' presentations introduced any problematic perspectives, as they both advocated a more diverse representation in the cultural sector; however, they both touched on the Muslim artists and their precarious relationship with visibility or marginalisation. When preparing the academic papers for the two events as well as when presenting, the author developed certain anxieties over how the presentations would be received, and how, as a researcher, the author would personally and professionally be perceived. Some of these anxieties were the outcome of the following considerations:

1. Due to the topic of the presentations, they might be marginalised within the programme of the events.
2. Questions about Islam in the UK are currently sensitive and challenging; therefore, speech concerning these questions should be measured and prudent.
3. The topic discussed in those presentations may inaccurately define the author/ presenter. These anxieties led to many revisions of the speech, unconscious self-censorship, a measured tone of delivery, and liberal choice of dress. All of which were in service of a performance of a coveted academic persona and a desire to appease the *invisible-incorporeal* stakeholders at the two events.

Edward Said (1996: 66) touched upon the self-silencing tendencies that intellectuals sometimes practise:

> You do not want to appear too political; you are afraid of seeming controversial; you need the approval of a boss or an authority figure; you want to keep a reputation for being balanced, objective, moderate; your hope is to be asked back, to consult, to be on a board or prestigious committee, and so, to remain within the responsible mainstream; someday you hope to get an honorary degree, a big prize, perhaps even an ambassadorship. For an intellectual, these habits of mind are corrupting par excellence.

Although Said (1996) reprimanded such intellectuals, his analysis excluded the interplay of power relations in the formation of an intellectual's identity. A reflective analysis of anxieties before and during the two academic events points to a correlation between the speaker's position and her ability to resist self-censorship. The author/presenter at the aforementioned events would, hesitantly, define personal and professional position as a self-decolonising, non-British, early-career, woman researcher. Such a position is idiosyncratic. Each of these subject positions typically acquires a persona that performs. Butler (1990) theorised how an identity is enacted through a set of practices rather than pre-given innate characteristics. Although Butler's (1990) focus is on gender, her conceptualisation of the performative nature of an identity could be applied to the daily practices through which we construct our varied identities, be it social, cultural, or professional. Identities are formed through "a stylised repetition of acts"; leading to a "constructed identity, a performative accomplishment which the mundane social audience, including the actors themselves, come to believe and to perform in the mode of belief" (Butler 1990:191–192). Perhaps the performance of an identity is rarely so much in the spotlight as when the speaker is centre-stage presenting to colleagues and general audience.

The persona – particularly that of an academic's – which a speaker performs at public events is all the more socially and politically nuanced when that speaker could be identified as not white, or "white, but not quite" (Samhan 1999). Mitchell and Miller (2011: 204) write, "The marginalization that women of color ... experience in their doctoral programs and then again in their faculty position fosters a guarded outward persona." They quote a professor, who is a woman of colour, stating, "[p]eople don't know what to expect from us. And when they don't know what to expect or don't know the real story behind us, they make it up" (cited in Mitchell and Miller 2011: 204). The professor speculates that she does not have the "benefit of the doubt" that some of her colleagues are bestowed with because she is culturally different, and, as such, she performs her "act to make them comfortable" (ibid.). The anxieties, felt by the author as a presenter and, no doubt, by others with similar identity formations, are a result of the cultural and political sensitivity surrounding speech on Islam in the UK juxtaposed by the subject position of the speaker. The question of who has the right to speak at such events is crucial. A collection of culturally diverse voices from speakers with different subject positions is more likely to negotiate cultural differences by bringing in new perspectives based on lived experiences. This could also potentially abate the aforementioned anxieties, limit the self-censoring attempts and help the speaker navigate the inhibitions prescribed by his/her subject position(s).

The speakers for the third event, the community-led 'Hubb Debate', were: a senior academic, spoken-word champion, and Mohammed Ali, a local and international-renowned artist. Respectively, the speakers were European, American, and British of a South-Asian descent. The event presented speakers, who were confident and less reluctant to address the issue of Islam in the UK even though the event was framed in a way aimed at debating the universal value of empathy. Perhaps the contextualisation of the event within the broader unproblematic topic of empathy enabled the speakers to present their ideas without courting controversy. The event was also structured as a debate with speakers presenting a ten-minute provocation, after which the audience responded. Such format allowed a more fluid and less restrictive environment for speech.

It is difficult to assess to what degree the speakers of the three events practised caution in approaching the topic of British Islam, and how this caution affected their speech and the event as an entity. But events are places of performance, where ethnicity, professional standing, gender, and culture are variables that prescribe the presenter's relationship with the topic he/she is presenting, the audience, and the political and social context of the event. Speakers, audiences, and organisers of politically or culturally sensitive events should be mindful of these correlations. For the sake of holding a constructive and diverse event, all three should support and encourage one another in the production of honest and inclusive speech, which would in turn influence positively the existing political and cultural context.

The audience

The speaker/presenter of an event prepares his/her speech for an audience in mind. Although the audience is still an imagined entity at that point, it greatly influences the materials to be presented. Indeed, audiences are powerful stake-holders in the event, influencing it in different ways at different stages. The audiences' number and engagement, for example, affect the event and can define its success. Moreover, audiences extend the event beyond its duration by carrying and distributing elements of it outside its temporal and spatial existence. The below analysis of audiences and their engagement at the three events is based on face-to-face interviews with members of the audience and field observation of the speaker-audience Q&A, which took place in all three events.

The audiences at the 'Co-Creating Cities and Communities' and 'TaPRA' conference comprised mostly of national academics and artists. The 'Hubb Debate' attracted an audience of similar calibre along with members of other professions, but with high representation from the local community. It must be noted that members of the 'Hubb Debate' audience were more ethnically diverse than audiences at the two academic events, and a number of them self-identified as Muslim. The subject-position of the 'Hubb Debate' audience members rendered the topic of discussion more personal, and, thus, politically and socially more immediate and urgent. Audience engagement with the issues raised at the debate was imbued with an activist and impassioned tonality. Unlike the two academic events, there was rawness to the interaction between the organiser, speaker, and audiences.

In the two academic events, the topic of British Muslim cultural participation drew initial hesitation, and then questions that evoked the theoretical and the abstract, or the politics of art in general. This was in stark contrast to the 'Hubb Debate' event, where audience members debated Muslim positioning in the UK, the Prevent Strategy, and even surveillance in a manner that elicited tears, laughter, anger, and sadness. Certainly, the different categories for which the three events belonged to, account for the difference in the 'feel' of each. An academic event is typically devoted to the exchange of ideas in service of theoretical advancement, while a community event is concerned with the suc-cesses or challenges of its community members (Mackellar 2014). However, the diverse ethnic composition of the 'Hubb Debate' audience members, some of whom expressed suffering from structural marginalisation, led to personal identification with the topic. This resulted in responses that were passionate and socially and politically cognisant.

Another consideration that could account for the difference in audience engagement at the three events relate to the influence of the *invisible-incorporeal* stakeholder on the public/private sphere. It can be argued that within a current political environment that governs the speech on Islam, audiences at public events are cautious in their engagement with the topic. All three events happened in the public sphere, but the 'Hubb Debate' took place within the confines of a community space, which is a private-public space. One wonders whether that community space offered its audience a sense of privacy in which they felt comfortable enough to debate issues on Islamophobia and Muslim surveillance more openly.

The setting itself for the 'Hubb Debate' event was designed to inspire a sense of trust and unity in its audience. Audiences were invited to sit in a circle that represented openness and absence of hierarchy. The lighting was intended to obscure rather than illuminate. To this end, the main lights were switched off, and the room was lit via a dim floor lamp. Intermittent smoke was used to convey both a sense of security (shielding the self) and mysticism. At the beginning of the event, the organiser, Mohammed Ali, introduced the topic of discussion and the format of the debate, and explained his rationale behind the choice of setting, light, and smoke. A pivotal moment occurred after the speaker finished his provocation; Ali then invited audiences to voice out their reflections and ideas. Ali further encouraged audience engagement by stating that the audience should feel absolutely free and safe to voice their thoughts. Jokingly, he asserted that there were no recordings or microphones operating, which would later be handed to the police. This comment elicited a riot of laughter.

The need to publicly announce that surveillance was not in operation, and the conscious decision to arrange the event's venue in a way that promises privacy and evokes security, convey powerful narrative about the anxieties that some Muslims feel in the UK in 2017. Haggerty and Ericson (2006: 19) state: "Resisting surveillance involves localized efforts to get by in the face of monitoring: to thwart a particular system, to live anonymously within its gaze, or to engage in any number of misdirection ploys." There were many manifestations in the event to signify an element of surveillance resistance or simply an awareness of it. As part of this research, a member of the audience was interviewed after the event. While the audience member was openly and warmly conversing outside the context of research, she became instantly reluctant when a notepad and pen were introduced to record the conversation. The simple recording device became a symbol of surveillance eliciting anxiety, reserve, and avoidance.

None of the topics discussed in all three events were controversial or particularly polemic. Although there was no prolonged discussion of the Prevent Strategy or an expression of one opinion about it in the three events, its invisible presence was hazily felt, especially in the community-led event, where Muslim members of the audience were present. At that event, one could discern a certain tension in regard to the permissibility of speech on Islam in public and how private and community concerns might be monitored under the Prevent mandate. In her conceptualisation of the relationship between the public and private sphere, Livingstone (2005: 170) advocates for the right to privacy:

> While granting the importance of the defence of the public sphere, there must be space within the debate for a defence of privacy. Conceptually, the notion of the private has a series of positive meanings easily lost within the public sphere debate. [...] Although government accountability is socially valued, so too is the right of individuals to privacy and civil liberties, thereby curtailing excessive state surveillance.

Surely, similar courtesy should be extended to public discussions about social and political challenges. Meaningful and constructive events are ideally organised in a way that encourages its audience to debate freely, but, as this analysis shows, there are contemporary hurdles to speaking about Muslim issues owing to the socio-political realities of our time. Perhaps the simple act of acknowledging the challenges that face Muslims in the UK, or jesting about the reality of surveillance in our suspicious time, could reassure the audience and encourage them to engage with the debate.

Conclusion

For the sake of a more diverse, inclusive, and harmonious society, more Muslim representation is needed. Such increased representation would address the epidemics of radicalisation and Islamophobia, and would represent a step towards eradicating both. However, speech on Islam in the UK is subject to political and social scrutiny. An event is an entity with many stakeholders at work, where speakers and audiences constitute powerful participants. Yet, they remain influenced by the *invisible-incorporeal* stakeholders (the socio-political contexts), which, at times, govern their access to the event as well as their speech. By acknowledging these influences, we can work towards finding a strategy to address the barriers that stand in the way of increasing Muslim representation in public events. Although this chapter explored the influences of the *invisible-incorporeal* on the *visible-corporeal* stakeholders, the relationship between the two is not linear. Counter influences by the speakers and audiences, for example, on their socio-political contexts are also powerful and worthy of future investigation. For the present, though, it is a cause for optimism when we can hold events that confront their audiences and socio-political environments with challenging questions and representations, such as in the three events discussed in this chapter. It is also positively constructive to have the critical space and tools to analyse and assess the stakeholders in these events, including one's own subject-position. Perhaps it is within the space of those diverse, inclusive events and spaces that we find solutions for our times of suspicion.

Questions for discussion

1. Identify the stakeholders in an event, including those that are *visible-corporeal* and *invisible-incorporeal*?
2. What are the challenges that face the presenters and audiences of politically and culturally sensitive topics?
3. What does the subject position of a speaker or an audience member mean? And how does it influence an event?

References

Ali, R. (2018). Homegrown censored voices and the discursive British Muslim representation. *Research in Drama Education: The Journal of Applied Theatre and Performance*, 23(3), 373–388.

Allen, C. (2017). Controversy: Is prevent harming universities? *Political Insight*, 8(1), 38–39.

Amnesty International. (2012). *Choice and prejudice: Discrimination against Muslims in Europe*. London: Amnesty International.

Barcan, R. (2016). *Academic life and labour in the new university: Hope and other choices*. London: Routledge.

BBC. (2017). Reality check: What is the prevent strategy? www.bbc.co.uk/news/election-2017-40151991.

Butler, J. (1990). *Gender trouble: Feminism and the subversion of identity*. London: Routledge.

Crespi-Vallbona, M. and Richards, G. (2007). The meaning of cultural festivals. *International Journal of Cultural Policy*, 13(1), 103–122.

Freeman, R. (1984). *Strategic management*. Boston: Pitman.

Graham, C. (2017). What is the anti-terror Prevent programme and why is it controversial? *The Telegraph*, 26 May 2017, www.telegraph.co.uk/news/0/anti-terror-prevent-programme-controversial/.

Haggerty, K. D. and Ericson, R. V. (2006). The new politics of surveillance and visibility. In K. D. Haggerty and R. V. Ericson (eds.) *The new politics of surveillance and visibility*. Toronto: University of Toronto Press.

Hall, C. M. and Rusher, K. (2004). Politics public policy and the destination. In I. Yeoman, M. Robertson, J. Ali-Knight, S. Drummond, and U. McMahon-Beattie (eds.) *Festival and events management*. Oxford: Elsevier, 217–232.

Independent Voices. (2015). Prevent will have a chilling effect on open debate, free speech and political dissent. *The Independent*, www.independent.co.uk/voices/letters/prevent-will-have-a-chilling-effect-on-open-debate-free-speech-and-political-dissent-10381491.html.

Livingstone, S. (2005). In defence of privacy: Mediating the public/private boundary at home. In S. Livingstone (ed.) *Audiences and publics: When cultural engagement matters for the public sphere*. Bristol: Intellect Books.

Mackellar, J. (2014). *Event audiences and expectations*. London: Routledge.

Maréchal, G. (2010). Autoethnography. In A. Mills, G. Durepos, and E. Wiebe (eds.) *Encyclopedia of case study research*. London: Sage Publications, 43–45.

Mitchell, A. N. and Miller, J. J. (2011). The unwritten rules of the academy: A balancing act for women of colour. In G. Jean-Marie and B. Lloyd-Jones (eds.) *Women of color in higher education: Changing directions and new perspectives*. Bingley: Emerald Group Publishing, 193–219.

Mitchell, R. K., Agle, B. R., and Wood, D. J. (1997). Toward a theory of stakeholder identification and salience: Defining the principle of who and what really counts. *Academy of Management Review*, 22, 853–886.

Nagle, J. (2016). *Multiculturalism's double bind*. London: Routledge.

Prevent Strategy. (2011). www.gov.uk/government/publications/prevent-strategy-2011.

Said, E. (1996). *Representations of the intellectual: The 1993 Reith Lecturel*. New York: Vintage Books.

Samhan, H. H. (1999). Not quite white: Race classification and the Arab-American experience. In M. Suleiman (ed.) *Arabs in America: Building a new future*. Philadelphia: Temple University Press, 209–226.

Soulcityarts. (2018). *The Hubb Debates – Soul City Arts*. www.youtube.com/watch?v=enqJlrmSqwo.

Turner, C. (2017). Kings College London admits to monitoring its students' emails in bid to root out potential extremists. *The Telegraph*, www.telegraph.co.uk/education/2017/01/20/kings-college-london-admits-monitoring-students-emails-bid-root/.

10 Performing advocacy

Caroline Gausden

Introduction

> The question of the political is given there as being the question that comes
> to us from the other, the foreigner.
>
> (Derrida and Dufourmantelle 2000)

Tanja Ostojić's 2016 performance of *Naked Life 6* at the Society of Advocates,
Aberdeen, Scotland, commissioned as part of a larger series on hospitality by the
Scottish Contemporary Art Network in collaboration with Dr Amy Bryzgel of
Aberdeen University, resonated in complex ways for its multiple participants. To
Ostojić, this particular performance, the sixth iteration in a series, beginning in
2004 and including participation in the *Call the Witness* Roma Pavilion of the
2011 Venice Biennale, felt important. Beyond the event, the video documentation
travelled east to the Seoul Biennale and west to the *Feminism is Politics!*
exhibition in the Pratt Manhattan Gallery, New York. To Sonia Michalewicz,
who brought with her Juliana da Penha, representative of the Govanhill-based
charity Romano Lav, simply travelling three hours north from Glasgow to
Aberdeen to offer a personal perspective on the issues raised was an equally
significant step. For artist/curator Jonathan Baxter, who coined the term 'performance advocacy' and shared his practice alongside Ostojić's performance, the
event provided a moment to think on how and where art can contribute to
different political futures.

This chapter is an attempt to represent these and multiple other perspectives on
a single event. It is also for the author, as co-curator of the event with Jonathan
Baxter, a way to relate something of the wider context that led to its production,
including creative and critical research practice, which offers a curatorial response
to questions of art and politics. The chapter works in three sections. The first
outlines choices made to link up different elements in the event and how these
choices relate to the wider research question. As an artist researcher, this section is
akin to a methodology, which works through the generative metaphor of feminist
manifesto to weave together theory and practice into an event structure. The second
section moves from planning and intentions to a description of the generated
discussion elements, which form live research findings. Finally, the last section

offers some conclusions relating these findings back to theoretical contributions on improvisation, voice, and politics.

The event's place as part of a larger commission by the Scottish Contemporary Art Network (SCAN), a member-led organisation committed to championing the contemporary art sector, should also be acknowledged. SCAN provides a platform for independent curatorial discussions in the region around relationships with power, institutions, artists, and audiences.[1] As part of this platform, the curators' brief was to support and highlight innovative local art practices by pairing them up with similar and pertinent international examples.

From this beginning, in the notion of generative cultural exchange, it was important to think through the specific geography of Aberdeen, listening carefully to the different narratives encountered. Conversations were initiated in an open way, not concealing an outsider perspective, instead, instead hosting from a position as guest and outsider. Playing this double host and guest role was part of a strategy to test similar artistic and curatorial methodologies at the core of the research. Through this process, it was striking the way Aberdeen itself mirrored the impulse in the series, combining a richness of incoming perspectives and rooted understandings of place. These complexities revealed by staged and un-staged encounters, within an economy that encouraged certain forms of migration if not others, led to theme the event series around conceptions of hospitality.

Feminist manifesto as method

This commitment to producing a contextual response reflects a larger interest in feminist praxis as the bedrock of the methodology for this research. The event, nestled in a larger series on hospitality, was designed as a practice-based test of the hypothesis that certain art practices and critical events could function as feminist manifestos thanks to their reception, function, and interpretation. Through research into the form, the aim was to produce a manifesto score that could be improvised in order to both produce events and think through their effects. This score acted as a generative metaphor through which to rethink the performance of art as a political act. It tested the manifesto's ability to voice missing and excluded histories, to be a doubled form that holds things in tension, and to be related to movement.

At first sight, it may not seem that the manifesto genre lends itself to a consideration of the altogether more accommodating field of hospitality; yet, the intersection between feminist critical concerns and a detailed study of the genre yielded insights to the contrary. In a certain light, manifestos could in fact be reconsidered as radical forms of hospitality.

As a form, the manifesto is in dialogue with accepted historical narratives, voicing missing histories of oppression. Manifestos often appear as unwanted guests or outsiders to the cultural and political sphere, voicing rage at the injustices of a given political system.[2] In this, Ostojić's performance is exemplary: entering the authoritative, sanctioned space of the Society of Advocates, framed by leather-bound tomes, she began by climbing the furniture, brandishing a handwritten statement (see Figures 10.1 and 10.2): "It's time to end the 'last acceptable racism' – racisms against Roma, Gypsies, and Travellers" (Ostojić 2016).

While holding up the sign, her heel stamped out a slow, insistent rhythm on the desk. When she speaks, she makes a vivid case, citing the startlingly high number of violent incidents and deaths among Travellers and highlighting the blindness of legal systems to these as racist attacks. Following the startling array of quotes and statistics is the heart-wrenching tale of deportation suffered by 15-year-old Leonarda and her family. Ostojić channels Leonarda asking questions about her perspective and relaying the emotive replies that describe a dreamed life and the contrastingly harsh reality she faces. As the catalogue of atrocities unfolds, Ostojić moves between speech and written assertions, drawing her material from a variety of sources including UK-based activist groups and empirical details of the treatment of Roma communities in United Nations Human Rights reports. Between each revelation, she takes off an item of clothing, so she is finally left naked and vulnerable (see Figure 10.3), exhibiting the female form[3] of *bare life* that Agamben (1998: 60) reframes as *Homo sacer:* "Life separated from the normal context of the living" outwith legal frameworks and without basic rights.[4]

Figure 10.1 Tanja Ostojić performs *Naked Life 6* (2016) at the Society of Advocates, Aberdeen, 2016.

Source: Photograph by Maja Zeco.

Figure 10.2 Tanja Ostojić performs *Naked Life 6* (2016) at the Society of Advocates, Aberdeen, 2016.

Source: Photograph by Maja Zeco.

Movement

The rage in Ostojić's performance coupled with its emotive effects asks us to reflect on the inhospitality of what Agamben (1998) refers to as the sovereignty of capitalist nation states. Not for the first time in Ostojić's practice, which offers a close-to-the bone bio-political critique of discriminatory systems within globalisation, we are asked to consider the borders that define political spheres and the people who occupy these threshold spaces.[5] In feminist manifestos, this threshold, which Agamben (1998) marks out as the place created by the state of exception embodied by the *homo sacer*, is also the primary ground for the manifesto, which enacts a movement between insider and outsider worlds. In this way, as well as rage, feminist manifestos embody different forms of movement. They are texts that move through the body into speech, written to incite a movement for change.

In keeping with this, Ostojić's position is both highly emotive and also on the move, between contexts and multiple accumulating narratives, like the Travelling community she advocates for. She stands outside as an angry guest knocking on the desk of exclusive frameworks. Yet, she does not stand outside alone; she gathers support through the moving dimensions of the performance. In gathering together, she hosts the multiple others that speak through her performance, offering them a different and growing home in political resistance. It is interesting how this form of hosting could relate to the underlying question posed by the event series, of curating

Figure 10.3 Tanja Ostojić performs *Naked Life 6* (2016) at the Society of Advocates, Aberdeen, 2016.

Source: Photograph by Maja Zeco.

as a form of radical hospitality, collecting outsider voices to contribute dialogues within a city that offered up its own challenges to the problems posed.

Guests who host

This less visible hosting dimension to the manifesto is one of the ways in which it is a double structure, playing both the guest and the host role. This double role offers an important reversal of the traditional paradigm of hospitality in which the head of the house, owning space, permits people to cross the threshold, setting up a whole chain of legal and administrative commands that must be fulfilled before entry is possible. In contrast to this, in a poetic commentary on two lectures by Derrida, published in a small text that lays out the impossibility and necessity of hospitality, Dufourmantelle speculates: "Perhaps only one who endures the experience of being deprived a home can offer hospitality" (Derrida and Dufourmantelle 2000: 56).

This suggestion, approached in the text, that the refugee/guest/outsider may be the only one in a position to offer hospitality is played out by the manifesto form, which hosts as an unwanted guest to political discourse. Through this reversal, manifestos perform a kind of showing of hands, revealing elements of invisible labour that structure hospitality – the many forms of preparation, cleaning, and care work that ready a space for occupation. This labour, or shadow work, is traditionally performed by the disenfranchised. In acknowledging these hosting outsiders, there is a paradigm shift away from power relations rooted in denial and exclusion, away from the kind of hosting that is close to hostility, and to Agamben's (1998) concept of national sovereignty.

In light of this shift, Derrida and Dufourmantelle (2000) suggest that in considering hospitality, we take a risk. Importantly, Derrida's conception of hospitality is something you cannot know in advance. In seeking hospitality by entering another language, an unknown territory, we may feel lost; yet, along with this, there is the possibility of new knowledge through loss. The writing suggests that this less than transparent knowledge, through risk-taking, is a kind of freedom, not just for the guests, but for the hosts as well. If we can move to less proprietorial modes of relationship, Derrida and Dufourmantelle (2000: 14) suggest: "One could dream about what could be the lesson of someone who didn't have the keys to his own knowledge…. He would give place to the place, leaving the keys to the other to unlock the words of their enclosure." She speculates on the knowledge derived from allowing a guest to host as a kind of freedom for both parties.

From rage to Utopia

Commenting on the form of the manifesto, Lyon (1999) repeats artist Jenny Holzer's astute remark that the manifesto combines an unlikely coupling of rage and utopia, holding the two in a difficult tension. Along with the rage of Ostojić's performance, the notions of utopia were fitted into the performative structure of the event. There was the desire for the event to move between critical and reparative positions, creating solidarity through this movement. For this reason, the author approached artist and curator Jonathan Baxter to be part of the conversation. Baxter has a social practice that involves him in long-term durational projects where he facilitates others (often outsiders to the art world) in producing just such utopian moments.

Baxter positions his social practice as a pre-figurative politics related to feminist methodologies like standpoint theory, which amongst other things values contextual and experiential knowledge and holds that outsider positions can create more objective accounts of the world (Harding 2005). The pre-figurative nature of this 'social work' is well illustrated in projects like *Dundee Urban Orchard* (DUO) where, with artist Sarah Gittins, Baxter co-ordinated a citywide art project to support communities in planting and caring for small scale orchards, setting in motion a vision for a more sustainable and co-operative urban environment. Each orchard and collaboration is a small-scale utopian moment; yet, embedded in these moments is an element of critique, which often works through pointing out the shadow labours that both hold up and are excluded from the increasingly corporate spaces of the city.[6]

Baxter's critique in this case offered a challenge to the terms of Ostojić's work through the suggestion that performing in an art venue, where shock is regularly sanctioned, would lessen the effect of the work. Added to this, he suggested that a follow-up dialogue would significantly increase that performance's effect. These observations led to the choice of Society of Advocates, suggested by Bryzgel and seconded by Baxter, whose work also interrogates the relationship between law and ethics, which is also fundamental to Ostojić's work. Through these interventions, Baxter moved from being a guest invited to speak on his outsider curatorial approach and its utopian possibilities, to a host, suggesting a call and response framework to differently honour the intentions of Ostojić's performance. This significant move to host as a kind of shadow curator enabled other shifts in the performative structure.

Performing advocacy

Through intervention, Baxter initiates new relational understandings within a given context. Rather than producing work for the consumption of passive spectators, there is a view of audience as an active provisional assembly, who speak back to the work moving it into the field of politics.[7] This view worked with the intention to initiate an open conversation on the possibility of radical hospitality. There was a joint curatorial concern for the effect of Ostojić's performance, a hope that, through its staging, effects could be channelled into activism.

To this end, the platform for discussion was positioned in relation not only to the situation for Roma populations in Scotland, but, more broadly, to the current refugee crisis. Local organisations working to support refugees were invited. In addition to this, Baxter suggested the discussion should involve respondents willing to talk about their experience of displacement as well as others who represent agencies in the city that support Traveller and asylum-seeking communities.

In order to achieve this provisional assembly, suggested by Baxter, various organisations that work with different Gypsy/Traveller communities in Scotland were approached, eventually receiving help and responses from Friends of Romano Lav in Govanhill and Aberdeen City Council's social work department.

Trust was a key issue in securing participation from a community member. The author's involvement in a network of activist groups and friendships proved decisive in eventually securing the participation of musician, dancer, and cleaner in a small Glasgow primary school, Sonia Michalewicz. Next to Michalewicz, social worker Jon Davidson, working for education services within the Aberdeen Traveller community, and Juliana da Penha, advocacy worker with Friends of Romano Lav, made up a responsive panel to the performance. Finally, Nigel Lamas from Aberdeen Solidarity with Refugees joined the group to give direct advice about actions and initiatives that people affected by the issues could join. With his network, we set up a temporary soup kitchen in the break-out space to the Advocates Library. After Ostojić's performance, audience members spilled into this space to eat together and reflect before regrouping to listen and be part of the response space. All donations towards the food were collected for the small Syrian refugee charity identified by the solidarity group.

After eating, Baxter welcomed us back to the space by offering a number of pertinent questions around the subject of hospitality and introducing the guest speakers. He attended to the details of the form of the event, ensuring that the formal and respectful feel of the first round of Ostojić's performance was carried through to embrace Michalewicz's contributions. He also provided considerable support to Michalewicz, who, in the discussion, elaborated on the risk she took in opening up her experience in public, including the possibility of social death through exclusion from the "Gypsy way of life" (Baxter and Michalewicz 2016).[8]

Call and response: putting the clothes back on

With Baxter's questions in mind, Michalewicz began the second half of the event with a moving personal response to Ostojić's performance, detailing many painful moments of persecution in her lifetime as well as stories from previous generations in different geographies. She spoke of everyday impossibilities for Gypsies in the UK, the need to mask their surnames and disassociate from their communities in order to gain and retain employment. She detailed the small everyday humiliations of being followed around shops and facing baseless accusations of theft. Then, in recounting a childhood where travel between countries to try to build a life and to attend to the lives of sick family members was necessary, the larger humiliations of deportation. These journeys, first between Poland and Germany, and later to the UK, seemed to be both impossible and necessary. In some cases, moving between these countries, something UK citizens still do freely, left her family branded as the worst kind of criminals.

Stuck between different threats of exclusion, from the rights of citizenship for her cultural identity and from her own community for turning outwards, Michalewicz nevertheless found some room for negotiation in thinking on history and what the future would remember. Michalewicz's story of *bare life*, to some extent, offered a reversal of Ostojić's performance in that it revolved around her

Figure 10.4 Jonathan Baxter and Sonia Michalewicz in *Performing Advocacy* (2016). Performed at the Society of Advocates, Aberdeen, 2016.

Source: Photograph by Maja Zeco.

activism, which could be seen as a deliberate putting back on of the clothes denied to her by these small and large acts of persecution.

From her own experiences, Michalewicz (2016) moved seamlessly to larger historical trajectories. She expressed pride in traditional Gypsy culture and identity stretching back to the forest camps, poetically termed as "a small country for us", that Polish and other governments started to destroy in 1969. Thinking on the travelling life that has been so persecuted and by way of reclaiming some forms of terminology that have fallen into negative perception, she also reclaimed Gypsy as a shared ground and proper name. Between the different institutional definitions, Roma, Sinti, and Traveller, she asserted, "We are all Gypsy. There is no distance between us" (Michalewicz 2016). She expressed a desire for her children to grow up with knowledge of these shared traditions, which fuels her activist commitments, including the performance of Roma culture with the all-female dance group Romane Cierhenia. In the discussion following her testimony, it became clear that the small charity, Romano Lav, works to support this kind of activity by producing celebratory festivals like the *International Roma Community Event*. Advocacy workers and members of the community, such as da Penha, who, representing the charity, helped Michalewicz to prepare her testimony, in this way form an important bridge by helping communities that may feel separated and isolated to have a voice in the places they live and through such events become hosts.

Missing histories

In Michalewicz's presentation, Roma history, preserved for the future through dance and song, was remembered alongside another significant and missing history: the half a million Roma victims of the Holocaust, identified and labelled in the concentration camps with a black triangle on their clothes and a 'z' tattooed on their bodies (Carolei 2015). Evocatively, Michalewicz (2016) relayed a first-hand testimony of one woman, a Roma grandmother, from the concentration camp:

> She described where they slept – it was bunk beds with different levels and she said even here before death people were divided, Roma people were sleeping on the ground and Polish people and Jewish people were sleeping in these bunk beds.

After these reflections, she led us to a minute's silence in collective memory. In this way, the space crossed a threshold, moving from the personal to the political, enacting a similar but different movement to Ostojić's earlier crossing of *bare life* with the legal setting.

In the discussions that followed, Agamben's (1998) vision of *homo sacer* returned with Nigel Lamas from Aberdeen Solidarity, reminding us that statelessness is the common point between refugees and Travellers. In relation to this stateless existence, Agamben (1998) asserts life that can be killed but not sacrificed is somehow beyond the sphere of human and divine law. It is hard to imagine a more evocative way to describe this place than the floor of a concentration camp. What's more, Agamben's (1998) account makes it clear that zones of exception, whether they be concentration camps, detention centres, or elsewhere, come about through an original act of casting out. This act is the foundation of sovereign power, which by drawing borders, creates an exclusion at the heart of all state power. What is startling about Agamben's

(1998) critique and equally Michalewicz's (2016) testimony are the links drawn between the past and the present. Through these stories and critical commentary, it is possible to see echoes of the Holocaust in the realities of life in this moment that we share.

Freedom

This question of our current bio-political reality also loomed large in the discussion and with it the accompanying question of freedom raised so clearly by the predicament of the Roma community. In educational settings, Jon Davidson stressed freedom as a value of the utmost importance to young people in a context where the state, of which education is a part, has, over generations, represented a stripping away of that freedom, particularly in relation to movement. Given the long history of persecution made vivid by Michalewicz's presentation, it became clear that to assimilate, or let the *gadjos* in, means the destruction of a way of life (Baxter and Michalewicz 2016).[9] Instead, Davidson emphasised passing on useful skills like literacy and numeracy rather than keeping them inside systems. Despite differences in ethnicity, between groups in Aberdeen and Glasgow, Davidson agreed with Michalewicz's reclaiming of the term Gypsy to acknowledge shared values that do not necessarily tie in with the systems that structure life in the UK, such as marriage customs.

Observations on these fundamental cultural differences led one member of the public to ask for greater openness from minority communities, which he described as acting like secret societies. He was insistent to the point that Baxter had to move the conversation on, but not before Ostojić offered a cutting observation on the increasing necessity for 'radical transparency', drawing on her own experiences of filling in visa applications as a non-EU national, as a prerequisite for being included as a visible citizen in neoliberal culture.

Between similarity and difference

This request for transparency led Michalewicz to elaborate the risk she took in presenting. Davidson (2016) related the importance of remaining separate as a matter of survival for some: "So, when they are being asked to assimilate into society the capacity, the empowerment they have had to find themselves, is threatened. So often the choice is not to." However, Michalewicz also motioned towards the politics of friendship, which was described as a step-by-step process, akin to Derrida's poetics of hospitality, that moves slowly and does not ask to know everything all at once. The discussion veered between the poles of similarity and difference. At times, Michalewicz emphasised very specific and different cultural practices, whilst at others, she made a clear call to acknowledge a common humanity. Lamas echoed this in his discussion of refugees, who could just as easily be us.

While on an abstract level expressions of common human nature are powerful, the conversation seemed to deal with too many complex realities, including questions of marriage, equality, cultural straitjackets, and freedom, to end there, in a place that Lamas did confess was beyond politics. In contrast, another audience member related psychoanalytical approaches to politics, explored by Volkan (1997), who observes that if real and perceived differences are denied, people actually experience a denial of their identity, which can lead to them becoming more entrenched. Instead, the audience member argued that through acknowledging difference, similarities could be recognised later by conflicting sides, once they were ready to think in those terms. Step by step. In this observation, along with the intrusive calls to reveal all, the violence of assimilation seemed to stand next to the opposite violence of total exclusion. For a good analysis of these extremes of violence in relation to the politics of the stranger, Ahmed's (2000) work is pertinent.

Conclusions on poetic experiments

Writing on Agamben's (1998) treatment of *bare life* and its blind spots, Ziarek (2008: 93) registers this question of difference as inherent to the very process of producing *bare life* which emerges: "As the aftereffect of the destruction of symbolic differences of gender, ethnicity, race, or class – differences that constitute political forms of life." This realisation can be closely linked to Davidson's assertion that preserving differences in cultural identity is a form of survival. Ziarek (2008) goes on to suggest that what is missing from Agamben's (1998) analysis are conceptualisations of resistance and the question "as to whether bare life itself can be mobilised by oppositional movements". Ziarek (2008) answers this with an example from the history of feminism, citing the suffragettes' use of the hunger strike as an act that both repeats and exposes the irrational violence of sovereign power. In relation to the militancy of the hunger strike, which turns the prison into a new ground for resistance, we can see the feminism of Ostojić's practice, which operates a similar symbolic exposure. Ziarek (2008: 98) writes that this transformational power lies in "the negation of existing exclusions from the political followed by the unpredictable and open-ended process of creating new forms of collective life – a process that in certain respects more closely resembles an aesthetic experiment".

While Ostojić's act represents a negation that works through rage, Michalewicz's response, triggered by the moving dimensions of this act of hospitality, represents the second part of Ziarek's (2008) formulation, marking the whole process of the event rather than any particular part as the aesthetic or creative intervention.[10] It is the particular nature of this creative intervention that will form the focus of my conclusion. After inviting us to share silence, Michalewicz, with Baxter's support, offered a song in her own language to commemorate the missing histories her testimony brought to light.

It is possible to hear this song in the full recording of Michalewicz' testimony, as its emotive potential is beyond what can be expressed here. But, if it could be conceptualised, it might be as the sound of someone who is guest becoming host.

Her song, a spontaneous act in public space, prefigures Lamas' comments on art as a bridge between difficult territories. It also mirrors Peters' (2009) conception of improvisation as an engagement with the past that imagines it not as something closed, that simply repeats itself, but as something the improviser re-opens and reimagines in the present. This opening is a conversation that invites multiple voices without resolving the tensions between perspectives. Instead, as with manifesto forms, tension is reimagined as a generative force, a point of departure.

Mother tongue

The extent to which the song holds tension in its poetics is also the point at which the event reconnects with the aforementioned conception of feminist manifestos as a movement between opposed but connected elements. Through the dimension of voice in song, Michalewicz both departs and yet remains with her important written testimony, offering something in excess of the stark meanings it relates. Writing on the politics of voice as a minor form in *For More than One Voice* (2005), Cavarero registers this excessive quality of voice as a subversive, rhythmic undercurrent to repressive symbolic structures. It is through Cavarero's (2005) reading of voice that it is possible to reframe, but not resolve this tension, in the discussion between similarity and difference. Where the manifesto holds guest and host positions as well as rage and utopia in tension, voice, Cavarero (2005) argues, also sits between uniqueness and relatedness, making it the perfect medium for the manifesto's moving intentions.

First, citing Kristeva's materialist critique, Cavarero (2005) explores the relatedness of voice through a connection between the history of voice and the mother, who offers a first voice and of course the first form of non-proprietorial hosting. This mother tongue opens up the relational joy of passing pre-symbolic sounds back and forth, making generative connections that Michalewicz also relates in sharing song and dance with her daughters. This play of sound occurs prior to becoming an individual within symbolic systems of language. The acoustic sphere of primary care, normally performed by the mother, consequently offers a first experience of relational proximity, delivered through voice and rooted in the rhythmic drives of the body. This experience is defined by Kristeva's *Revolutions in Poetic Language* (1984) through her exploration of the semiotic *chora*, drawn from Plato's definition, in *Timaeus*, of a territory outside of the city or politics. In Kristeva's (1984) writing, the *chora* is both a foundational, unconscious support for systems of language and a disruptive excess that can be traced through the pleasure of reverberating sounds in poetic texts. Where the structure of language often works through difference, poetry contrastingly plays with the similarities between sounds. Consequently, in these poetic spaces, "voice and writing come together against a certain systemic and normative concept of language" (Cavarero 2005: 132). The invisible work performed by Plato's *chora*, a primal form of hospitality, finds voice in Kristeva's (1984) analysis. Sounds emerging from the semiotic *chora* remind us that we are more than isolated individuals and this reminder, played out in political spaces like the society of advocates, disrupts fixed systems of power. We are related, our voices meet and sound off each other to create an ethics of proximity. This memory is of significant importance to the politics of manifestos, which also attempt to engender collective resistance to oppressive systems and change. Through song, Michalewicz bridges the distance between us. This move to connect is achieved not by the erasure of her unique voice but by its emphasis.

Despite the call to belonging and collectivity offered by voice, Cavarero (2005) insists meaning is altered by each voice and by each location. Though the unconscious rhythms of voice suggest we are more than ourselves, the specific sounds of voice, travelling through specific bodies, ensure we remain unique. In this way Cavarero (2005) frames voice as the medium for a politics that avoids the abstract and universal categories that Agamben (1998) argues lead to the proposition of *bare life* in the first place. She argues that this politics is conceptualised by Arendt (1958) as a field of action. Arendt (1958) argues that while thought is solitary, speech occurs between particular bodies. Speech consequently requires a non-generalisable ethics that is responsive to the particular context and individuals within a field of action. To Arendt (1958) and Cavarero (2005), politics is not actually the rigid bordered terrain defined by sovereign power but a moving contingent space, generated by interaction. It is this contingent and importantly malleable space that the manifesto as event reaches for and creates through its forms.

In speaking at the event, da Penha (2016) reminds us of the driving motivation behind the small advocacy charity, Romano Lav: "In working with Roma and non-Roma, our main idea is to support people to speak for themselves."[11] In this spirit, it seems right to give Michalewicz the last words. Before singing, Michalewicz stressed the importance of this small improvisation and moment of sharing in a way that both sums up its personal importance and consequences for solidarity beyond stateless existence and for a different kind of politics that resonates with Arendt's (1958) philosophy:

> The music and our language unites us – when we sing and play we feel free and happy – this is the most precious moment for us – it makes us feel that for this moment we are in our small country. In this point, just this point, we are very poor because we don't have a country – so sometimes I still think about where is the place for me for my family because I don't know maybe today tomorrow or after one month they're going to deport us again – so but in this moment I know where my house is.

Questions for discussion

1. Can critical events function as feminist manifestos, advocating for social change and gathering an empowered audience around key issues?
2. What does hospitality mean in both the local and global context, where concepts of national identity and sovereignty are increasingly put under pressure by the border crossings of migrant labour, war, and climate change?

3. Through events, can we interrogate the position of guest and host, initiating an open conversation on the possibility of radical forms of hospitality?
4. What is the role of artists and curators in the performance of advocacy?

Notes

1 For more details see: https://sca-net.org/what-is-scan/.
2 This perspective on the manifesto as voice of missing history is in part derived from Janet Lyon's pivotal study *Manifestos: Provocations of the Modern*, which offers many examples of manifestos that seem to speak as outsiders, even from historical time itself.
3 In an article of the same title, Susana Milevska refers to this female form of *bare life* as *Femina Sacra*. The article also provides an interesting contextual study of Ostojić's work on migration.
4 More broadly, *bare life* refers to a conception of life as exclusively biological without consideration for quality or the way life is lived.
5 Prior to and co-existent with the work around Roma persecution, Ostojić's practice consists of many personal experiments with crossing the borders between former Eastern bloc states and EU nations. Perhaps the most notorious of these involved marriage, as an artwork, in the five-year durational performance, *Looking for a Husband with an EU Passport* (2000–2005).
6 For more on DUO: https://dundeeurbanorchard.net/.
7 The term provisional assembly is borrowed from the BAK (*basis voor actuele kunst)* publication, *Future Publics*, edited by cultural producer and curator Maria Hlavajova and Ranjit Hoskote. As director at BAK, Hlavajova was responsible for commissioning the Venice Biennale performance of *Naked Life* for the Roma Pavilion.
8 This quote is taken from Michalewicz's full testimony that can be found online along with an introduction by Baxter at: http://feministmanifesto.co.uk/content/performing-advocacy.
9 *Gadjos* is the term Michalewicz uses to refer to those outside of Gypsy communities, consequently relaying their own terminology to define insides and outsides.
10 After the event, Michalewicz confessed that Ostojić's performance, a moment of sharing, had been a trigger for her to express many things about her life for the first time in front of her daughters, who were present.
11 This quote can be found in the recording of the event discussion at: http://feministma nifesto.co.uk/content/performing-advocacy.

References

Agamben, G. (1998). *Homo sacer: Sovereign power and bare life*. California: Stanford University Press.
Ahmed, S. (2000). *Strange encounters: Embodied others in post-coloniality*. London: Routledge.
Arendt, H. (1958). *The human condition*. Chicago: The University of Chicago Press.
Baxter, J. and Michalewicz, S. (2016). *Performing Advocacy*. http://feministmanifesto.co. uk/content/performing-advocacy.
Carolei, D. (2015). *The most persecuted minority in Europe: An assessment of Roma rights in Europe*. Glasgow: Global Minorities Alliance.
Cavarero, A. (2005). *For more than one voice*. California: Stanford University Press.
Derrida, J. and Dufourmantelle, A. (2000). *Of hospitality*. California: Stanford University Press.

Harding, S. (2005). Rethinking standpoint epistemology: What is 'strong objectivity?' In A. E. Cudd and R. O. Andreasen (eds.) *Feminist theory: A philosophical anthology*. Oxford: Blackwell Publishing.

Hlavajova, M and Hoskote, R. (2014). *Future publics: A critical reader in contemporary art*. Amsterdam: Valiz.

Kristeva, J. (1984). *Revolutions in poetic language*. New York: Columbia University Press.

Lyon, J. (1999). *Manifestoes: Provocations of the modern*. London: Cornell University Press.

Milevska, S. (2009). Femina sacra, Intergration impossible? The politics of migration in the artwork of Tanja Ostojić. In P. Allara, M. Bojadzijev, M. Grzinic, M. (eds.) Berlin: Argobook.

Ostojić, T. (2016). *Naked Life 6. (Film)*. Aberdeen: Aberdeen University & SCAN.

Peters, G. (2009). *The philosophy of improvisation*. Chicago: University of Chicago Press.

Volkan, V. (1997). *Bloodlines from ethnic pride to ethnic terrorism*. Colorado: Westview Press.

Ziarek, E. P. (2008). Bare life on strike: Notes on the biopolitics of race and gender. *South Atlantic Quarterly*, 107(1), 89–105.

11 Conceptualising events of dissent

Understanding the Lava Jato rally in São Paulo, 5 December 2016

Ian R. Lamond

Introduction

The Swedish free market think-tank Timbro has, in recent years, produced an annual index that marks changing trends in support for what it calls authoritarian populist parties from across Europe. Findings reported in July 2017 (Timbro 2017) suggest vote share for such political movements has been relatively stable at just below 20% since 2015; however, this marks an almost 150% increase from ten years before, where the 2005 share was closer to 8%. In the introduction to its 2016 index, its principle compiler wrote: "Today, populist parties are represented in the governments of nine European countries and act as parliamentary support in two others. Hence, one third of the governments of Europe are constituted by or dependent on populist parties" (Timbro 2016: 4–5), arguing that "the authoritarian strain in these parties... is dangerous and threatens the values and principles that have been at the core of European democracy for more than half a century."

But the growth of political populist movements has not been confined to Europe. Around the world, the electorate in democratic states seems to be moving towards a more populist position. Examples might include Donald Trump's election as the 45th President of the United States, the rise of the One Nation party in Australia, and the expansion of populism across democracies in South America, including the increasing support for forthcoming presidential candidate Jair Bolsonaro in Brazil, to name but a few. In this chapter, the primary concern is with an event of dissent associated with the populist right in Brazil.

But what is populism? A full discussion of that term would lead this chapter in a direction other than that which is intended, but some basic consideration of it is essential. At its most basic, populism is an appeal to *the people*; but, it is more than simply that, it also contains aspects of anti-establishmentism and anti-elitism (Bosteels 2016). Muller (2017) suggests that we do not yet have anything approaching a theory of populism, and as such it is an essentially contested political concept; one which carries, at its core, a paradox. As a political position, it makes substantial claims to be the voice of *the people*, defending their interests, and articulating their concerns. Yet, by suggesting that the "people" are unified and univocal construes them as singular, which undermines the significance of diversity at both an axiological and ontological level. As such, the "people", within populism, becomes constituted not by what it stands for but that to which it is opposed. As the Tunisian activist, Sadri Khiari, argues, "The question 'What is the people?' must naturally be answered by another question: against whom are the people constituted?" (Khiari 2016: 88). Through homogeneity, populism becomes an exclusionary principle; one that clothes itself in the trappings of democracy whilst ignoring its substance.

This chapter reflects on a demonstration by populist Right groups in support of the on-going anti-corruption investigation *Operação Lava Jato* (Operation Car Wash), which was observed by the author in São Paulo on 5 December 2016. The principle aim of this chapter is to develop a richer conceptual understanding of mass demonstrations as events of dissent by presenting a synthesis of approaches that suggest a theoretical framework with which we can begin to grasp, and, in the case of authoritarian populism, confront such events. Thus, rather than adopting a specific research method that attempts to establish a definitive conclusion, this chapter adopts a reflexive ethnographic perspective, with an orientation rooted in critical event studies (CES), which suggests insights that can be derived from the application of the theoretical frameworks it pulls together. Consequently, it becomes more important to see how the proposed confluence of ideas can develop understanding than whether it can establish authoritative findings.

The proposed synthesis draws on ideas from Stebbins, and others, around different forms of leisure practice, and the descriptive model of policy change that has grown out of the work of Sabatier, referred to as the Advocacy Coalition Framework (ACF). By bringing these two theoretical perspectives into CES, the aim is to gain richer understanding of populist events of dissent and, in so doing, enable others to develop strategies for confronting populism's assault on diversity and its implicit counter-democratic agenda of exclusion in democratic participation (Rosanvallon 2008).

Beginning with an outline of understanding of what it means to adopt a CES orientation to the study of events, and why it is of value to the study and analysis of events of dissent, this chapter proceeds to describe the anti-corruption demonstration the author observed in São Paulo. The reflection on the event then follows two paths. First, there is consideration of how activism can be understood as a form of leisure activity, and, thus, how the varieties of participant engagement observed during the event can be construed from a perspective of diverse leisure practices. Second, events of dissent are positioned to be a form of seeking policy change, framing the observed demonstration as the articulation of coalitions advocating the formation or revision of an existing policy framework. Thus framed, questions around how coalitions are formed, sustained and, potentially, how they can be challenged and confronted, can be raised. In conclusion, the two theoretical perspectives can be drawn together to highlight how they have enabled a richer understanding of events of dissent whilst also suggesting pathways for developing strategies for confronting the growth of authoritarian populism.

CES and the study of events of dissent

CES emerges from a broad-spectrum dissatisfaction with how events are studied within the aligned fields of event management and events studies. One approach has been to address this dissatisfaction by proposing an expansion of the curriculum associated with the field in order for wider social sciences to play a greater part (for example, Andrews and Leopold 2013; Moufakkir and Pernecky 2014). An alternative approach, which is adopted by this chapter, has been to begin by problematising the concept of *event* within the field, and then move from that reconceptualisation to show how wider concerns and topics become drawn into the purview of events research (Spracklen and Lamond 2016). In the case of the former, events become contested because of the context in which they occur; for the latter, contestation becomes a central characteristic of what constitutes the referent of 'event'. This is a much bolder claim, as it effectively flips the former perspective; instead of the social science being central to event studies, the study of events becomes a significant concern for the social sciences.

In *Being and Event*, Badiou (2007) draws on the idea of event as a rupture that exposes *the real*; as such, it has had a long philosophical tradition. If, for example, considering Heidegger's discussion of Plato's myth of the cave from the "Republic" (Heidegger 2010), it could be argued that such a construal of *event* dates back almost 2500 years. What is helpful in Badiou's (2007) construal, however, is, for him, the rupturing is understood as an outpouring of possibilities and potentialities. Event *is* the sudden eruption of possibility, the disruption of discursive routines; consequently, it is best conceived as multiple rather than singular (Badiou 2007). At a phenomenological level, the group experience of *events* in, for example, festival attendee experience, can be conceptualised as a multiplicity of multiplicities. Thus conceived, it becomes tenable how contestation emerges from *event*.

Whilst an event can be seen as singular, in fields such as event management, this needs to be taken as an abstraction that facilitates discourses of resource management, financial control, publicity and marketing, etc. In adopting a more critical stance to the study of *event*, the referent is closer to its disruptive multiplicity. It, therefore, makes more sense to conceptualise its object of study less as an *event*, and more like an evental site. As such, the referent becomes more textured and layered in highly complex and nuanced ways. To study *events* within a CES orientation thereby becomes an interest in them as multiplicities and how those multiplicities are co-ordinated, channelled, sustained, mediated and, in some cases, mitigated. Preceding 'event' with an indefinite or definite article (for example, to refer to either *an* event or *the* event), may make things simpler; however, it is ultimately misleading.

Events of dissent do not fit comfortably into frameworks established in much mainstream events research. In the typology of events developed in Getz's (2007) foundational work in event studies, events of dissent do not appear and would seem to fall somewhere between political events and what he refers to as "unplanned events". Whilst protest does appear in a table of "Forces, trends and issues related to planned events" (Getz and Page 2016: 29), in the most recent edition of his book, they are primarily associated with some form of instability and characterised by their negative impact.

> There always seem to be factors such as conflicts, terrorism, disease or civic unrest that impact tourism – and on event tourism in particular – affecting the stability of environments in which to host events…pressure to deal with climate change (for example) results in carbon taxes and, potentially, other measures that could increasingly act to slow growth or impose specific barriers to travel and events.
>
> (ibid.: 30).

In this quote, it seems clear that events of dissent (in his example, pressure to deal with climate change) are not to be studied as events but are considered something which has an impact on events considered worthy of study. Protests, captured here as being part of a family that suggests a resonance with, for example, terrorism and disease, he suggests, need to be handled correctly, as they may otherwise carry the potential of resulting in barriers to the development of *planned events* (Getz 2007). This is very different from an approach rooted in CES, especially from the perspective outlined earlier. In their discussion of leisure activism and protests as event, Spracklen and Lamond, (2016) argue it is of value to study and subject to scrutiny such *events* in their own terms, and not merely as coeval, concomitant, or contemporaneous, to other events. As such, the conceptual grounding of CES makes it especially suitable for such research. Having established the orientation to the study of events that this chapter adopts, and indicated its relevance to the identified topic, it is important to now provide an outline of the exemplar event.

The anti-corruption demonstration in São Paulo, 5 December 2016

Operação Lava Jato is an ongoing investigation being conducted by the Brazilian federal police under the direction of the state judge, Sérgio Moro. The investigation began in March 2014, following an earlier inquiry into money laundering which, itself, came to light when allegations were made in 2008 of the unlawful use of money transfer services at a petrol station in Brasilia (Connors and Magalhaes 2015). *Lava Jato* has gone beyond that original inquiry to encompass an aligned investigation into allegations of corruption associated with the state-controlled oil company, Petrobras, the Brazilian-based construction company, Odebrecht, and the São Paulo based meat-processing business, JBS.

Though the inquiry is not, ostensibly at least, partisan, with allegations crossing multiple party lines, much of the Brazilian media has focused its attention on groups on the left and centre-left of the political spectrum. Those media narratives have keyed into a growing anti-government and anti-establishment feeling being articulated by Brazil's populist and evangelical Christian right (Fortes 2016; Leahy 2016).

The anti-corruption demonstration observed for this chapter took place along the Avenida Paulista in São Paulo – a long, straight, road that lies at the financial and commercial heart of the city. Alongside shopping malls, high-end stores, and designer outlets, sit the headquarters for many of the largest companies in Brazil. As a space, it is known as being one of the primary arenas where mass expressions of dissent are articulated, not just in São Paulo, but in Brazil itself. Most weekends see some form of organised demonstration take place along all, or part, of the Avenida. The city authorities are geared up for such events of dissent with simplified arrangements for establishing, effectively booking a time and date for a demonstration, and a highly co-ordinated system for returning the road to its former state once the demonstration has finished. Figure 11.1 illustrates this through a photograph taken at the end of a demonstration observed in São Paulo on 18 June 2017. The clean-up team took little more than 30 minutes to clear up after a demonstration of over three million people along the Avenida. A similar, though smaller, team followed the demonstration on 5 December 2016.

Whilst it can be argued that such routinisation of protest challenges the symbolic capital of social movements in their articulation of otherness (Lamond

Figure 11.1 Cleaning up the Avenida Paulista after an event of dissent, São Paulo, June 2017.

Source: Photograph by the author.

2018), it also illustrates the operative structures the city can deploy in its strategic management of events of dissent.

Initial impressions of the anti-corruption demonstration observed was one of conviviality. Street vendors lined much of the street, selling food and what looked like craft goods. Figure 11.2 shows one of those street units selling snacks to people gathering near one of the event's floats.

On the Avenida, families and friends gathered together as they set up impromptu picnic areas. Children carried balloons, many of which were of a character known as Super Moro, the name the media and many on the populist Right use to refer to the judge currently leading the *Lava Jato* inquiry. There was a lot of laughter, and the general atmosphere seemed calm, friendly, and very informal. A colleague was the one who first pointed out what was a much more sinister current. The ubiquity of the Brazilian flag and the shirt of the national football team was not a surprise; but, when alerted to the almost complete absence of non-whites in the crowd and the preponderance of members of more politically peripheral communities staffing the stalls, the event took on a different shape. The limited instances where white people, who also appeared to be more affluent, were standing near a stand, it would be to seek support for a diverse

Figure 11.2 Street vendor at the anti-corruption demonstration, December 2016.
Source: Photograph by the author.

range of politically right-leaning agenda. Requests for a return to a military Junta, in place of an apparently systemically corrupt democracy, along with demands for reforms designed to limit the perceived degeneracy emerging from the government's *loose grip* on dealing with immigration, abortion, 'radical Islam'. and LGBT rights.

One float (see Figure 11.3) was covered in a banner which suggested that it was democracy, tarnished by the left, that was the problem, and only a return to military rule could provide a solution. Placards, banners, and chants, proclaimed that *Lava Jato* was routing out the lies that parties of the left were supposedly circulating, which were also, apparently, undermining what it meant to be truly Brazilian. Replacing them with the self-declared 'truths' of a populist and evangelical Christian right which, they suggested, was the only way the country could return to strength and take up its true place in the world.

One inflatable (see Figure 11.4) was of a generic corrupt politician wearing underwear stuffed with money; the badges adorning that underwear were all parties on the left.

The juxtaposition of apparent conviviality with such sentiments of hatred and anger, were highly disturbing to experience. Yet, the state and national media that reported on the event described it, almost exclusively, as a peaceful and friendly demonstration. Some field notes from the experience:

> It is unusual for me to feel intimidated whilst being amongst a large group of people; however, while I was there, I found myself deliberately masking some of the badges I wear that demonstrate my link to the LGBT community. I felt

Figure 11.3 One of several campaign floats at the demonstration, December 2016.
Source: Photograph by the author.

Figure 11.4 Generic 'corrupt politician' inflatable at the demonstration, December 2016.
Source: Photograph by the author.

very vulnerable and threatened, as I was someone that did not seem to fit in with the stock view of humanity that was being articulated by this purportedly 'polite' crowd. The diversity of participation and engagement I observed led me to realise that if I hoped to gain a greater understanding of this event, to confront it and challenge it, I would need to move away from considering it as something graspable in the singular and instead try to understand its multiplicity; i.e. less as an event and more as an eventual site.

Protest participation and leisure

For most of those participating in the demonstration on 5 December, it was something that they had undertaken in their spare time; it formed part of what could be considered a "free-time activity" (Stebbins 2011: 239). Whilst that might not apply to everyone there, the majority of attendees were there in non-work time, participating as a result of a choice made by themselves or some social unit of which they are a part, such as young people attending with members of their family. As such, at that very base level, their participation can be construed as a leisure activity (Lamond and Spracklen 2015). However, that does not, nor could it, simplify their engagement, for leisure is "multilayered and therefore quite complex" (Bouwer and van Leeuwen 2017: 15). Shared participation in leisure suggest forms of communicative rationality (Spracklen 2011) and relationship (Habermas 1991) that, following Stebbins, can be conceptualised as occurring within three broad forms (Stebbins 1992): *casual*, *project-based*, and *serious*.

Much of Stebbins' work has been to examine the rich variety and articulation of these forms of leisure (Veal 2017). To elucidate a detailed empirical account of how they were embodied within an event of dissent would reach far beyond the remit of this chapter, and somewhat diverts from the point it aims to make, as it is a more conceptual discourse. The main point from personal observation of the anti-corruption demonstration is those three forms of leisure appeared to be present. Some clarification of these forms of leisure is thus required.

For Stebbins, casual leisure was initially "cast in a residual role" (Stebbins 1997: 17) to serious leisure. Its position being a contrast to, and opposite of, the pursuit of a leisure activity that takes a more *serious* form. There are early hints of this in his work around defining the amateur (Stebbins 1977) and the differentiation between "amateur" and "hobbyist" in the study of leisure (Stebbins 1980). That early work concentrated on conceptualising *serious leisure*, which he set out in his conceptual statement of 1982 (Stebbins 1982), which relegated *casual leisure* to a position of minor significance. However, by 1997, he asserts that engagement in casual leisure is far more complex than being merely residual (Stebbins 1997), suggesting that it encompasses at least six different types. As a broad definition he suggests, "casual leisure can be defined as an immediate, intrinsically rewarding, relatively short-lived pleasurable activity requiring little or no special training to enjoy it" (ibid.: 18). He concludes; "to treat casual leisure as a residual whose only use is to further the definition of one aspect or another of serious leisure is to miss the opportunity to explore a leisure world rich in unique properties of its own" (ibid.: 4).

More recently, Stebbins has argued for a connection between *casual leisure* and loose, short-lived, participation as social actors in neo-tribal groups (Veal 2017), even if that participation is relatively ephemeral. Such a formulation resonates with many of the small groups and families observed at the demonstration, which seemed to drift in and out of the event. People were interspersing their time with shopping, having a picnic, or going for a meal with friends, not as something to do pre- or post-protest, but as part of a mixed range of activities that only seemed to incorporate the event at various points. They could be seen sauntering along the street in Brazil football shirts for a little while before going for a coffee with some friends, joining the crowd and chanting before exiting to visit the Riachuelo department store, returning to cheer on someone speaking over a PA system, before setting out an impromptu picnic.

Stebbins (2005: 2) has defined *project-based leisure* as a "short-term, moderately complicated, either one-shot or occasional, though infrequent, creative undertaking carried out in free time…(which) requires planning effort, and sometimes skill or knowledge". He first recognises this as a form of leisure in his 2005 paper for *Leisure Studies*, "Project-based leisure: theoretical neglect of a common use of free time". Interestingly, he splits it into two main sub-categories: one-offs and occasional projects. Where the former are realised through the undertaking of an activity to produce a unique outcome, occasional projects "contain the possibility of becoming routinised" (ibid.: 6). He argues that such projects contain that possibility because, even though they include "a sense of obligation", it is one that is experienced as agreeable to the person undertaking the project, who, in turn, anticipates that the completion of the project will be fulfilling (ibid.: 2). Bailey and Fernando (2012) found in their study of more than three hundred college students that such routinised occasional projects facilitated the formation of significant relationships and wider social engagement. Such intermittent participation draws on ready-to-hand skills and requires an element of planning, preparation, and potentially collaborative working to a shared outcome. It operates as a form of social capital that draws people together within and beyond a specific leisure activity.

Though less easily observable, a suggestion of such leisure practice could be discerned in the engagement of some participants at the demonstration. It is more difficult to identify occasional project-based leisure as a characteristic, as it relies on the sense of fulfilment experienced by the social actor who irregularly engages in the activity. However, a range of behaviours, such as prolonged engagement with the event, the appearance of a greater level of preparation, specifically associated with the theme of the protest (such as small, apparently non-aligned, group production of simple home-made banners), a more thorough representation of association with key messages of the event, and so forth, act as indicators of participation somewhere along a spectrum towards an engagement at the level of serious leisure.

The literature that connects *serious leisure* and activism is substantial. Stebbins' work itself draws on earlier studies of voluntary action (for example, Bosserman 1975) that incorporated involvement in the political and civic sphere, where "volunteers get involved in citizens' movements, social advocacy, social action and political functions" (Stebbins 1982: 264). He defines *serious leisure* as:

> the systematic pursuit of an amateur, hobbyist, or volunteer core activity that people find so substantial, interesting and fulfilling that…They launch themselves on a (leisure) career centered (*sic*) on acquiring and expressing a combination of its special skills, knowledge, and experience.
>
> (Stebbins 2011: 239)

As already suggested, Spracklen (2011) has argued for a strong connection between serious leisure, close communicative relationships, and the construction of identity. A close association of one's identity with the leisure practices with which one engages, Stebbins (2011) argues, facilitates what he refers to as the durable benefits of such activity. Those participants at the protest that had laboured hard to produce complex banners, co-ordinate the use of the huge Brazilian flag that adorned the centre of the road for a few hundred metres, staffed stalls seeking signatories for petitions, who, with what seemed to be tireless stride, had promenaded along the Avenida, some with mega-phones, leading chants and call/responses, in elaborate and highly decorated outfits that mirrored the events' focus were engaged with it to an extent that far exceeded that of many others present. It was their presence, participation, and voice that formed the eidetic heart of that event of dissent.

Given the variety of participation, interaction, and articulation encountered whilst observing the protest along the Avenida, it is suggested that a consideration of Stebbins' tri-partite conceptualisation of leisure can facilitate a richer understanding of the diversity of engagement at such an event of dissent.

Protest, policy change, and the Advocacy Coalition Framework

The relationship between collective protest and policy takes just a moment's reflection. People engage in events of mass dissent because they are either demanding a new policy, or they wish to protect an existing one. In a similar fashion, it seems reasonable to conclude that such demonstrations arise from a position of not being able to individually effect policy change. Protest is not the seeking of the acquisition of power per se, as that would be either revolution or, possibly, electioneering. Whilst a few banners, chants, stalls, and floats at the demonstration were pushing that agenda (one of the event's facets that the author found most disturbing), this omits a consideration of the broader spectrum of protestful participation and, thereby, neglects the wider connection between dissent and policy. To grasp that, it is suggested that consideration be given to the Advocacy Coalition Framework (ACF).

Initially developed by Paul Sabatier, ACF was developed as a response to perceived shortcomings of top-down models, which concentrated on prescribing structures through which policymakers should develop policy, and bottom-up approaches, which focused more on implementation and the filtering up of learning from the application of policy to those that made it (Sabatier 1988). In collaboration with Jenkins-Smith, ACF became an evolving and adaptive framework that would, through ongoing empirical study into actual policy change, be regularly reviewed and updated (Jenkins-Smith and Sabatier 1994; Weible, et al. 2011). Despite its longevity (almost 30 years) Pierce, et al. (2017) argue that ACF is still a useful tool in understanding the empirics of the policy process. They go on to suggest that rather than ACF being a framework that guides policymakers, it constitutes a shared language that supports policy process research. Key to this are several core concepts from which, with regard to participation in events of dissent, can be identified as *advocacy coalitions* and *belief systems*, as those elements of the framework that are most relevant.

Following Weible, et al. (2011) and Jenkins-Smith, et al. (2014), pressure for policy change occurs when there is some form of shock encountered in a prevailing policy domain. That systemic shock may be internal to a regime, external to it, or both; wherever it emerges it is through a move from prior stability to contestation. How it is apprehended and articulated will be bounded by a range of parameters which include, for example, broad public opinion on the issue, the prevailing socio-economic climate, and where it sits within institutional cycles of change and renewal (for example, elections or the nomination of board members). Coalitions, both formal and informal, form around possible responses to that shock and adopt a range of strategies to articulate their position. The belief systems of coalition members vary through a combination of what they know (the diverse epistemic communities and modes of epistemic framing that they are part of, according to Meijerink 2005), and their world view (the degree of ontological cohesion around how the shock has impacted their ontic orientation, according to Matti and Sandström 2013). The membership of coalitions fluctuate as different agents, whether individual or institutional, acquire new knowledge or the ontological ties that formally bound them to a coalition are no longer found to be tenable. As the issue emergent from the system shock remains unresolved or unacceptably addressed, coalitions become more apparent; their epistemic and ontic foundations become increasingly evident (Pülzl and Treib 2007); consequently, they become more stable (Weible 2006).

Such degrees of ontic and epistemic attachment could, at a surface level at least, be observed within the varied formal/informal, fluid, and transient social and organised groups that were participating in the anti-corruption demonstration; though more research would be required to confirm, empirically, whether such groupings were actually present. As such, the demonstration was the single voice of a coalition advocating a clear and unified policy position. Instead, it would be more plausible to grasp it as evental, that is, a site of multiplicity and contestation. The demonstration would be a bringing together of multiple coalitions, each connected through the range of epistemic and ontic associations between them. As participants in the event of dissent, those present would exhibit a wide spectrum of engagement. Some agents' core beliefs may demonstrate dedication to radical systemic change (for example, those participants calling for a return to a military junta and a general repatriation of non-Brazilians), and others with a less committed political/cultural position simply feel aggrieved by the current state-of-affairs, who may, given changes in their level of knowledge, drift from one coalition to another, and even potentially away from the overarching populist right position that dominated the demonstration.

Conclusion and recommendations: bringing leisure and ACF together

Drawing together a tripartite conceptualisation of *leisure* and the understanding of coalition formation and sustainability, it is possible to present in ACF through a consideration of the way identity, epistemic framing, and ontic cohesion converge and become articulated as a world view (Filardo-Llamas, et al. 2016). How might that be achieved?

As was argued earlier, leisure, especially serious leisure, forms a vital element within the construction and expression of identity (Spracklen 2011), which is made manifest through the ontic and epistemic structures that constitute communicative relationships that are bound up with participation in leisure activity (Stebbins 1980). It would seem to follow that such variation in ontic and epistemic attachment would represent differences in the expression of identity (deixis); the more tightly bound these elements are, the more likely that engagement in an activity can be expressed as serious leisure. The looser they are, the closer it can be to casual leisure. Though, it should be noted, this is not arguing for a causal relationship. Whilst deixis is manifest through the ontic and epistemic, they, in turn, are manifest through deixis.

A similar situation is encountered when considering the extent to which an individual might associate with a coalition's position. In considering the stability of a coalition, and the likelihood of migration from one policy position to another, as was apparent in the arguments of Meijerink (2005) and Weible (2006), the degree of ontic and epistemic attachment was central. Depending on the scale of the system shock, those less attached to a coalition will migrate; whilst others, with stronger ontic and epistemic bonds, may use it to consolidate their attachment.

What does this amount to? In effect, the argument is when we consider engagement in activism as a form of leisure and understand protest as a way of articulating a policy position, there is a continuum of participation from those that are loosely connected to a coalition, which display that association as casual leisure to those firmly attached to it, and who articulate their relationship to a coalition as serious leisure. The variety in the ways people participated in the demonstration observed was a manifestation of the breadth of different forms of diversity and inclusion associated with individual and group leisure practice and attachment to a policy coalition.

If there is a desire to challenge the rise of such populism, whilst still confronting governmental corruption, we are thus led to a conclusion that suggests such multiplicity can only be contested in a multi-modal way. Presenting people with 'the facts' only has an impact on the casual leisure participant, whose attachment to a coalition is weak. Those same 'facts' may be twisted and turned against us by the serious leisure activist, who may epistemically re-frame our position as evidence of the correctness of their own. To overturn such entrenchment might require drawing such people into a position of system shock, where the challenge is profound at an epistemic, ontic, and deictic level. Such confrontation may risk violence (at least at a symbolic level). This means that for people whose natural pre-disposition is towards nonviolent direct action (NVDA), we are left with a significant problem; how are we to overcome such entrenched positions whilst maintaining a commitment to NVDA. It may be that it is here that the use of creativity, humour, and the arts deployed to celebrate diversity and inclusion can play a crucial part.

Questions for discussion

1. Why might CES be a more helpful orientation to the study of events of dissent than perspectives derived from familiar approaches in event studies?
2. Within the chapter, two ways of approaching critical event studies are outlined: how do they differ, and what are the implications of those differences?
3. One way of understanding the implication of putting 'critical' before field (such as critical tourism studies, critical disability studies etc.) is that it indicates that field is to be of value as a means of confronting power and

facilitating emancipation. What does this mean for event studies, and is an emancipatory event studies even possible?

4. How might the approach to CES presented in this chapter be applied to an event of dissent of your own choosing?

References

Andrews, H. and Leopold, T. (2013). *Events and the Social Sciences*. London: Routledge.

Badiou, A. (2007). *Being and Event*. London: Continuum.

Bailey, A. W. and Fernando, I. K. (2012). Routine and project-based leisure, happiness, and meaning in life. *Journal of Leisure Research*, 44(2), 139–154.

Bosserman, P. (1975). Some theoretical dimensions to the study of social time. *Society and Leisure*, 7(1), 21–44.

Bosteels, B. (2016). This people which is not one. In: A. Badiou and J. Gladding (eds.) *What Is a People*. New York: Columbia University Press.

Bouwer, J. and van Leeuwen, M. (2017). *Philosophy of Leisure: Foundations of the Good Life*, Vol. 2. London: Routledge.

Connors, W. and Magalhaes, L. (2015). How Brazil's 'Nine Horsemen' cracked a bribery scandal. *The Wall Street Journal*, 6th April, www.wsj.com/articles/how-brazils-nine-horsemen-cracked-petrobras-bribery-scandal-1428334221.

Filardo-Llamas, L., Hart, C., and Kaal, B. (2016). *Space, Time and Evaluation in Ideological Discourse*. London: Routledge.

Fortes, A. (2016). Brazil's neoconservative offensive: How right-wing forces co-opted and redirected popular discontent in Brazil to oust democratically elected President Dilma Rousseff. *NACLA Report on the Americas*, 48(3), 217–220.

Getz, D. (2007). *Event Studies: Theory, Research and Policy for Planned Events*. Oxford: Butterworth-Heinemann.

Getz, D. and Page, S. J. (2016). *Event Studies: Theory, Research and Policy for Planned Events*. 3rd ed. London: Routledge.

Habermas, J. (1991). *The Theory of Communicative Action. Vol. 2: Lifeworld and System*. Cambridge: Polity Press.

Heidegger, M. (2010). *Being and Time*. Albany: State University of New York Press.

Jenkins-Smith, H. and Sabatier, P. (1994). Evaluating the advocacy coalition framework. *Journal of Public Policy*, 14(2), 175–203.

Jenkins-Smith, H., Silva, C. L., Gupta, K., and Ripberger, J. T. (2014). Belief system continuity and change in policy advocacy coalitions: Using cultural theory to specify belief systems, coalitions, and sources of change. *Policy Studies Journal*, 42(4), 484–508.

Khiari, S. (2016). The people and the third people. In: A. Badiou and J. Gladding (eds.) *What Is a People*. New York: Columbia University Press.

Lamond, I. R. (2018). The challenge of articulating human rights at an LGBT 'mega-event': A personal reflection on São Paulo Pride 2017. *Leisure Studies*, 37(1), 36–48.

Lamond, I. R. and Spracklen, K. (2015). *Protests as Events: Politics, Activism and Leisure*. London: Rowman & Littlefield International.

Leahy, J. (2016). Brazil's evangelicals push politics to the right. *Financial Times*, 24th October, www.ft.com/content/7430b300-98fe-11e6-b8c6-568a43813464.

Matti, S. and Sandström, A. (2013). The defining elements of advocacy coalitions: Continuing the search for explanations for coordination and coalition structures. *Review of Policy Research*, 30(2), 240–257.

Meijerink, S. (2005). Understanding policy stability and change: The interplay of advocacy coalitions and epistemic communities, windows of opportunity, and Dutch coastal flooding policy 1945–2003. *Journal of European Public Policy*, 12(6), 1060–1077.

Moufakkir, O. and Pernecky, T. (eds.) (2014). *Ideological, Social and Cultural Aspects of Events*. Wallingford: CABI International.

Muller, J. (2017). *What Is Populism?* London: Penguin.

Pierce, J. J., Peterson, H. L., Jones, M. D., Garrard, S. P., and Vu, T. (2017). There and back again: A tale of the advocacy coalition framework. *Policy Studies Journal*, 45(1), 513–546.

Pülzl, H. and Treib, O. (2007). Implementing public policy. In: F. Fischer, G. J. Miller, M. S. Sidney (eds.) *Handbook of Public Policy Analysis: Theory, Politics, and Methods*. Florida: CRC Press, 89–107.

Rosanvallon, P. (2008). *Counter-Democracy: Politics in an Age of Distrust*. Cambridge: Cambridge University Press.

Sabatier, P. A. (1988). An advocacy coalition framework of policy change and the role of policy-oriented learning therein. *Policy Sciences*, 21(2–3), 129–168.

Spracklen, K. (2011). *Constructing Leisure: Historical and Philosophical Debates*. London: Palgrave.

Spracklen, K. and Lamond, I. R. (2016). *Critical Event Studies*. London: Routledge.

Stebbins, R. A. (1977). The amateur: Two sociological definitions. *Pacific Sociological Review*, 20(4), 582–606.

Stebbins, R. (1980). 'Amateur' and 'hobbyist' as concepts for the study of leisure problems. *Social Problems*, 27(4),413–417.

Stebbins, R. A. (1982). Amateur and professional astronomers: A study of their interrelationship. *Urban Life*, 10(4), 433–454.

Stebbins, R. A. (1992). *Amateurs, Professionals and Serious Leisure*. Québec: McGill-Queen's University Press.

Stebbins, R. A. (1997). Casual leisure: A conceptual statement. *Leisure Studies*, 16(1), 17–25.

Stebbins, R. A. (2005). Project-based leisure: Theoretical neglect of a common use of free time. *Leisure Studies*, 24(1), 1–11.

Stebbins, R. A. (2011). The semiotic self and serious leisure. *The American Sociologist*, 42 (2–3), 238–248.

Timbro (2016). *Timbro Authoritarian Populism Index: 2016*, Sweden.

Timbro (2017). Timbro Authoritarian Populism Index: 2017. https://timbro.se/allmant/ timbro-authoritarian-populism-index2017/.

Veal, A. J. (2017). The serious leisure perspective and the experience of leisure. *Leisure Sciences*, 39(3), 205–223.

Weible, C. M. (2006). An advocacy coalition framework approach to stakeholder analysis: Understanding the political context of California marine protected area policy. *Journal of Public Administration Research and Theory*, 17(1), 95–117.

Weible, C. M., Sabatier, P. A., Jenkins-Smith, H. C., Nohrstedt, D., Henry, A. D., and DeLeon, P. (2011). A quarter century of the advocacy coalition framework: An introduction to the special issue. *Policy Studies Journal*, 39(3), 349–360.

Part III

Sporting events

12 Rio 2016 Paralympics and accessibility

Breaking barriers in urban mobility?

Silvestre Cirilo dos Santos Neto, Ailton Fernando Santana de Oliveira, Vinicius Denardin Cardoso, and Marcelo de Castro Haiachi

Introduction

The history of the Paralympic Movement begins remotely with World War II, when the war wounded were sent to Stoke Mandeville Hospital. Dr Ludwig Guttman recognised the physiological and psychological value of sports in the rehabilitation of these patients (Brittain 2010; Legg and Steadward 2011; Brittain 2012). In this way, Guttman brought those patients to life, while rehabilitation worked as a factor of social integration, especially when it was perceived that sports provided good results in medical treatment. This protocol adopted by Dr Guttman led in 1948 to the realisation of the Stoke Mandeville Games, regarded as the origin of the Paralympic Movement as we know it today. This integration between medicine and sports has had a direct impact on disability sports.

In 1951, with the spread of this medical rehabilitation protocol in British hospitals, patients from other countries began to take part in these Games, beginning their internationalisation process, which culminated in the realisation of the First Paralympic Games in Rome 1960 (Brittain 2010; Legg and Steadward 2011; Brittain 2012). Just as Guttman held the first Stoke Mandeville Games on the same day as the opening of the 1948 Olympic Games held in London, the proposal was made to hold the Paralympic Games in the same host city as the Olympic Games. In the 1960 and 1964 editions, Guttman achieved this goal, but, because of the second-class treatment given to this event, the Olympic and Paralympic Games were finally only hosted in the same city in 1988 (Brittain 2010, 2012).

Through the signing of a Memorandum of Understanding in 2000, basic principles and relationships between the International Olympic Committee (IOC) and the International Paralympic Committee (IPC) were established, ensuring resumption of their organisation in the same city. This obligation was included in the Host City Contract. In 2001, the second part of the Agreement was signed, protecting the future of Paralympic Games, and, since then, many extensions of this agreement have occurred, formalising the 'One Bid, One City' concept (Brittain 2010; IPC 2014). However, even though the agreement provides greater financial support, brand protection for the Paralympic Movement, and includes further co-operation in a range of other areas, the Paralympic Games still suffer from a lack of funding, with a lesser degree of importance given by society in general, as well as the complexity in the relationship between the Committees and the difference in philosophical and ideological foundations.

This chapter aims to investigate how the accessibility, mobility, and urban regeneration policies proposed for the city of Rio de Janeiro had an impact on the lives of the disabled population due to the Rio 2016 Games. This is a case study which, as pointed out by Yin (2015), through evidence from multiple sources, allows for data to demonstrate a contemporary phenomenon in the context of real life. Through a multi-method approach, the research has been carried out through a triangulation method. The first part is an analysis of official documents from Rio 2016 since the bid, conducted as a critical analysis from the contextual point of view. According to Rother (2007: 7), "This type of review does not describe the methodological approach that would permit reproduction of data, nor an answer to a specific quantitative research question." Second, a media analysis through the qualitative approach has been made by content analysis, consisting of a contextual review of news articles relevant to the scope of this study.

From different points of view, bringing the world of disabled people into the discussion, it is possible to move forward to the understanding of the diversity involved in hosting a mega-event. We bring to the discussion some crucial elements linked to the theme. Urban regeneration and the mega-events explain the catalyst effect over the Host City under the light of the Paralympic Movement. The second topic approaches urban mobility and accessibility, focusing on disabled people. Then, the Rio 2016 Paralympics case is presented, crossing the views from media agenda and the official documents, and positioning these elements in the Games that were held to answer the question stated above.

Background

Urban regeneration and mega-events

Coaffee (2011) argues that the importance of urban regeneration has been growing in the last 50 years, while, at the same time, the advantages of hosting a sports mega-event, for promoting community development and a sports infrastructure, have just recently come to be appreciated. But how does the Paralympic community see the theme? Schantz and Gilbert (2012), analysing the two movements (Olympic and Paralympic), stated that they are in a binary opposition, explaining the hierarchical nature between movements. Meanwhile, the Paralympic Movement, by itself, looks for two conditions: health and human rights (Blawuet 2005), focusing on the person instead of the development of the host city as generally used as an argument by the 'Olympic' candidature. Notwithstanding, according to Blawuet (2005), inaccessibility of sports facilities is one of the main reasons that lead disabled people not to have access to the necessary spaces to engage in physical activity. Through this paradox, and considering the positioning of the Paralympic Games inside the bidding planning, the benefit of urban regeneration has been stressed as the main counterweight to the high costs of hosting the Games.

Also, IPC has a vision of urban development as the way to make the city accessible overall (IPC 2017a). But, LERI (2007) pointed out an absence of available data about the impact on disabled people. In this way, urban regeneration with its all aspects (city infrastructure, mobility, accessibility, etc.) is, in fact, closely associated with the Olympic Games. Thus, the Local Organising Committee of the Olympic Games (LOCOG), since the early plan, adopted standardised rules for accessibility and, under political and cultural interests, the drawing of a new city or neighbourhood in terms of mobility and new use for existing land.

Questions to consider are: Do the Paralympic Games have the same importance for the urban regeneration bidding planning as the Olympics? Are the benefits that the Games bring in greater than the money spent? How do disabled people influence the bidding planning? Keeping with the focus of the study, the following section continues with the explanation about urban mobility and accessibility.

Urban mobility and accessibility

Urban mobility can be interpreted as the ability of individuals to move from one place to another within cities (Cardoso 2008). It is also related to the time and agility in the movement of these individuals, regardless of whether they have limitations or not. Initially, the analysis of urban mobility contemplated mainly questions of the road network and the flow and conditions of passenger transportation. Subsequently, the concept was expanded, involving socioeconomic aspects related to the way of life in the cities. Rio de Janeiro has the greatest metropolitan region in Brazil. Urban mobility in Rio de Janeiro has always been one of the most problematic issues in the city and has always faced critical problems related to infrastructure for disabled people. Since the choice to host the Rio 2016 Games, there were significant differences in the city of Rio de Janeiro.

In the area of transportation, the works motivated by the Rio 2016 Games included the construction of Line 4 of the Metro, exclusive lanes for Bus Rapid Transit (BRT) and the light rail vehicle (VLT). Until 2009, fewer than 18% of the city's inhabitants were served by mass transit. In 2017, approximately 63% of the population were able to use the high-capacity network, a combination of exclusive corridors of BRT, VLT, ferries, trains and metro (Portal Brasil 2016). Galindo (2009) emphasises that issues of urban mobility must always be considered in tandem with accessibility, making it critical to plan and set priorities, in addition to avoiding unnecessary spending. The VLT is 100% accessible and combines high technology and safety. The floor is 100% low, allowing access by wheelchair users. The stations have smooth and non-slip ramps that facilitate access and tactile floors (suitable for the visually impaired) in all their extensions. They still lack sound stimulation for the hearing impaired (Portal Brasil 2016).

After having been almost considered abandoned, the port region of Rio de Janeiro was revitalised for the 2016 Games. The Porto Maravilha Urban Opera-tion has transformed the region and can be considered one of the most important structural legacies of the city. The new system favours collective public trans-port, with new spaces created for pedestrians for leisure options and physical activities, and also providing accessibility resources for disabled people (Haiachi, et al. 2017). Places such as the Museu do Amanhã, Museu de Arte Moderna (MAR), Sambódromo, beaches and the general surroundings of the sports facilities are also worth mentioning when we approach accessibility. These places were inaugurated or were revitalised to allow anyone with disabilities to make use of the facilities. But it should be noted that the term accessibility does not only mean that disabled people participate in activities that include the use of products, services, and information (Sassaki 2005). It relates to the concept of citizenship, in which individuals have rights guaranteed by law that must be respected (Manzini 2005).

The Rio 2016 Paralympic Games is analysed in the next section with regard to accessibility and the urban mobility area.

Rio 2016 Paralympics

The study on the Rio 2016 Paralympic Games refers to the understanding of the catalytic effect on the city, from the studied scope and through the analysis of the official documents and the analysis of the media and its discourse on accessi-bility and urban regeneration. Thus the question of the study can be answered, bringing to light the real effects of the Games on the city of Rio de Janeiro.

Analysis of the official Rio 2016 documents

> The Olympic and Paralympic Games are a spectacular sporting festival but also provide an ideal opportunity to promote the social inclusion of all people in the Host City and leave a lasting accessible legacy for the Host City and the Host Country.
>
> (IPC 2017b: 16)

The researchers carried out an analysis of the relevant official documents from the applicant city questionnaire up through the legacy plans, some common points having been observed in terms of urban mobility and accessibility. In the applicant city questionnaire, the points analysed in the study reveal a plan focused on making the city's transportation systems accessible to disabled people. But, if the main concern was a lack of coordination among transport mode operators, the plan would create accessibility in the transport elements, and at the same time one of the objectives in the operational area would be that of increased public transport modal share. In addition, the BRT was expected to ensure accessibility across the entire line (CO-RIO 2007). As explained in the Candidature File, LOCOG "is committed to providing a fully accessible Games" (CO-RIO 2009: 103). This was promised through the adoption of national accessibility laws, and this condition was considered a bid legacy. In addition, a review would be made by international experts of the infrastructure projects and the general city environment.

When an accessible environment is to be created, generally the governments apply the local building code requirements to define accessibility standards. However, this code only ensures the minimum parameters. At the same time, these minimum requirements do not ensure the breaking of all the barriers faced by people who need an accessible environment (IPC 2017b). In 2009, the city of Rio de Janeiro had a transport infrastructure assessed as partially accessible, but the local laws required that transport become totally accessible in five years. Thus, the key element in this area was the "accessibility in the neighbourhood" programme, also to work as a transformer element to the city. National and international standards for accessibility were to be complemented by the parameters of IPC Accessibility Guidelines and the Convention of United Nations for the Rights of Persons with Disabilities. Thus, the Paralympic Vision had an aim to make Rio a friendly city to disabled people (CO-RIO 2009).

On the existing transport infrastructure, permanent works were required for a major urban arterial network (upgrading the length of road lanes), the metro and suburban rail system (renewal of the support system and upgrading stations) and the airport gateway (capacity improvement). Alongside all this, planned and additional transport infrastructure would be opened, highlighting the extension of Metro Line 1 (currently called Line 4) and BRT corridors (CO-RIO 2009). If accessibility was considered a bid legacy in the applicant city document, Rio de Janeiro's public transport system has been regularly tested in major events held in the city since. Thus, through the adoption of a regulatory framework, the Games would bring accessibility for persons with restricted mobility and ensure connectivity through the city zones (CO-RIO 2009).

During the Games, with the launch of the Legacy Usage Planning, the document outlined an approach to urban mobility in the Olympic and Paralympic venues. Two lines of the BRT system (Transcarioca and Transolímpica) were contemplated for Barra cluster and, in addition, urban renewal would make improvements and new urban facilities surrounding Barra Olympic Park, offering accessibility in this area and also linking urban facilities to the public transport system (APO 2016). In Deodoro cluster, an urbanisation process was observed, aiming to facilitate access and circulation of the athletes in local venues. Two main programmes were applied to ensure easy access at the Deodoro X-Park: Bairro Maravilha and Asfalto Liso, with improvements to the road system and the surrounding neighbourhood. For urban mobility, the BRT Transolímpica allows the link among transport modes, ensuring connectivity through the entire city. Besides, the Deodoro cluster is mainly stocked by the rail system, which was renewed for the Games, ensuring standards of accessibility, at least in those localised surroundings of the sporting venues (APO 2016).

Media analysis

Media analysis allows us to know the concerns that are highlighted by media companies. This is known as 'media agenda' and is largely influenced by the media power over public opinion, conditioning the political and institutional agendas. Secchi (2011: 36) defines agenda as "the set of problems or themes understood as relevant". For the media analysis, the newspapers *o Globo* (Rio de Janeiro) and *Folha de São Paulo* (São Paulo), with almost 550,000 units daily (print and digital), were chosen. The criteria adopted were to search for accessibility terms, analysing those items that relate to the scope of this chapter and which were published in the main sections of the papers. From early on, a pattern in the approach to this news was observed. Almost 75% of the stories involved an evaluation of accessibility by disabled people on the way to sporting venues and directly linked to the Games. The remaining items focused on accessibility with the cultural equipment (Rio de Janeiro and São Paulo). The analysis indicated a negative agenda, inclusive if separated by periods (pre-, during and post-Games). In the pre-Games days, reports were made to assess accessibility. Through three different ways, a lack of complete accessibility was found, mainly over the transport systems, both public and private.

a) França (2016) pointed out that disabled people walked through the city of Rio de Janeiro from many points to sporting venues. They used rail, bus, metro, BRT and VLT system. The one mode of transport that was totally accessible was the VLT. All the others showed problems that compromised the free access of those people to transportation. In the rail stations there was a gap between the train and the platform. In the BRT system, a lack of tactile indicators was observed. The Metro presented a failure in the tactile indicators, and buses presented failures on the elevators; the buses were also found to lack low floor chassis.

b) Label (2016) described the experience of a wheelchair user in air travel from São Paulo to Rio de Janeiro. Many difficulties were found at the airport, from a lack of information (one passenger missed a flight because of a change of boarding gates without any company assistance) and an inadequate elevator that provoked a delay in boarding.

c) Vasconcelos and Bustamante (2016) assessed the accessibility of Rio de Janeiro for a person with visual impairment and a wheelchair user. The test was carried out around the city and problems of accessibility in the public transportation were observed, as well as in the urban infrastructure that did not allow for total autonomy by disabled people.

d) Alves (2016) was responsible for the one positive news story analysed, talking about the adaptations made in the Rio de Janeiro museums and, consequently, the increase of levels of accessibility, highlighting the condition of there being yet a lot more to do to make the city really accessible.

During the Games, accessibility was put to the test. While Ferro and França (2016) described the nuisance caused by a broken elevator at the Maracanã rail station, causing serious difficulty to wheelchair users and other people with impairments on the day of the opening ceremony, Furtado (2016) showed an experience of the photographer Loren Worthington, a wheelchair user who, while working at the Rio 2016 Olympics, had a problem with the shuttle service because of the driver's lack of training over how to operate the bus lift. The attention turned to daily problems faced by disabled people. Candida (2016) pointed out the situation of a wheelchair user with palsy who cannot go to college because the railway station to which he has access, like more than 80 others in the Rio de Janeiro rail system, is not accessible. On the other hand, Gentile (2017) reported the refurbishment of the Museum of Ipiranga, in São Paulo; however, the local government not provide equipment to meet the required standards of accessibility.

Is Rio 2016 Paralympics breaking barriers?

After decades of neglect in relation to urban interventions, the city of Rio de Janeiro made some gains with the Rio 2016 Games, despite being far from ideal. Even receiving thousands of people with impairments during the games, the hotel network, transport system and cultural and leisure spaces (museums and restaurants) still need to pay greater attention to this segment of the population (Mendonça 2016). Haiachi (2017: 100–101) interviewed a Brazilian Paralympic athlete who showed his vision of how accessibility is treated in Brazil:

> It's our fault, I always tell people with disabilities, it's the fault of not having an accessible Brazil, a large part is ours, of us disabled people, that we did not leave home, by the time everything was being built, everything was being assembled, because the public power is there. The guy is going to do a project, I'm going to build a gym, do you have a wheelchair to use there? No. If you have a wheelchair, if you have a handicapped person to use, you will have accessibility. That was one of the legacies, for me, the most important, of Rio 2016. It was not even the buildings that are staying, everything that was changed in Rio, is the change of mentality of the public power that makes projects and the improvements in the city. Any project that is going to be done now will be made accessible, if there is a person with a disability to use or not, because the mentality of the people has been changed, with the coming of the international projects, because everything that was done for the Olympics, is used for the Paralympics, was made accessible and the public, municipal, state and federal power had to do this. They had to do the works, so there you may have asked yourself, 'but why am I going to make it accessible here if the wheelchair will not use it?'

It will be there, all places have to be accessible, for all people. So this was the important legacy because the public power makes the changes in society that people in general have been using.

This statement is corroborated by the former mayor of city of Rio de Janeiro, Eduardo Paes, who noted that the Games were always thought to improve the city. He added that the city has not always been friendly to people with disabilities, but today it is possible to travel through the entire city, showing a breakthrough in this area (Ramalho, Motta and Gianotti 2016). This is complemented by the IPC (2017b: 87), for whom "accessible transport is the single most important aspect for creating an inclusive urban environment". Improvements in accessibility have focused on tourist spots, transportation, and sports facilities and missed the opportunity to promote action more widely throughout the city (Rezende 2016).

Conclusions

One of the main legacies expected for the Rio 2016 Paralympic Games was accessibility for disability people, not only in the sports facilities that were part of the Games but also throughout the city of Rio de Janeiro. With regard to the accessibility of Rio de Janeiro we could say that improvements were made before, during and after the Games. We understand that, although positive, these changes are still far from meeting the high standards required to attend all the impairments in the entire city; however, advances were perceived in this area. In this way, we must think of accessibility as a long process of transformation in our society where attitudes, behaviour and a change of perception towards disabled people can be a tangible legacy that the Games left for Rio de Janeiro. Even when the media agenda had been negative, bringing to light the problems found in the accessibility of transportation infrastructure, yet it created a positive scenario through a series of discussions with the society and the politicians, influencing other agendas.

Therefore, is very fair to say that the Games allowed for transformations in the city, as largely shown above. But, we must pay attention to the level at which these changes were made. In the case of the Rio 2016 Paralympics, it was observed that most of the changes occurred in the Games axis, thinking first of serving the customers of the event. Logically, the 'common citizen' will use the full range of services offered to disabled people in the Games period, working as a legacy, promised since the applicant city period. Despite that fact, and as frequently commented above, the Games brought improvements to accessibility and urban mobility, improving the levels before the candidature. But, it is far from serving disabled people in the entire city, and we are missing the opportunity to continue evolving and offering autonomy to these people. Answering the title question, the Rio 2016 Paralympics broke barriers in urban mobility and accessibility only partially, not taking full advantage of the catalytic effect of the mega-event.

Questions for discussion

1. Discuss if the Paralympic Games have the same importance for urban regeneration as observed in the Olympic Games?
2. How can urban regeneration, urban mobility and accessibility be influenced by a mega-event?
3. Discuss why a mega-event does not ensure a totally accessible city?
4. How is it possible to break barriers in urban mobility by hosting a mega-event and creating a totally accessible city?

References

Alves, M. E. (2016). A arte de fazer sentir. *O Globo*, 4 (September), 18.

APO. (2016). *Planejamento de Uso do Legado*. Rio de Janeiro.

Blawuet, C. (2005). *Promoting the health and human rights of individuals with a disability through the Paralympic Movement*. www.sportanddev.org/sites/default/files/downloads/62__the_paralympics___promoting_health_and_human_rights_through_sport.pdf.

Brittain, I. (2010). *The Paralympic Games explained*. London: Routledge.

Brittain, I. (2012). *From Stoke Mandeville to Sochi: A history of the summer and winter Paralympic Games*. Illinois: Common Ground.

Candida, S. (2016). Escadaria de trem levou futuro advogado ao tribunal. *O Globo*, 1 (October), 21.

Cardoso C. (2008). *Análise do transporte coletivo urbano sob a ótica dos riscos e carências sociais*. Tese (Doutorado em Serviço Social). São Paulo: PUC.

Coaffee, J. (2011). Urban regeneration and renewal. In J. R. Gold and M. M. Gold (eds.) *Olympic cities: City agendas, planning, and the world's Games 1896–2016*. London: Routledge, 180–193.

CO-RIO. (2007). *Candidature acceptance application for Rio de Janeiro to host the 2016 Olympic and Paralympic Games*. Rio de Janeiro: Bid Commission Rio 2016.

CO-RIO. (2009). *Candidature file for Rio de Janeiro to host the 2016 Olympic and Paralympic Games*. Rio de Janeiro: Bid Commission Rio 2016.

Ferro, M. and França, R. (2016). Filas, um legado incômodo. *O Globo*, 8 (September), 4.

França, R. (2016). Uma corrida de obstáculos rumo aos Jogos. *O Globo*, 4 (September), 19.

Furtado, T. (2016). A esperança foi a última a subir. *O Globo*, 9 (September), 2.

Galindo E. (2009). *Análise comparativa do entendimento do transporte como objeto do planejamento*. Tese (mestrado em transportes). Brasília: UnB.

Gentile, R. (2017). Museu do Ipiranga, interditado há 4 anos, ainda nem iniciou a reforma. *Folha de São Paulo*, B1.

Haiachi, M. (2017). *O curso de vida do atleta com deficiência: a deficiência e o esporte como eventos marcantes*. Tese (Doutorado em Ciências do Movimento Humano). Porto Alegre: UFRGS.

Haiachi, M. C., Santos Neto, S. C., Cardoso, V. D., and Oliveira, A. F. S. (2017). The Paralympic city of Rio de Janeiro and the challenges of hosting mega multi-sports events. In L. Mataruna and B. G. Pena (eds.) *Mega events footprints: Past, present and future*. Rio de Janeiro: Engenho, 1263–1278.

IPC. (2014). *First IPC-IOC agreement*. Rio de Janeiro.

IPC. (2017a). *IPC handbook*. Rio de Janeiro.

IPC. (2017b). *IPC accessibility guide*. Rio de Janeiro.

Label, F. (2016). Viagem turbulenta. *Folha de São Paulo*, 22(August), B20.

Legg, D. and Steadward, R. (2011). The history of the Paralympic Games. In D. Legg and K. Gilbert (eds.) *The Paralympic legacies*. Illinois: Common Ground, 13–20.

LERI. (2007). *A lasting legacy for London: Assessing the legacy of the Olympic Games and Paralympic Games*. London: University of East London.

Manzini, E. J. (2005). Análise de artigos da Revista Brasileira de Educação Especial (1992–2002). *Revista Brasileira de Educação Especial*, 9(1), 13–23.

Mendonça, A. V. (2016). Paralimpíada deixa Rio mais acessível para pessoa com deficiência. http://g1.globo.com/rio-de-janeiro/olimpiadas/rio2016/noticia/2016/06/paralim piada-deixa-rio-mais-acessivel-para-pessoa-com-deficiencia.html.

Portal Brasil. (2016). Integração urbana é um dos maiores legados da Rio 2016. 16 June, Governo do Brasil. www.brasil.gov.br/esporte/2016/06/integracao-urbana-e-um-dos-maiores-legados-da-rio-2016.

Ramalho, R., Motta, P., and Gianotti, R. (2016). Entrevista Eduardo Paes. *O Globo*, 21 (August), 15.

Rezende, C. (2016). Acessibilidade continua sendo grande problema na 'cidade olímpica. *O Estado de São Paulo*, 5 September. http://esportes.estadao.com.br/noticias/jogos-olim picos,acessibilidade-continua-sendo-grande-problema-na-cidade-olimpica,10000074049.

Rother, E. T. (2007). Revisão sistemática × revisão narrativa. *Acta Paulista de Enfermagem*, 20(2), 5–6.

Sassaki, R. K. (2005). *Inclusão: Construindo uma sociedade para todos*. Rio de Janeiro: WVA.

Schantz, O. J. and Gilbert, K. (2012). The Paralympic movement: Empowerment or disempowerment for people with disabilities? In H. J. Lenskyj and S. Wagg (eds.) *The Palgrave handbook of Olympic studies*. Basingstoke: Palgrave Macmillan, 358–380.

Secchi, L. (2011). *Políticas públicas – Conceitos, esquemas de análise, casos práticos*. São Paulo: Cengage Learning.

Vasconcelos, G. and Bustamante, L. (2016). Rio tem apenas ilhas de acessibilidade. *Folha de São Paulo*. www1.folha.uol.com.br/esporte/olimpiada-no-rio/2016/08/1807102-prestes-a-sediar-a-paraolimpiada-rio-tem-apenas-ilhas-de-acessibilidade.shtml.

Yin, R. (2015). *Estudo de caso: Planejamento e métodos*. Porto Alegre: Bookman.

13 Volunteering and wellbeing

Case study of the Glasgow 2014 Commonwealth Games volunteer programmes

Briony Sharp

Introduction

Recent studies have highlighted the potential volunteering holds to support a more multi-dimensional and interrelated legacy from major events, suggesting improvements in volunteer activity numbers, social inclusion in volunteers, contribution to the economy and development of a skilled volunteer workforce (Nichols and Ralston 2012). With regard to research surrounding this topic, typical major event volunteer research findings are concerned with the experience, likelihood to re-volunteer in the future (Jones and Yates 2015) and motivations and satisfaction (Kristiansen 2015); however, there is scope to widen this research to explore further the links between major event volunteering and individual wellbeing and confidence.

McCartney, et al. (2013) propose volunteering opportunities may lead to direct health, social and wellbeing impacts. Similarly, Minnaert (2012) suggests volunteering has been used as a tool for the reduction of social exclusion, development of urban communities and reduction in crime as well as an opportunity for the host cities of sporting events to realise the potential to create long-term social legacies.

There are a number of ways in which volunteering can be categorised: informal or formal, episodic or discrete, continuous or successive, collective or unconditional (McGillivray, et al. 2013). Each of the volunteer categories provides routes for participants' contributions to society in a satisfying and important way. These routes include using existing skills, developing new skills, positively contributing to the lives of others and developing community engagement (Jones and Yates 2015; Kristiansen 2015). Sadd (2010: 269) proposes that sport and social regeneration "is more about participation and especially the role the voluntary sector can play in that". As well as being used by policymakers to enhance social inclusion and cohesion (Kristiansen 2015), volunteering also had been found to have a positive impact on personal health, with research suggesting encouraging results in wellbeing, life satisfaction, mortality and depression (Jones and Yates 2015). Furthermore, Lee, et al. (2014) suggests participating in volunteer activity increases community and individual wellbeing in addition to generating feeling of self-satisfaction, accomplishment and enhance self-confidence (Morrow-Howell, et al. 2003; Brown, et al. 2012).

Research context

Links between volunteering and wellbeing are evident within the literature in a number of different areas, including promoting social inclusion and wellbeing through arts programmes (Secker, et al. 2011), formal volunteering and self-reported health and happiness (Borgonovi 2008) and the relationship between volunteering, wellbeing and public policy (Binder and Freytag 2012). The majority of this research reports increased levels of wellbeing in people who participate in regular volunteer activities (Binder and Freytag 2012). Nichols and Ralston (2012), in their review of volunteer legacies, highlight that only Manchester 2002 Commonwealth Games had a positive influence on volunteering in sport, which could be attributed to the creation of the Manchester Event Volunteers (MEV) directly after the event that enabled the pool of volunteers to be accessed for future volunteering opportunities. The increased interest in providing a lasting legacy has led Games hosts, public policymakers and academics to embrace the growth in research concerning legacy and social legacies; however, the potential has yet to be researched fully with regard to the large number of volunteers and possible legacy of such programmes (Downward and Ralston 2006; Nichols and Ralston 2012). The growth in research concerning voluntary work and wellbeing continues to develop. This is much like the growth in the emerging body of literature on legacy potential of major sporting events. The overlap within these academic fields with regard to large numbers of volunteers and potential legacy of such programmes, provides a research opportunity yet to be fully studied.

Minnaert (2012) highlights the potential social legacy through skills enhancement including employment and volunteering opportunities. McCartney, et al. (2013: 25) also acknowledges this subcategory as a critical pathway for generating a positive health, wellbeing and social impact in Glasgow from hosting the Commonwealth Games, "where members of the community would gain new skills and confidence by being valued for the voluntary input during the event". Volunteer programmes are commonly employed to encourage economic and social regeneration for local communities (Smith and Fox 2007). They offer training and employment experience, which aims to provide volunteers with the environment to nurture new skills, in turn offering an occasion for individual and community development (Doherty 2009).

Case study

In November 2007, Glasgow was announced as the city that would host the 2014 Commonwealth Games. From the bidding stage, a partnership between Glasgow City Council and the Scottish Government made a concerted effort to demonstrate the potential benefits for the host community from hosting such an event. Drawing from established and emerging research combining major events with post-industrial regeneration, place marketing and social impacts, the bid included a variety of possible legacies across infrastructure, employment and health (Christie and Gibb

2015). The Organising Committee for the Games, Glasgow 2014 Ltd, brought Commonwealth Games Scotland, the Scottish Government and Glasgow City Council together into the partnership responsible for delivering the bid documents. Glasgow as a case study of event-led regeneration and legacy research has generated a considerable amount of academic interest (see Matheson 2010; Rogerson 2016; Christie and Gibb 2015; Misener, et al. 2015). The links between post-industrial cities and event-led regeneration as well as Glasgow's history as an events city are examined in combination with the emerging area of major events' potential to create a social legacy.

From the outset of Glasgow's bidding documents, the emphasis on both economic and civic development is evident. Not only from the newly designed city-wide branding, "People Make Glasgow", but also the pre-Games vision of: "Glasgow 2014 will help achieve a healthier, more vibrant city with its citizens enjoying and realising the benefits of sport and the wider, longer term economic, social, cultural and environmental benefits that Glasgow 2014 can help deliver" (Glasgow City Council 2009: 4). Here, Glasgow City Council demonstrates the wide reaching aspirations the hosting of such an event would enable. The holistic nature of this vision is aligned with the shifting paradigm of major event research to include more focused attention on the longer-term impacts of major events (Smith 2012; Misener, et al. 2015). Due to the wide-ranging nature of potential benefits and ability to examine the social legacy potential, this case study has enabled a focused approach concerning the social legacy for individuals from volunteering at a major sporting event.

Delivered in collaboration with city volunteering developments, the Games volunteer programmes provided opportunities for people to get involved with the Commonwealth Games. Figures from Glasgow 2014's (2015) post-Games report state an estimated 12,500 Clyde-siders and 1,200 Host City Volunteers participated in Games volunteering initiatives. The Clyde-sider programme saw Glasgow embark on its largest peacetime volunteer project, "with a record 50,811 volunteer applications" received (Glasgow 2014, 2015: 15). Volunteers within Glasgow 2014 also played a crucial part for Glasgow within the Queens Baton Relay project, pre-Games Frontrunner volunteer programme, and ceremonies Cast Member volunteers. From post-Games figures, an approximate 3,000 volunteers took part in the opening and closing ceremonies. In addition to this, Glasgow Life, part of Glasgow City Council, also established the Host City Volunteer programme. This programme "supported volunteers from part of the community least likely to take up volunteer opportunities as part of a 3-year project" (Misener, et al. 2015: 458). Glasgow Life describe the purpose of the Host City Volunteer project as:

> The HCV project was designed to form the first part of a wider Host City Glasgow programme which is planned to run from Dec 2013 until Dec 2016. Its aim is to enable Glasgow's communities to engage better with the delivery of future major event opportunities, building on the experiences from the Commonwealth Games and supported by a programme of flexible learning, citizenship, and volunteering. The programme intends to achieve the following outcomes:

- increased learning opportunities for Glaswegians to understand, develop and sustain local and city-wide concepts of identity and civic pride;
- increased awareness of and engagement with the city's cultural and sporting assets;
- increased uptake and active participation by Glaswegians in volunteering and delivery opportunities associated with major cultural and sporting events.

(Rogerson, et al. 2016: 6)

The large numbers of people involved in Games-related volunteer initiatives allows for critical research to be undertaken concerning social legacies. Volunteer populations are essential to the success of any major event (Nichols and Ralston 2012); therefore, it is important to develop further understanding of the potential social outcomes from being involved in major event volunteering.

The quantitative findings for this chapter are based on responses to an online survey made available to every volunteer who participated in a Glasgow 2014 Commonwealth Games related volunteer initiative. Two focus groups with Games volunteers were carried out in Glasgow as a pilot to decide upon the online survey questions. The volunteer sample (n=229) in this study was not from a specific region or place; rather, the targeted sample required a general sample of volunteers required only to have volunteered as part of a Glasgow 2014 related programme. The largest group of Games volunteers were the Clyde-siders; the Commonwealth Games official Games time volunteers. Also included were the Baton Bearers, Cast and Ceremonies volunteers and Frontrunners, the latter being the pre-Games volunteers who were responsible for interviewing, training, protocol, mascots and PR events. Further to these groups, Glasgow Life, implemented a Host City Volunteer programme.

The online survey was made available online ten months post-Games in June 2015. This decision was made in an attempt to avoid the "feel-good" factor (see Porsche and Maennig 2008; Smith 2009) commonly reported in research conducted directly after a major event. It was found that an online survey would reach a wider sample and not be restricted by location or ability to attend a focus group (Case, et al. 2013). The mix of questions is supported by evidence suggesting that when participants fill out open-ended questions they tend to use more words and provide more in-depth answers. Furthermore, the survey called for respondents to be reflective; therefore, it needed to be some time after the event in order to allow for capacity to reflect on past experiences (Woodall, et al. 2016). It was advertised through social media (for example, Facebook volunteer groups, Twitter) as well as posted on Volunteer Scotland's website. The survey information and weblink was also published in Volunteer Scotland's newsletter twice, complemented by a blog written by the author highlighting the importance and potential impact of this research on major event volunteer legacies. The survey remained open for six months until December 2015.

The survey comprised qualitative open-ended questions, supported by demographic information questions and the use of the Edinburgh Warwick Mental

Health Wellbeing Scale (WEMWBS) to provide quantitative data from this sample. Questions included 'Can you describe your experience in being involved in the Glasgow 2014 Commonwealth Games?', 'What impact will the Games have on your life? For example, has it changed anything for you? Or not? Do you do anything now you didn't before or are planning on?'. The WEMWBS was selected due to its personal wellbeing focus and the inclusion of measures such as confidence and positivity. Defined in the user guide, the WEMWBS:

> is worded positively and together they cover most, but not all, attributes of mental wellbeing including both hedonic and eudaimonic perspectives. Areas not covered include spirituality or purpose in life. These were deemed to extend beyond the general populations' current understanding of mental wellbeing and their inclusion was thought likely to increase non-response.
>
> (Stewart-Brown and Janmohamed 2008: 3).

Aligned with the growing research interest in wellbeing measurement (Pawlowski, et al. 2014), the measurement of perceived wellbeing improvement was used to determine if volunteering at Glasgow 2014 Commonwealth Games has the potential to leave a social legacy.

With regard to the self-reported, retrospective wellbeing scale (WEMWBS) (see Table 13.1), the participants were asked to fill out a portion of demographic questions followed by the scale while thinking about how they thought and felt before taking part in a Games-related volunteer programme. The use of the retrospective survey can be seen to be used within similar studies of health and wellbeing (Graham, et al. 2014), the impact of the Commonwealth Games on Glasgow's health (McCartney, et al. 2013), volunteering (Wahrendorf, et al. 2016) and resident social cohesion and interactions (Zhu, et al. 2014). From previous research, it is suggested retrospective surveys may be subject to error when remembering past experiences, possible honeymoon effect (Zhu, et al. 2014) or recall bias (Wahrendorf, et al. 2016). Despite these limitations, this study addressed important gaps in research concerning major event volunteering and its potential legacy. The respondents were then asked to reflect on their experience of being involved in a volunteer programme and fill out the WEMWBS scale for the second time. That was followed by questions regarding their thoughts on the impact for Glasgow and Scotland, on their life and their overall satisfaction of their involvement. The use of the scale was intended to show how the participants feel about themselves pre- and post-Games having been part of a volunteer programme. This was completely anonymous.

As suggested by the WEMWBS user guide, the data is presented, firstly, as a mean score for the sample with 95% confidence interval. By analysing the mean score from this data sample, it enabled a useful comparison between quantitative data collected in this study and the wider population mean score. As this research is concerning differences between scores of the same group at different times, the user guide suggests statistical testing is employed; therefore, paired-samples t-

Table 13.1 Warwick Edinburgh Mental Wellbeing Scale.

Statements	None of the time	Rarely	Some of the time	Often	All of the time
I've been feeling optimistic about the future	1	2	3	4	5
I've been feeling useful	1	2	3	4	5
I've been feeling relaxed	1	2	3	4	5
I've been feeling interested in other people	1	2	3	4	5
I've had energy to spare	1	2	3	4	5
I've been dealing with problems well	1	2	3	4	5
I've been thinking clearly	1	2	3	4	5
I've been feeling good about myself	1	2	3	4	5
I've been feeling close to other people	1	2	3	4	5
I've been feeling confident	1	2	3	4	5
I've been able to make up my own mind about things	1	2	3	4	5
I've been feeling loved	1	2	3	4	5
I've been interested in new things	1	2	3	4	5
I've been feeling cheerful	1	2	3	4	5

tests were conducted to compare each before-and-after thoughts and feelings. A basic statistical tool, t-tests measure group variances by investigating the difference and mean in each group (Andrew, et al. 2011).

The representative demographic from the data collected (n = 229) in this study contained: 59% Clydesider volunteers, 16% Frontrunners, 10% Ceremonies Cast Members, 7% Host City Volunteers, 4% Queens Baton Relay and 5% stating 'other' to include team assistants and casting support; 75% female, 24% male, <1% transgender and prefer not to say; 8% 16–24 year old, 23% 25–44 year old, 60% 45–64 year old and 9% 65 years old and over; 49% employed/self-employed, 28% retired, 9% student, 7% volunteer, 4% unemployed and 3% job-seeking.

Findings and discussion

Despite existing theoretical links between events volunteering and wellbeing (Pi, et al. 2014), quality of life (Binder and Freytag 2012), employment and work production (Li 2013), Horne (2007) suggests research varies vastly in rigour and quality often being carried out prior to the event. Therefore, while the emerging dialogue on maximising the potential positive legacies has stimulated a more cohesive approach to assessing said impacts, currently there has been inadequate measurement of post-event outputs as well as inputs, particularly social or "softer" impacts, which are arguably more difficult to measure (Swart, et al. 2011).

This research presents an area for further research aligned with wider volunteering and wellbeing research (Borgonovi 2008; Secker, et al. 2011; Binder and Freytag 2012). It is suggested by the findings in this research that wellbeing improvements from volunteering at a one-off event present potential to create a social legacy similar to recognised volunteering benefits from longer-term volunteer commitment. The implications of such a notion highlight the emergence of a broader volunteer legacy to include additional themes on top of volunteer motivations and likelihood to continue to volunteer.

McCartney, et al. (2013) proposed volunteering as a critical pathway for generating a positive Games legacy. They suggest that by providing volunteering opportunities as a key ingredient for change, potential direct impacts include increased future volunteering, increased skills and health, wellbeing and social impacts. The premise behind compiling self-reported survey data for this research was to gain access to a broad and varied sample and provide insight into the reach of potential social legacy on a personal level. To analyse the wellbeing element of Games legacy, the WEMWBS provides an average self-reported wellbeing score (scoring valued from 1 to 5, minimum 14 and maximum 70 total) with a 95% confidence interval. From the data collected in this research before the Games provided a mean score of 52 (51.6); this is representative of the average population score of 51 (Stewart-Brown and Janmohamed 2008). Therefore, it provides a reliable base line assessing self-reported wellbeing levels. The mean score when the participants were asked to consider their wellbeing level post-Games has increased by 5 points to 57 (56.7); hence, the data in this study suggests a significant increase on the population average in wellbeing levels from participating in a Games volunteer programme. Additionally, the increase in perceived wellbeing level post-Games is further confirmed by a more stable standard deviation result. The post-Games value of 8.1 standard deviation informs the analysis of a standard range ($\pm$ 8.1) either side of the average wellbeing score. Therefore, the participants were more similar and sure of an increase in wellbeing when reporting their feelings and thoughts post-Games, compared to pre-Games standard deviation of 9.3 +/− range below or above the average score which suggests a slightly more uncertain feeling surround their perceived wellbeing.

The table below provides data regarding the presented results (Table 13.2). This is consistent with suggestions made by McCartney, et al. (2013) that volunteering opportunities have the potential to encourage wellbeing improvements; this data demonstrates encouraging results from Glasgow's volunteer programmes.

From the WEMWBS user guide, Stewart-Brown and Janmohamed (2008) suggest when examining before-and-after feelings, further statistical analysis should be employed. Therefore, the analysis in this chapter adopted established practice from the literature. When analysed using paired-samples t-test through

Table 13.2 Survey data representing 'before' and 'after' wellbeing results.

	Before	After
Average	51.6531532	56.7612613
Standard Dev	9.38090213	8.10796682
Sample Size	222	222
Confidence	1.23	1.06655576
Margin of Error	0.77441406	0.58038883
Upper Bound	52.4275672	57.3416501
Lower Bound	50.4231532	56.1808724
Max	70	70
Min	14	14
Range	56	56

SPSS, the overall basic results demonstrated each element of the WEMWBS reported a strongly significant improvement in overall self-reported wellbeing; P < .005. The following section details the analysis conducted for each wellbeing indicator. Paired-samples t-tests were conducted to compare each before-and-after thoughts and feelings to assess the likeliness of the results happening by chance. The table below (Table 13.3) includes each element and the corresponding data analysis results. There was a significant difference in the scores for reported for all before and after. Table 13.3 details the paired-sample t-test for each element including the statistical data of each mean (M), standard deviation (SD), total sample (t) and significance indicator (p). Importantly, the statically significance is interpreted due to the 'p' value being less than 0.05 in each of the wellbeing indicators. Furthermore, a 'p' value of less than 0.05 is also small enough to justify the rejection of an insignificant hypothesis (Higgins and Green 2011).

By splitting the data into the age groups (16–19, 20–24, 25–34, 35–44, 45–54, 55–64, 65+), the specific wellbeing results can be seen to differ in each age category. The age groups were specified by the Scottish Government's definition of adult age as 16 and aligned with Glasgow 2014 Commonwealth Games welcoming applications from aged 16 and over (Legacy 2014, 2015). Firstly, participants aged 16–19 only reported significant wellbeing increases in 4 of the 14 indicators (29%). The areas that did significantly improve for this age group were optimism, interested in other people, feeling good about myself and confidence. Interestingly, this age group of 16–19 year olds reported the least impact in wellbeing improvement post-Games. This is perhaps due to the small sample gathered. In the next age category (20–24), a greater wellbeing impact was reported post-Games. From the paired sample t-tests, 50% of wellbeing indicators presented a significant increase including: feeling useful, interested in other people, dealing with problems well, feeling close to other people, confident, able to make up my own mind, and cheerful. With regard to the next age

Table 13.3 T-test analysis WEMWBS results.

Thoughts and feelings	T-test analysis results
Optimism	Before the Games *(M = 3.68, SD = 0.873)* and after *(M = 3.97, SD = 0.766); t (221) = −5.825, p < .001*
Feeling useful	Before the Games *(M = 3.68, SD = 0.837)* and after *(M = 4.12, SD = 0.636); t (220) = −8.747, p < .001*
Feeling relaxed	Before the Games *(M = 3.44, SD = 0.763)* and after *(M = 3.83, SD = 0.748); t (221) = −7.943, p < .001*
Interested in other people	Before the Games *(M = 3.97, SD = 0.826)* and after *(M = 4.27, SD = 0.664); t (221) = −6.385, p < .001*
Having energy to spare	Before the Games *(M = 3.45, SD = 0.833)* and after *(M = 3.82, SD = 0.788); t (220) = −7.053, p < .001*
Dealing with problems well	Before the Games *(M = 3.62, SD = 0.859)* and after *(M = 4.00, SD = 0.709); t (219) = −8.212, p < .001*
Thinking clearly	Before the Games *(M = 3.78, SD = 0.791)* and after *(M = 4.01, SD = 0.724); t (221) = −5.056, p < .001*
Feeling good about myself	Before the Games *(M = 3.60, SD = 0.859)* and after *(M = 4.08, SD = 0.685); t (221) = −9.212, p < .001*
Feeling close to other people	Before the Games *(M = 3.58, SD = 0.841)* and after *(M = 4.02, SD = 0.716); t (220) = −9.136, p <.001*
Confidence	Before the Games *(M = 3.58, SD = 0.909)* and after *(M = 4.10, SD = 0.680); t (220) = −9.395, p < .001*
Able to make up my own mind	Before the Games *(M = 3.96, SD = 0.822)* and after *(M = 4.23, SD = 0.698); t (220) = −6.320, p < .001*
Feeling loved	Before the Games *(M = 3.66, SD = 0.924)* and after *(M = 3.97, SD = 0.788); t (219) = −6.622, p < .001*
Interested in new things	Before the Games *(M = 3.89, SD = 0.872)* and after *(M = 4.62, SD = 0.677); t (220) = −6.828, p < .001*
Feeling cheerful	Before the Games *(M = 3.79, SD = 0.812)* and after *(M = 4.10, SD = 0.661); t (219) = −6.622, p < .001*

group (25–34), an increased wellbeing impact was reported after the Games compared to the youngest participants, but slightly less of an impact than 20–24. Out of the 14 wellbeing indicators 5 reported a significant increase post-Games (36%); these included: feeling useful, interested in other people, feeling good about myself, feeling close to other people, and confidence. Participants aged 35–44 reported a significant improvement in 12 out of a possible 14 wellbeing indicators after the Games (86%), only optimism and having energy to spare did not display a significant improvement. Respondents from the age group of 45–54, interestingly, reported a strongly significant improvement in all of the wellbeing indicators, therefore presenting a 100% increase in overall wellbeing after participating in a Games volunteer programme. While slightly lower, participants aged 55–64 reported an improvement in 13 of the 14 wellbeing indicators (93%). The only element not reporting a significant improvement was interested in other people. Lastly, participants aged 65+ reported an overall positive improvement with 10 of the 14 wellbeing indicators displaying a significant improvement post-Games (71%).

An interesting finding across all age groups is the significant increase in reported confidence after the Games. The results from this study are in agreement with similar findings reported by Woodall, et al. (2016) in their examination of volunteer impacts and the Glasgow 2014 Commonwealth Games. This is reflected in the data collected in this study as each age group did report an increase in overall wellbeing at some level across each indicator. More specifically, when analysing the reported confidence level, confidence was the only wellbeing indicator that conclusively increased regardless of age. Thus, there are links between volunteering and increased wellbeing impact. Similarly, 80% of participants in this study reported a significant increase in confidence as well as an interest in trying new things. Although this early stage research may not be definite, this area of research presents many future study opportunities to explore the evident themes proposed by studies of Games time volunteering and increased in overall wellbeing impacts.

While there remains a lack of evidence to directly relate regeneration or sporting success to improved wellbeing of the host nation, an improvement within mental health, wellbeing and confidence for the population was an aspiration noted in the bid document submitted by Glasgow for the Commonwealth Games (Glasgow 2014, 2005). The above data suggests the major event volunteer initiatives may be a pathway that requires further attention for future host nations wishing to enhance national wellbeing and in particularly confidence levels across all age groups of the population.

The following section discusses the data collected from the online survey while spilt into non-volunteers and participants who have volunteered previously. In addition to results previously examined, the data collected for this study demonstrates further agreement that states there are links between volunteering and wellbeing (Morrow-Howell, et al. 2003; Brown, et al. 2012; Lee, et al. 2014). This affirmation is clearly displayed in both groups (those who had and those who had not volunteered before the Glasgow 2014 Commonwealth Games). Table 13.4. shows that the group who had not volunteered before increased significantly post-Games with the majority of levels going up in the WEMWBS scale. Similarly, Table 13.5 shows those who had previous volunteer experience also increased post-Games; however, that group had a notably higher starting point with the vast majority of the starting levels being similar to the first group's post-Games reported levels. This is consistent with previous studies (Borgonovi 2008). It should be noted that the second group, Table 13.5, were also the majority of the sample (n= 169, 74%), which also supports the claim that individuals with higher wellbeing levels are more likely to participate in volunteering.

These findings suggest that wellbeing does increase and a one-off large event volunteer experience does have an impact on reported wellbeing levels, including confidence, optimism and usefulness. Furthermore, results from this study

Table 13.4 Responses from non-volunteers.

Feelings and thoughts	Before	%	After	%
Optimistic about the future	Some of the time	45	Often	49
Useful	Some of the time	40	Often	61
Relaxed	Some of the time	52	Often	43
Interested in other people	Some of the time	37	Often	56
Energy to spare	Some of the time	36	Often	48
Dealing with problems well	Some of the time	36	Often	48
Thinking clearly	Some of the time	42	Often	47
Feeling good about myself	Some of the time	35	Often	56
Close to other people	Some of the time	38	Often	49
Confident	Some of the time	31	Often	50
Able to make up my own mind	Often	37	Often	49
Loved	Some of the time	35	Often	43
Interested in new things	Often	31	Often	55
Cheerful	Some of the time	36	Often	63

demonstrate that having previous volunteer experience does have an impact upon wellbeing levels since a person who had no previous volunteer experience reported a lower starting level of wellbeing. This study is consistent with the findings of Brown, et al. (2012) in proposing that an increase in wellbeing did not show a direct correlation with the amount of time spent volunteering. However, regarding a formal volunteer commitment, this is contradictory to Borgonovi's (2008) findings that demonstrate that an increase in frequency of volunteering did increase the level of reported wellbeing. Therefore, it can be suggested that volunteering at a major event does differ in experience than a formal volunteer commitment; however, both volunteering types present opportunities to enhance an individual's wellbeing with event volunteers suggesting wellbeing improvements from a shorter involvement. The difference may originate from the different circumstances for the studies being completed.

In addition to examining self-reported wellbeing impact after the Games, the survey participants were asked to predict how long they expected the feeling of wellbeing improvements (if any) would last. Overall, concerning the entire sample, the majority of responses predicted their wellbeing impacts to last years (32%). When only considering respondents who had previously volunteered, the consensus was less sure with 35% of participants reporting they were 'unsure' how long these changes would last. With that being said, 29% and 27% of previous volunteers did report expecting these improvements to last 'years' or 'longer', respectively. Analysis of the participants who were first time volunteers displayed a different picture. From these results, the majority of first volunteers expected their wellbeing changes to last years (36%), closely followed by 'longer' (35%). Interestingly, this group reported much less uncertainty in their

Table 13.5 Responses from previous volunteers.

Feelings and thoughts	Before	%	After	%
Optimistic about the future	Often	50	Often	58
Useful	Often	47	Often	64
Relaxed	Some of the time	43	Often	54
Interested in other people	Often	48	Often	51
Energy to spare	Often	43	Often	54
Dealing with problems well	Often	44	Often	62
Thinking clearly	Often	52	Often	60
Feeling good about myself	Often	47	Often	63
Close to other people	Often	47	Often	57
Confident	Often	43	Often	61
Able to make up my own mind	Often	53	Often	53
Loved	Often	40	Often	51
Interested in new things	Often	49	Often	53
Cheerful	Often	47	Often	60

expectations with only 22% of responses selecting 'unsure' how long these changes would last. This is perhaps an expected finding due to the research substantiating the links between volunteer activity and increased wellbeing (Morrow-Howell, et al. 2003; Brown, et al. 2012; Jones and Yates 2015; Liu 2016) and the higher levels of reported wellbeing within previous volunteers from this study. Moreover, the potential wellbeing legacy impact proposed in this study further emphasises the need for more long-term focus research in this area of Games volunteering legacy. Table 13.6 illustrates the impacts that volunteers think the Games will have on their lives.

From the qualitative data collected, common themes identified when considering the impact of the Games upon the respondent's future were volunteering, more opportunities that are new, and friends. The findings in this research are consistent with Jones and Yates (2015) and with Woodall, et al. (2016) research on the Glasgow 2014 Clyde-siders programme, which proposed that Games volunteering provided participants with a valuable opportunity to meet and build relationships with people from differing cultures and backgrounds.

Conclusions

From the preceding discussion, it is clear that volunteering initiatives engender an increased level of self-reported wellbeing, skills increase and social opportunities. Furthermore, the data mirrored previous findings from Jones and Yates (2015) concerning the reported likelihood to continue to volunteer post-Games and, therefore, that an increase in future volunteering activities is likely. The data collected also confirmed previous research that suggests people who volunteer at

Table 13.6 Volunteer survey answers of impacts of Games.

Volunteer	What impact will the Games have on your life?
10	"I will continue to volunteer. Alongside some of the big sporting events still being attracted to the city I am also doing community based volunteering for instance I am now a mentor for Project Scotland, and will be helping out at Pride Scotland. In addition, it has given me additional skills to put on my CV"
15	"I found my best friend at G2014, and made other good friends too. G2014 has improved my life more than I ever imagined. . ."
222	"put me in contact with volunteering networks (not directly but through FB contacts I made during the games"
150	"Contact with people from different backgrounds from different parts of the world"
164	"it helped me in my aim to build on my experiences volunteering and to meet people and come out of my shell"
87	"It increased my confidence and I met people who will remain in my life for a long time and became really good friends"
32	"It gave me a load of new friends from all walks of life. Has given me the confidence to pursue a new career path"
200	"I have a host of new friends, have joined a social media site and volunteer even more often than I did before. I am ready to try out new sports and events and have so many opportunities to volunteer I have to be selective. It's a great way to spend my retirement, from small charity events to major sporting ones"
90	"Another social group to enjoy meeting and sharing stories with"
56	"Now part of a group made up of ex-Clydesiders and host city volunteers, call Vamos 2014. We connect on Facebook and volunteering opportunities are available almost daily. Between Vamos and Glasgow Life, I could be busy 7 days a week"
76	"Have signed up for more volunteering. Made life-long friends who have shared in this experience. Have many memories to pass on to kids etc. Possibly could use this experience to further my career"

sporting events place an importance on social connections and interactions (Lee, et al. 2014. Furthermore, this research highlights the importance placed on individual self-development through sport event volunteering and, as Downward and Ralston (2006) highlight, the need for organisers to recognise the ability sport event volunteering has to increase confidence, wellbeing and skills.

On an individual level, it is argued that volunteering is a pathway to generate a positive social legacy, as suggested by McCartney, et al. (2013). In addition, there is evidence to suggest an increase in social capital amongst Games volunteers. The links between Games volunteering and social capital would benefit from further analysis of a larger and varied sample. It is argued that fostering social capital enables wider cultural and social understanding; therefore, it is recommended this concept is utilised to develop understanding within bridging and bonding social capital containing different community, volunteer and social groups. This, notably, also shares links with community development strategies and fosters stronger communities through shared experiences and new networks. The evidence presented in this research is considered in the early stages and should be utilised as a starting point to develop possible avenues where major events can generate a social legacy in areas such as social capital, increased skills, improved wellbeing, and continued volunteering.

Questions for discussion

1. What other ways could volunteering at a major event benefit the individuals involved?
2. By exploring social capital further, how could this concept help identify wider volunteering legacies?
3. Discuss other intangible legacies that host cities may consider including in their legacy initiatives.

References

Andrew, D. P., Pedersen, P. M., and McEvoy, C. D. (2011). *Research methods and design in sport management.* Leeds: Human Kinetics.

Binder, M. and Freytag, A. (2012). *Volunteering, happiness and public policy.* Jena: Max Planck Institute of Economics.

Borgonovi, F. (2008). Doing well by doing good: The relationship between formal volunteering and self-reported health and happiness. *Social Science & Medicine*, 66(11), 2321–2334.

Brown, K. M., Hoye, R., and Nicholson, M. (2012). Self-esteem, self-efficacy, and social connectedness as mediators of the relationship between volunteering and wellbeing. *Journal of Social Service Research*, 38(4), 468–483.

Case, R., Dey, T., Lu, J., Phang, J., and Schwanz, A. (2013). Participant spending at sporting events: An examination of survey methodologies. *Journal of Convention & Event Tourism*, 14(1), 21–41.

Christie, L. and Gibb, K. (2015). A collaborative approach to event-led regeneration: The governance of legacy from the 2014 Commonwealth Games. *Local Economy*, 30(8), 871–887.

Doherty, A. (2009). The volunteer legacy of a major sport event. *Journal of Policy Research in Tourism, Leisure and Events*, 1(3), 185–207.

Downward, P. M. and Ralston, R. (2006). The sports development potential of sports event volunteering: Insights from the XVII Manchester Commonwealth Games. *European Sport Management Quarterly*, 6(4), 333–351.

Glasgow 2014 (2015). *Glasgow 2014 Commonwealth game final report.* Glasgow.

Glasgow City Council (2009). *Glasgow 2014 legacy framework.* Glasgow.

Graham, C. L., Scharlach, A. E., and Price Wolf, J. (2014). The impact of the 'village' model on health, well-being, service access, and social engagement of older adults. *Health Education & Behavior: The Official Publication of the Society for Public Health Education*, 41(1Suppl), 91S–97S.

Higgins, J. P. and Green, S. (2011). *Cochrane handbook for systematic reviews of interventions.* London: John Wiley & Sons.

Horne, J. (2007). The four 'knowns' of sports mega-events. *Leisure Studies*, 26(1), 81–96.

Jones, R. and Yates, G. (2015). *Pre-games expectations and past volunteering experiences of Glasgow 2014 Clyde-sider applicants*. Glasgow: Glasgow Centre of Population Health.

Kristiansen, E. (2015). Competing for culture: Young Olympians' narratives from the first winter Youth Olympic Games. *International Journal of Sport and Exercise Psychology*, 13(1), 29–42.

Lee, C., Reisinger, Y., Kim, M., and Yoon, S. (2014). The influences of volunteer motivations on satisfaction, attitudes, and support for mega-event. *International Journal of Hospitality Management*, 40 37–48.

Legacy 2014 (2015). *An evaluation of legacy from the Glasgow 2014 Commonwealth Games: Post-Games report*. Scottish Government: Legacy Partnership.

Li, S. (2013). Large sporting events and economic growth: Evidence from economic consequences of event infrastructure and venues. *Event Management*, 17 425–438.

Liu, D. (2016). Social impact of major sports events perceived by host community. *International Journal of Sports Marketing and Sponsorship*, 17(1), 78–91.

Matheson, C. M. (2010). Legacy planning, regeneration and events: The Glasgow 2014 Commonwealth Games. *Local Economy*, 25(1), 10.

McCartney, G., Hanlon, P., and Bond, L. (2013). How will the 2014 Commonwealth Games impact on Glasgow's health, and how will we know? *Evaluation*, 19(1), 24–39.

McGillivray, D., McPherson, G., and Mackay, C. (2013). Events and volunteerism. In: R. Finkel, D. McGillivray, G. McPherson, P. Robinson (eds.) *Research themes for events*. Oxford: CABI, 31–43.

Minnaert, L. (2012). An Olympic legacy for all? The non-infrastructural outcomes of the Olympic Games for socially excluded groups (Atlanta 1996–Beijing 2008). *Tourism Management*, 3(2), 361–370.

Misener, L., Taks, M., Chalip, L., and Green, B. C. (2015). The elusive 'trickle-down effect' of sport events: Assumptions and missed opportunities. *Managing Sport and Leisure*, 20 (2), 135–156.

Morrow-Howell, N., Lee, Y. S., Mccrary, S., and Mcbride, A. (2003). Volunteering as a pathway to productive and social engagement among older adults. *Health Education & Behavior: The Official Publication of the Society for Public Health Education*, 41 (1Suppl), 84S–90S.

Nichols, G. and Ralston, R. (2012). Social inclusion through volunteering: The legacy potential of the 2012 Olympic Games. *Sociology*, 45(5), 900–914.

Pawlowski, T., Downward, P., and Rasciute, S. (2014). Does national pride from international sporting success contribute to wellbeing? An international investigation. *Sport Management Review*, 17(2), 121–132.

Pi, L., Lin, Y., Chen, C., Chiu, J., and Chen, Y. (2014). Serious leisure, motivation to volunteer and subjective well-being of volunteers in recreational events. *Social Indicators Research*, 19(3), 1485–1494.

Porsche, M. and Maennig, W. (2008). *The feel-good effect at mega sport events: Recommendations for public and private administration informed by the experience of the FIFA World Cup 2006*. Hamburg contemporary economic discussions, No. 18 Hamburg.

Rogerson, R. J. (2016). Re-defining temporal notions of event legacy: Lessons from Glasgow's Commonwealth Games. *Annals of Leisure Research*, 19(4), 497–518.

Sadd, D. (2010). What is event-led regeneration? Are we confusing terminology or will London 2012 be the first Games to truly benefit the local existing population?. *Event Management*, 13(4), 265–275.

Secker, J., Loughran, M., Heydinrych, K., and Kent, L. (2011). Promoting mental well-being and social inclusion through art: Evaluation of an arts and mental health project. *Arts & Health*, 3(1), 51–60.

Smith, A. (2009). Theorising the relationship between major sport events and social sustainability. *Journal of Sport & Tourism*, 14(2–3), 109–120.

Smith, A. (2012). *Events and urban regeneration: The strategic use of events to revitalise cities*. London: Routledge.

Smith, A. and Fox, T. (2007). From 'event-led' to 'event-themed' regeneration: The 2002 Commonwealth Games legacy programme. *Urban Studies*, 44(5–6), 125–1143.

Stewart-Brown, S. and Janmohamed, K. (2008). *Warwick-Edinburgh mental wellbeing scale. User guide*. Coventry: University of Warwick.

Swart, K., Bob, U., Knott, B., and Salie, M. (2011). A sport and sociocultural legacy beyond 2010: A case study of the Football Foundation of South Africa. *Development Southern Africa*, 28(3), 415–428.

Wahrendorf, M., Blane, D., Matthews, K., and Siegrist, J. (2016). Linking quality of work in midlife to volunteering during retirement: A European study. *Journal of Population Ageing*, 9(1–2), 113–130.

Woodall, J., South, J., Southby, K., Kinsella, K., May, E., Bagnall, A., and Coan, S. (2016). *Exploring the experiences and impacts of volunteer applicants for the Glasgow 2014 Commonwealth Games*. Project Report Glasgow: Glasgow Centre for Population Health.

Zhu, X., Yu, C., Lee, C., Lu, Z., and Mann, G. (2014). A retrospective study on changes in residents' physical activities, social interactions, and neighborhood cohesion after moving to a walkable community. *Preventive Medicine*, 69 S93–S97.

14 Post-humanist investigation into human–equine relations in event landscapes

Case of the Rodeo

Paula Danby and Rebecca Finkel

Introduction

Human attitudes towards animals have changed considerably from anthropo-centric ontologies in the early pre-modern period, where humans regarded themselves as the central element of the universe and realities were exclusively interpreted in terms of human values and experiences. In this way, humans consumed animals for their own purposes, and relations with animals originally were through modes of domination (Franklin 1999). In the postmodern period, there has been a prominent shift from such philosophical thought, which is evident within this study, whereby human society has, for the most part, adopted a bio-centric ontology towards animals. This considers all forms of life as having intrinsic value and acknowledges non-human life as a fundamental element of the universe, which has led to the formation of more sentient and compassionate relationships with animals through a sense of equality and moral consideration. Although this is not universal, it has become much more prevalent, and this research recognises the existence of intimate relations between humans and animals in events contexts. Intimacy within the human–animal relationship is understood in this study as a two-way relationship implying a degree of affective mutuality (Knight 2005). This has implications for the leisure, tourism, and events fields by repositioning animals as partners in the co-creation of cultural experiences.

It is important to acknowledge the diversity of research disciplines with an interest in human–animal relations. Research has been conducted within disci-plines including sociology, anthropology, psychology, veterinary science, zool-ogy, socio-biology, environmental studies, political science, and, to a lesser extent, leisure, tourism, and events. An additional area of study concentrates on animal ethics, and each subject looks at the issues surrounding human–animal relationships based on their own agendas (Franklin 1999). For example, Fennell's (2017) work on the animals' roles in tourism has been significant in furthering understanding about moral issues in past and current practice. However, pre-viously, much of the literature surrounding the human–equine relationship is rooted in veterinary science and psychology (Rollin 2006; Hallberg 2008).

From a veterinary science perspective, the research relates to equine physiology and welfare, reinforcing the bio-centric stance; whereas, the psychology literature discusses the psychological and wellbeing effects of human–animal relations that mostly take an anthropocentric stance. These two theoretical approaches towards human–animal relations underpin the basic concepts towards human interactions with animals that illustrate an appreciation of animals and an interest in their differences to humans with an understanding of their own value and welfare.

This research attempts to bring together this divide between the two approaches by specifically exploring human–equine relations and lived experiences within event landscapes with a particular focus on rodeo, where the relationship is viewed for the first time through a post-humanist lens. Although there are studies concentrating on the ethical dimensions of rodeo (Rollin 1996; Arluke and Bogdan 2014), the focus of this chapter is more explicitly on how human–equine interactions and multi-species experiences are investigated and evaluated by adopting post-humanist approaches. Until very recently, theoretical frameworks involving human–animal relations in event landscapes have mainly been anthropocentric, signifying how humans interact with animals for their own pleasure, as animals hold some form of entertainment value for humans. Previously, animal domestication was seen as one of the main qualities and practices that distinguished humans from animals. Within existing literature, there are limited accounts demonstrating how animals are able to evade subordination to be dominant over humans; rather, animals have mainly been regarded as a relatively powerless and a marginalised 'other' partner in human–animal relations (Philo and Wilbert 2000). However, this research aims to progress this concept by investigating human–equine relationships to re-conceptualise the human–animal divide from one of oppositional dualism into networks of interdependencies focused on partnership (Wilbert 2009). Moreover, findings in this study illustrate an equalling of power within the human–equine relationship, acknowledging that both human and horse respect and trust each other to be able to interconnect effectively within the relationship, and, in doing so, achieve outcomes that are more successful and rewarding. Although findings do identify a conscious 'othering' between humans and horses in some respects, in contrast to Philo and Wilbert's (2000) statement categorising animals as marginalised 'others', it also is revealed that the humans within this study have taken a post-humanist approach to interactions with their horses. Indeed, human rodeo performers indicate that they have to view the world through the lens of a horse to be able to understand its behaviour and to communicate and co-operate together effectively. Therefore, it can be argued here that the horse in this situation could instead be regarded as a 'powerful other'.

This study supports the notion that humans want to share their leisure time with a diverse range of non-humans for mutual benefit, and, without such interactions, perhaps their lives would be very different and less enjoyable. Furthermore, the horse becomes a fundamental actor within the events environment, acting as a performer, athlete, and motivator for equestrian-related leisure, tourism, and events. Experiential equestrianism provides an opportunity for humans to gain knowledge associated with equine culture as well as creating a stage for social interactions for humans to showcase their animals and exhibit their performances through interconnectedness and cross-species communications (Danby 2013).

This chapter begins by illustrating the historical context of human–animal relations and the changes in interaction over time. It then goes on to examine the shift in adopting post-humanist theoretical approaches as an attempt to explore "new, imaginative ways of understanding relations between lives" (MacCormack 2012: 1). The findings of this research reveal human–equine interactions, and experiences encountered within a rodeo environment are indicative of how equine spaces work as landscapes co-constituted between tourism and events, revealing that successful encounters between humans and horses provide highly emotional and embodied experiences.

The post-humanist shift in human–animal relations

Human attitudes towards animals have changed considerably from anthropocentric views of the early pre-modern period, where Christian theological orthodoxy maintained a view that God gave humans the right to use animals as they saw fit, which basically entailed human sustenance and labour (Franklin 1999). For example, Thomas (1983) acknowledged that most farm animals, such as cattle, pigs, horses, sheep, and poultry were not kept for sentimental reasons; they were there to work, be eaten, or both. Due to the close proximity of humans and animals living in a rural existence, their lives were interlinked, which provided a systematic interrelation between humans and the natural world (Franklin 1999). Anthropocentrism was undermined by the emergence of the natural and biological sciences which created classifications in relation to differences between species. This had the outcome of expanding the human universe (Franklin 1999). Humans began to see the universe through a different lens and realised that it was not just human–orientated, which led to the adoption of biocentric notions in the sense that the world was made up of 'other' organisms which included animals and plants and became aware that humans played only a small role in a very large universe (Franklin 1999). O'Neal Campbell (2007) notes that humans increasingly modify landscapes, and animal habitats increasingly move beyond the 'natural' to encompass intensively occupied human spaces, whilst arguably suggesting that this has major consequences for both animals and humans to co-exist.

According to Franklin (1999), the modern period witnessed a fundamental shift in human–animal relations whereby humans began to sentimentalise their approaches to animal welfare, and the animals rights movement emerged. Following this, animals increasingly became a significant actant in human leisure. It can be argued that substantial changes in the economic, political, and cultural face of human relations with animals occurred in the twentieth century, where Western societies became less dependent upon animal power through industrial development and became more urbanised, creating a major shift in human–animal relations and attitudes; moreover, a pet-keeping culture was formed as a sphere of leisure activity (Franklin 1999). The growth of mass leisure surged the range and scale of human–animal encounters and associated relations.

Postmodern relations with animals are characterised by a stronger emotional and moral content, a greater range of involvement and a demand for more regulation and order. As Hurn (2012) acknowledges, many social scientists have documented the myriad ways in which relationships between humans and non-humans exist across geographical, historical, and cultural divides (Bekoff 2007; Sanders and Arluke 1993; Serpell 1996). Such an interest in human–animal interactions over the past decade has encouraged a much broader base of scholarly activity and an increasingly wide range of theoretical concepts for consideration (Hurn 2012). Post-humanism is often adopted as an effective approach for exploring human–animal relational being and the interconnectivity between humans and other animals (MacCormack 2012). Viewing the world through a post-humanist lens blurs boundaries between nature, society, humans and animals (Instone 1998). Bowes, et al. (2015) acknowledge that trans-species social bonds are driven by a variety of factors, including affection, kinship, and companionship, which promote wide-ranging benefits. Wilbert (2009) refers to this as understanding the human–animal divide from one of oppositional dualism into networks of intricate dependencies focused around companionship and kinship. Haraway's (2003) seminal work examines the ongoing processes of "becoming with" each other in natural cultural practices. Instead of seeing a nature-culture divide, Haraway (2003) proposes there are entanglements that are mutually interactive. Thus, interspecies interactions are viewed as potentially meaningful encounters (Bertella 2014).

The 'animal turn' has created a paradigm shift in thinking about ways in which humans and animals co-exist through such lived experiences. Much research has begun to consider animals as social actors in their own right as sentient beings, and adopt a more appreciative understanding of the cultural practices of non-human 'others'. The 'animal turn' encouraged more balanced considerations of the multifarious roles that animals play in human societies. The post-humanist recognition that other animals are indeed integral actors within social lives and worthy of anthropological attention in their own right has led to a move to 'bring in' the animal; that is, to consider human–animal interactions from the perspective of the non-human as well as the human (Hurn 2012). Such approaches have led to complex geographies of intra-action between humans and animals (Barad 2007), where sharing experiences results in both parties being changed as a result of the deep relationships and complex modes of attention and attachment established. This calls 'human centredness' into question and requires a re-thinking of "being, co-being, and wellbeing" (Maurstad, et al. 2013: 323); therefore, such perspectives are allied to post-humanism.

It is evident here that the human–animal relationship has taken a shift from an anthropocentric viewpoint towards a biocentric viewpoint, which asserted that animals are worthy of moral consideration and humans can effectively coexist with animals. Therefore, this relationship has transformed in the postmodern period from viewing the human–animal relationship through a humanistic lens towards a post-humanistic lens, demonstrating that humans acknowledge the instrumental role of co-existing with animals. The nature of the relationships formed depends upon the species of animal and the types of interactions humans have with them. A common issue relating to post-human approaches to human–animal relations is associated with the conceptual placing of animals. A key debate linked to such relations surrounds the concept of boundaries; that is, where do we draw the line between humans and non-humans (Haraway 1992; Philo and Wilbert 2000; Whatmore 2002). The notion that there are clear boundaries becomes blurred due to the association of imaginative geographies of animals, where animals should be kept close to humans, and, by doing so, humans and animals share spaces and have the potential to interconnect. It can be argued that there is no such thing as pure human and pure non-human due to the complex associations and entanglements of ecologies (Game 2001). The notion to bring nature back into social theory is becoming common place within the literature associated with critical animal studies; however, much of the existing research is linked to wild animals and the association with zoos and wildlife parks or popular domestic animals such as dogs and cats (Philo and Wilbert 2000; Markwell 2015). There is very little acknowledgement of horses despite their close proximity to natural spaces. Also, perhaps surprisingly, there is very little acknowledgement in the literature of horses in human intimate spaces as well. Although there is still a 'pet culture' in contemporary society, where humans form closer relationships with animals and welcome them into more intimate human spaces, horses are not often viewed as pets per se. This may be due to their size and their location outside of the human household. Additionally, there still exists the traditional association of horses with labour. However, given advances in technology, which have decreased the need for working horses, the majority of horses in the Western world have become more and more associated with human leisure activities, where closer kinship relations and strong emotional connections have developed.

Dashper (2017) similarly acknowledges that once the horse was considered a vital partner to humans with regards to agriculture, warfare, and transport; whereas, nowadays, it is predominantly a partner in sport and leisure. However, a dominant view in leisure and tourism literature positions animals as passive rather than active actors (Bertella 2014). It is argued here that in order to achieve meaningful multi-species encounters, humans and animals need to be involved in the co-creation of experiences. An initial and important step towards achieving this is the co-creation of relationships to achieve multi-species connectivity. As Ghiringhelli (2016: 460) argues,

> Domesticated horses have an advanced ability to assess a human's emotional wellbeing, having been side by side with humans for centuries. Horses 'know' humans and will attempt to trust and partner with humans to form relationships. Relationships between humans and horses are co-constructions of both parties.

Although many leisure activities involving animals are rooted in humanist heritage and traditions, and, thus, prioritise the human in the relationship, consumers in recent times have more awareness of and empathy for animal wellbeing, cognition, and affect (Despret 2004). Emotional connections as part of the audience experience are increasingly becoming popular (Bertella 2014). Although this may not be a conceptually informed decision to shift cultural viewpoints, it can be seen in practice that more post-humanist approaches are being demanded and adopted in human–animal leisure sites. This is evident within this research, where we demonstrate how human–equine interactions and relations have developed and have been incorporated into events landscapes, in this case, an exemplar being the rodeo.

Research methods

This chapter draws on research focused on a case study of the Austin Rodeo in Texas, USA. A qualitative approach has been adopted, as it provides an opportunity to be flexible and sensitive to contextual factors during research as well as explore symbolic dimensions and social meaning more effectively (Bryman 2001). Case study design has been selected because it is viewed as the best means to obtain a holistic understanding of systems of action, which are sets of interrelated activities in which actors in a social situation are engaged (Tellis 1997). This study employs in-depth semi-structured interviews with ten key event stakeholders, such as rodeo event managers, performers, such as barrel racers and bull riders, and animal specialists. Purposive sampling was selected, as in-depth interviews with experts in the subject of enquiry can aid in the exploration of how key themes of this research are embedded in the social structure (Lofland and Lofland 1995). Themes drawn out from the questions include issues pertaining to events destination strategies, cultural identity, heritage tourism, and human–animal relationships and performances. Ethnographic approaches, including rich field notes, visual methods, and participant (as an audience member) and direct observation at rodeo events also inform the study. Ethnography is considered an effective method when studying event spaces, as the observation and recording of lived experiences can complement other methods to increase the validity and reliability of the findings (Finkel 2006). An obvious limitation of researching non-humans is the inability to interview animals and have them give human language accounts of their views and experiences. Yet, horses display strong bodily cues to express their feelings and signal behaviour to communicate effectively with humans. Brandt (2006) refers to high levels of body-to-body contact between a human and a horse through interaction, which act as a basis for haptic communication. Through a co-created embodied system of cues, Brandt (2006) reveals that shared meaning is possible due to the absence of spoken verbal language. Thus, to overcome verbal language barriers and focus on interpreting embodied communication as much as possible in order to take into account animals' perspectives, visual approaches were adopted (Rose 2013). This included interpretation of photographs and videos to provide better understanding of animal body language and human–animal interactions. By studying still photographs and re-playing videos, nuances in behaviour, physical communication, and non-verbal signals were able to be closely observed and evaluated to draw convincing conclusions about animals' viewpoints and experiences in this rodeo environment.

Case of the rodeo

When analysing human–equine relations in leisure, tourism, and event settings, rodeo is a fitting case study example. The origins of rodeo are rooted in the frontier and ranching heritage of the North American West, which relied on non-human animal interactions for both commercial and occupational purposes. As Arluke and Bogdan (2014: 32) suggest, "The rodeo is a metaphor for our attempt to tame the wild with all the inherent contradiction that such a struggle entails. Those who participate, both competitors and spectators, are there to see this struggle acted out." Cowboys (and, to a certain extent, cowgirls) have gained an almost mythic symbolism in the North American heritage narrative, representing the so-called 'rugged individualism' of the West and exemplifying traditional values (Stoeltje 1981). The image of the cowboy in popular culture is that of a loner; however, he is never without his horse. The cowboy and his horse are viewed as a team, relying on each other for survival, labour, and companionship. This links to post-humanist dimensions of human and animals having to think and work together. Hallberg (2008) reminds us that the Western riding movement originated around the late 1700s out of necessity due to the harsh conditions and lifestyle of the American West. At this time, the horse was honoured and respected and treated much as a family member, as it was the horse that made life possible. A partnership between cowboy and horse was a necessity to move thousands of cattle across thousands of acres in all weather. The horse was a companion, often staying in houses during cold spells, and the only being a cowboy had to talk to for days or weeks on end (Hallberg 2008).

In keeping with Helgadóttir's (2006) suggestion that horse-based tourism is reminiscent of a rich cultural and historical heritage intermingled with the nostalgia of the romantic past, rodeos are the performance aspect of this particular and now idealised way of 'Wild West' frontier life. Lawrence (1984) referred to rodeo forms of social theatre which show the range of human–animal relations. These events originated in the nineteenth century as a way of bridging the urban and rural divide through popular entertainment drawing upon pioneer ideology (Boatright 1964). This supports Franklin's (1999) argument regarding urbanisation and disconnection from animals in everyday life and the need to recreate this in performance settings. As Stoeltje (1981: 125) argues, "Rodeo does re-enact the Western frontier experience by presenting the popular hero of that experience, the cowboy, in a live performance." It follows, then, that animals associated with the ranching way of life also were brought into the sporting performance arena.

In many respects, these animals went from working 'tools' on the ranch to working 'actors' in a spectator sporting event. Horses retain their companion role and are present in all rodeo events except bull riding. This emphasises the importance of horses in achieving rodeo success, whether calf roping, steer wrestling, or barrel racing. As Lawrence (1984: 123) suggests, "Most contestants say that they consider the rodeo livestock to be athletes in their own right and highly respect them for doing their jobs well." Aligned with the post-humanist principles set out by Barad (2007) and Haraway (2003), where humans and animals are entangled in ongoing processes of "becoming with" each other through intra-action encounters, riders and horses in rodeo settings can be seen to co-create a shared language through embodied communication. Using a reciprocal set of cues and symbolic movements with their bodies, humans and horses can adapt and accommodate each other physically and mentally, thus developing a world of co-being (Maurstad, et al. 2013). Brandt (2004: 300) recognises the "significance of the body as a vehicle for expression" in order to "facilitate the creation of shared meaning". Such co-operation beyond the individual self is imperative for the co-creation of the human–equine relationship, and, thus, successful performances in the rodeo arena. As Ghiringhelli (2016: 463) states,

> Neither can have a communication without the other responding... The relationships between human and horses are co-constructions of both parties... Parties intra-act, and, respectively, are changing and attuning to each other in order to communicate well and engage in their activities in meaningful ways.

In practice, a barrel racer interviewee (R2) supports this by stating:

> Animals are a part of you. You know each other very well. Your horse knows your mood and feeds off how you are. You're partners and become one. You get to know your horse and feel better, so you perform better. It's rewarding to compete with a horse you know. There's a bond, a reciprocal relationship. You can be a good rider, but if you're not on a good horse, you're not at the top. You're reliant on each other and have to work together.

Indeed, barrel racing is the only rodeo event in which women compete and which only involves horses. It is an event focused on speed and agility rather than strength and brawn. Based on visual methods for this research, there is evident interspecies fluidity when barrel racers are riding, as there appears to be a blurring of beings as they move through the arena. At times, it is difficult to know where the human ends and the horse begins, as their bodies are entwined and their movements are correlated, both looking the same way, leaning forward in tandem, and set on accomplishing their goals together. This supports Brandt's (2006) explanation that horsewomen speak of an awareness of the experience of sensation, or "feel" as a source of information to guide their interactions with horses. She refers to sensations as being an essential part of communication, which occur when horses pick up sensations through body-to-body connections with humans (Brandt 2006).

This also relates to Game's (2001: 2) arguments about the interconnectedness of humans and horses; she states, "different species attune to each other, live with and through each other." This kind of trusting mutual relationship between human and horses is evident within rodeo. Horses are the only animals that performers can bring to rodeos, so they are the only animals that are known to their human counterparts before the events. All the horses observed for this research at the Austin Rodeo were healthy weight and size with smooth, shiny coats. Through the use of visuals, we examined horse body language at various events. The overwhelming majority of horses had relaxed heads and tails before events began, and their ears were forward and alert throughout. These are understood to be signs of contentment. Almost none of the horses appeared to be upset by the activities they were doing or disturbed by the environment they were in. Many horses were observed snorting and nuzzling their humans, which are signs of being comfortable and affectionate and indicate positive interspecies relationships. The main exception to this human–equine partnership is the bucking bronco event, where a man tries to dominate a horse. This has origins in the horse breaking skills required on a working ranch and demonstrates the pre-companion stage of the human–equine relationship, where men felt the need to conquer the wild.

In terms of the other animals involved in rodeo events, this also reflects work on a cattle ranch to a large degree, so mastery over calves and other livestock features heavily. Stock contractors provide the other animals for the rodeo events, such as calves, bulls, mutton, goats, and other livestock. This can be seen to influence human–animal relations, and, thus, there is a hierarchy of animal performance roles in rodeo. Arluke and Bogdan (2014: 18) suggest, "This array of relationships falls on a continuum; one end is defined by human–animal co-operation, harmony, tameness, and control while the other end by conflict, violence, and unruliness." Also, an argument can be made that the size and type of animal is linked to constructions of masculinity of the cowboy. For men, Toth (2000) argues, horses usually move them physically; whereas, for women, horses move them emotionally. For example, bull riding is seen as the top echelon of 'macho' performance given the fierceness of the animal. Mutton busting is an event for children and could be seen as a training ground for performing with animals within the rodeo arena. Masculinity is tied up with the skill in controlling the animal, as it was crucial for ranch work and survival on the range. In this way, human interactions with animals are exemplary of a particular way of life, cultural heritage, and reflection of self-identity.

It is apparent how humans benefit from the relationship with animals at rodeos. Cowboys and cowgirls demonstrate their skills and have the potential to win large monetary prizes. Audiences of rodeo events are entertained in a colourful, exciting setting that can reinforce community belonging and con- nections to a storied past. Along with these meaningful experiences associated with negotiating heritage and tradition, rodeo also provides educational bene- fits for humans regarding animal welfare. Throughout the rodeo site, there are opportunities for attendees to interact with and learn more about livestock, such as Texas Longhorns, goats, lambs, dairy cows, and so forth, as well as a petting zoo for children with pony rides and pig races. As for the animals, the benefits of being a rodeo performer are more nuanced but still convincing. Although there are still traditional narratives of human dominance in rodeo events, it can be argued that human–animal performance relationships are symbiotic. Similar to the survival necessity of the range and the ranch, both actors need and rely upon each other in order to succeed in the rodeo arena. There is a case that the animal does not have a choice in the matter, but this can be said of much of an animals' agency in a still human–centric world. However, animals in rodeo are cared for well (often better than their ranch working contemporaries), get attention and companionship, exercise, work only for short intervals, and are well fed. They are significant actors in the relationship; therefore, their welfare is a core priority.

Still, there have been protests and controversies by animal rights activists surrounding rodeo. The main controversy is with the bucking broncos, where a flank strap is tightly tied around the horse's lower belly to cause bucking. An animal specialist interviewee for this research (R4) states, "There are oversights on this, as it is a regulated sport which takes place in public during a competition. Also, these performing horses have lighter work schedules than other working horses." Rodeo is a spectator sport, so there is sensitivity to audiences' feelings in terms of animal welfare and wellbeing, as contemporary audiences would not stand for cruelty in this public arena. This is illustrative of the 'animal turn' and shift toward animal sentimentalisation. According to R4, being spectator-driven contributes to oversight and fewer problems with regard to the wellbeing of animals participating in rodeo, and most policing happens within the sport itself. Furthermore, many rodeo animals, especially horses and bulls, are worth large sums of money and have had large sums of money invested into their welfare. For example, barrel racing horses are considered partners in the sport by their riders, but they are also huge investments and well-known barrel racing horses are in high demand (R2).

Rodeo can be viewed as an expression of historic ranching ethos and human–animal alignment in sport. These relationships developed from a work environment into performance roles, which has mainly shifted human–equine relationships from dominance/subjugation to co-operation and co-creation. Moreover, rodeo provides opportunities for the public to experience more informed, less threatening encounters with animals in an event and tourism setting. As Lawrence (1984: 270) suggests, "Rodeo is essentially a ritual addressing itself to the dilemma of man's place in nature, exploring the boundary lines between people and other forms of life." Human–equine interactions are intimate, which incur embedded powerful emotions providing a feeling of human–equine connection and euphoria by instilling a sense of togetherness and natural harmony (Danby 2013).

Conclusions

The human–equine relationship has changed drastically over time due to the increased consumption of leisure activities (Dashper 2017). This study reveals the close encountering, blurring of boundaries between humans and horses through furthering an understanding of how both species can develop trustworthy and close bonded relationships to interconnect and create meaningful experiences. Furthermore, the example of the Austin Rodeo illustrates how a heritage sporting event rooted in human–centred traditions is being rehabilitated to reflect contemporary concerns for animal welfare surrounding human–animal performances within event landscapes. Here, this study recognises the entanglements associated with the 'animal turn' in reconstructing and renegotiating non-human animals' places in human society. The research assembled draws on Haraway's (2003: 16) "ongoing processes of 'becoming with' each other in natural cultural practices". Although this is not necessarily generalisable to all rodeo events, it is evident within this case study how the relationships between humans and horses are enriched by the fluidity and interconnectedness of both species through knowledge, skill, companionship, performance, and wellbeing. This contributes to interdisciplinary understanding of how post-humanist approaches can aid in the co-creation of successful relations with horses in experiential environments. As Bertella (2014: 123) argues, "The tourism experience that includes the use of animals would then be seen as an encounter where the privileged subjects use their power not to dominate the other but to help the other to fulfil his/her potentials." By adopting an animal perspective, it could lead to more meaningful encounters and harmonious coexistence, particularly in leisure, tourism, and events environments. Indeed, as Game (2001) suggests, humans need to forget their human self, blur their boundaries, and adopt an inbetween-human-and-horse way of being in order to effectively co-exist. Thereafter, both species are transformed as a result of their encounters and mutual understanding.

Questions for discussion

1. How does post-humanism theory enhance the inclusion of and co-creation between humans and non-humans within events environments?
2. How can post-humanist perspectives be applied to other events?
3. What would be involved in making the co-creation of events experiences between humans and non-human animals successful for the wellbeing of all species?
4. How can rodeos be improved to be more non-human animal-centric?

Acknowledgements

The field work conducted at Austin Rodeo was made possible by a research grant from the Carnegie Trust for the Universities in Scotland.

References

Arluke, A. and Bogdan, R. (2014). Taming the wild: Rodeo as a human–animal metaphor. In J. Gillett, and M. Gilbert (eds.) *Sport, animals, and society.* London: Routledge, 15–34.
Barad, K. (2007). *Meeting the universe halfway: Quantum physics and the entanglement of matter and meaning.* Durham, NC: Duke University Press.

Bekoff, M. (2007). *The emotional lives of animals: A leading scientist explores animal joy, sorrow, and empathy – and why they matter.* Novato: New World Library.

Bertella, G. (2014). Co-creation of animal-based tourism experience. *Tourism Recreation Research*, 39(1), 115–125.

Boatright, M. (1964). The American rodeo. *American Quarterly*, 16, 195–202.

Bowes, M., Keller, P., Rollins, R., and Gifford, R. (2015). Parks, dogs, and beaches: Human–wildlife conflict and the politics of place. In N. Carr (ed.) *Domestic animals and leisure: Leisure studies in a global era.* London: Palgrave Macmillan.

Brandt, K. (2004). A language of their own: An interactionist approach to human–horse communication. *Society and Animals*, 12(4), 299–316.

Brandt, K. (2006). Intelligent bodies: embodied subjectivity human–horse communication. In D. V. Waskul (ed.) *Body/embodiment, symbolic interaction and the sociology of the body.* Hampshire: Ashgate Publishing, 141–152.

Bryman, A. (2001). *Social research methods.* Oxford: Oxford University Press.

Danby, P. (2013). *A critical investigation into human–equine motivations, interactions and associated experiences as a leisure and tourist activity within the North East of England.* Unpublished PhD Thesis.

Dashper, K. (2017). *Human–animal relationships in Equestrian Sport and Leisure.* Oxford: Routledge.

Despret, V. (2004). The body we care for: Figures of anthropo-zoo-genesis. *Body & Society*, 10(2–3), 111–134.

Fennell, D. (2017). *Tourism and animal ethics.* London: Routledge.

Finkel, R. (2006). Unicycling at Land's end: Case study of the Lafrowda Festival of St Just, Cornwall. *Leisure Studies*, 2(92), 129–145.

Franklin, A. (1999). *Animals and modern cultures: A sociology of human–animal relations in modernity.* London: Sage Publications.

Game, A. (2001). Riding: embodying the centaur. *Body and Society*, 7(4), 1–12.

Ghiringhelli, B. (2016). The 'First' Horse. *Sociology and Anthropology*, 4(6), 459–465.

Hallberg, L. (2008). *Walking the way of the horse: Exploring the power of the horse–human relationship.* New York: iUniverse.

Haraway, D. (1992). Otherwordly conversations: Terran topics; Local terms. *Science as Culture*, 3(1), 64–98.

Haraway, D. (2003). *The companion species manifesto: Dogs, people and significant otherness.* Chicago: Prickly Paradigm Press.

Helgadóttir, G. (2006). The culture of horsemanship and horse-based tourism in Iceland. *Current Issues in Tourism*, 9(6), 535–548.

Hurn, S. (2012). *Humans and other animals: Cross-cultural perspectives on human–animal interactions.* New York: Palgrave Macmillan.

Instone, L. (1998). The coyote's at the door: Revisioning human–environment relations in the Australian context. *Cultural Geographies*, 5(4), 452–467.

Knight, J. (ed.) (2005). *Animals in person: Cultural perspectives on human–animal intimacies.* Oxford: Berg.

Lawrence, E. (1984). *Rodeo: An anthropologist looks at the wild and the tame.* Chicago: University of Chicago Press.

Lofland, J. and Lofland, L. (1995). *Analysing social sciences: A guide to qualitative observation and analysis.* Belmont, CA: Wadsworth.

MacCormack, P. (2012). *Posthuman ethics.* Surrey: Ashgate.

Markwell, K. (2015). *Animals and tourism: Understanding diverse relationships.* Bristol: Channel View Publications.

Maurstad, A., Davis, D., and Cowles, S. (2013). Co-being and intra-action in horse–human relationships: A multispecies ethnography. *Social Anthropology*, 21(3), 322–335.

O'Neal Campbell, M. (2007). An animal geography of avian ecology in Glasgow. *Applied Geography*, 27(2), 78–88.

Philo, C. and Wilbert, C. (2000). Animal spaces, beastly places: An introduction. In C. Philo, and C. Wilbert (eds.) *Animal spaces, beastly places, new geographies of human–animal relations*. London: Routledge, 1–34.

Rollin, B. (1996). Rodeo and recollection: Applied ethics and western philosophy. *Journal of the Philosophy of Sport*, 23(1), 1–9.

Rollin, B. (2006). Reasonable partiality and animal ethics. *Ethical Theory and Moral Practice*, 8(1–2), 105–121.

Rose, G. (2013). *Visual methodologies*. London: Sage.

Sanders, C. and Arluke, A. (1993). If lions could speak: Investigating the animal–human relationship and perspectives of nonhuman others. *Sociological Quarterly*, 34(3), 377–390.

Serpell, J. (1996). *In the company of animals*. Cambridge: Cambridge University Press.

Stoeltje, B. (1981). Cowboys and clowns: Rodeo specialists and the ideology of work and play. In R. Bauman and R. Abrahams (eds.) *'And other neighborly names': Social processes and cultural image in Texas folklore*. Austin: University of Texas Press, 123–151.

Tellis, W. (1997). Introduction to case study. *The Qualitative Report*, 3, 2.

Thomas, K. (1983). *Man and the natural world*. London: Pantheon.

Toth, D. (2000). The Psychology of Women and Horses. In R. Berman (ed.) *Of Women and Horses*. California: Bow Tie Press, 31–41.

Whatmore, S. (2002). *Hybrid geographies: Natures, cultures, spaces*. London: Sage Publications.

Wilbert, C. (2009). Animal geographies. In R. Kitchin and N. Thrift (eds.) *International encyclopedia of human geography*. London: Elsevier, 122–126.

Part IV

Conferences

15 Measuring accessibility in MICE venues

The case of the Euskalduna Conference Centre (Bilbao, Spain)

Ainara Rodríguez-Zulaica and Asunción Fernández-Villarán Ara

Introduction

The region of the Basque Country in Spain contains several conference venues; the most important ones are the Palacio Europa in Vitoria, the Kursaal in San Sebastian, and the Euskalduna Conference Centre in Bilbao. This chapter focuses on the results of the measures the Euskalduna Conference Centre has already overcome in terms of accessibility and those that must be fulfilled in order to be able to demonstrate 'total accessibility' in this venue.

From literature reviews about the study and application of accessibility in specific tourism spaces of a destination (World Tourism Organization, 2014, 2015), we can conclude that there are few studies focused on the application of inclusive strategies in sites related to MICE (Meetings, Incentives, Conventions and Exhibitions) events and, furthermore, to conference centres. We are aware that some main accessibility issues are common to all type of infrastructures, but we can also note that there are others specific to the event industry. We therefore believe it is essential to make an in-depth analysis of these infrastructures and their needs in terms of inclusiveness.

The main concern for conference centres is how to guarantee access to the building itself, and to its services and equipment. With the application of the concept of 'total accessibility', measures are applied that guarantee an adequate environment in terms of capacities, needs and expectations of all potential users, no matter what the degree of their capability is. DALCO (Ambulation, Apprehension, Location and Communication) criteria is used when having to measure infrastructure accessibility, corresponding with the characteristics of the buildings; thus, everyone can participate in the actions of ambulation, apprehension, location and communication that are linked to all processes related to these environments, especially in case of emergency.

Even so, our study goes far beyond the evaluation of the sites (conference centres in this case). Total accessibility must refer not only to the moment of the event itself, but also to the whole value chain; that is, from the beginning of the need to participate in the event until the attendee is back home. For this reason, together with the analysis of the accessibility of the environment, we have considered as fundamental the analysis of the web page of the conference centre and of the event organisers, as main information sources in the first stage of the pre-event phase.

To do so, the Web Content Accessibility Guidelines (from now on, WCAG) are applied. Their main purpose is to provide a single shared standard for web content accessibility that meets the needs of individuals, organisations, and governments internationally. In summary, in order to be able to assure that a MICE venue allows everyone to access, communicate and participate completely in any event that takes place on site, different levels of performance must be applied (Gorbeña et al., 2002). These levels are:

a) physical accessibility: understood as the elements that event infrastructures and equipment help people to access, enter and exit, and use these spaces.
b) communicative accessibility: defined as all aspects considered in information support (videos, brochures, web pages) and in the signage (panels, posters, maps) of the venue.
c) social accessibility: referring to those measures that allow citizens to participate in any event that takes place in the venue with independence of their capabilities. This level includes programming inclusive events, having a marketing strategy that shows diversity as a value, training employees in how to attend special needs, and hiring disabled people.

All these levels and its indicators will be analysed applying two basic research tools: 1) observation; and, 2) in-depth interviews with the managers of the sites.

MICE tourism in the Basque Country

MICE tourism is a sector of the wider tourism and events industries. Also known as business tourism, it encompasses: conferences and meetings, exhibitions and trade fairs, incentive travel, corporate events, outdoor events and business travel. This segment has grown incredibly in past years and, looking ahead, it has an encouraging future. And so, it is logical that Spanish cities have been 'put to work' in building adequate infrastructures that can give service to this segment. In fact, in recent years, we are witnessing an expansion in the number of conference centres throughout Spain, changing the urbanism of the cities with modern buildings that have put Spain on the map as the world's fifth largest destination for business tourism, close behind USA, Germany, UK and France. Spain can offer top-level facilities in cities such as Madrid, Barcelona, Valencia, and Bilbao. The first two comprised 61% of all international conferences held in Spain in 2016.

The evolution of Spain as a MICE destination has been well documented. According to the study *Business Tourism in Spain* published by Ostelea (2015), School of Tourism & Hospitality, Spain was the fourth country in the world in 2015 in the number of international conferences held (572) which represents 2% more than in 2014. A total of 3.8 million attendees were registered, 3.4% more than in the previous year, which generated a total economic impact estimated at almost 5.200 million euros in 2015 (3% more than in 2014). In 2016, Spain climbed up to fifth place; moreover, in city ranking, two Spanish cities are listed among the top ten: Barcelona, being number three, and Madrid, number eight, both improving their positions from previous years. Of the three Basque cities (Vitoria, San Sebastian, and Bilbao), the only one that is mentioned in this ranking is Bilbao, 170th in the world and 91st in Europe.

Business tourism in the Basque Country has generated an economic impact of almost 56.3 million euros in 2014, of which 31.4 million corresponds to the city of Bilbao, 21.9 million to San Sebastián and 2.9 million to Vitoria, according to the Ibiltur MICE Report 2014 (Basque Tourism Observatory, 2014), carried out by Euskadi´s Tourism Observatory (2015). This report highlights some of the main characteristics of MICE tourism including the following:

- It complements the leisure tourism sector, relying on much of the same physical infrastructure and bringing business to destinations such as seaside resorts which would otherwise be dependent upon a relatively short summer season for their economic health and prosperity.
- Investments in MICE tourism facilities leads to the regeneration of urban and inner city areas.
- Many of the investments in a destination's infrastructure designed primarily for the MICE tourist (hotels, transport and communications facilities, restaurants, attractions and amenities, even conference auditoriums) provide benefits which can also be enjoyed by the leisure tourist and the local population.
- Research suggests that approximately 40% of MICE travellers will return with their families as leisure visitors to destinations they have enjoyed visiting on business.
- The MICE industry involves other non-tourist industries through outsourcing, which is the way of organising and managing most events.

As said before, accessibility is a prerequisite for active participation of people with disabilities in society. It is therefore advisable to take into account the measures needed to ensure the accessibility of all type of buildings, establishments and facilities. In this sense, it is crucial that MICE venues also become accessible infrastructures.

Reference standards on environment accessibility

One crucial element in order to achieve the goal of becoming an accessible destination is the existence of a legal framework, which ensures that people with disabilities have the right to access tourism facilities and services and to encourage tourism professionals to adopt related measures. Standards are documents that establish a basis or principle linked to uniform units of measurement. Compulsory standards are enforced through national legislation while voluntary standards suggest best practice (Theobald, 2005). Several governments have passed comprehensive legislation to protect the rights of persons with disabilities. Others are in various stages of adoption, formulation and planning such legislations. Countries which have already adopted the legislation enact additional laws and regulations or amend existing ones to further protect the rights of persons with disabilities in specific areas. Among these are numerous regulations revised to include mandatory requirements for the implementation of specific measures covering areas such as access to the built environment and public transport, positive mass media portrayal of persons with disabilities, and closed captioning (for deaf persons). The vast majority of the available accessibility guidelines are formulated either as general design principles or low-level specific recommendations. They are usually based on past experiences and best practice, while experimental evidence is typically rare.

In Spain, the transfer to the Autonomous Communities of Competencies for accessibility and tourism matters has informed policies and set out a clear purpose of removing architectural barriers for those with disabilities. This can be found in practically all communities' standards throughout the country. However, it has also highlighted a distinct lack of approval for much of the actual built environment. Therefore, Spain has developed a National Accessibility Plan, which represents a strategic framework for action to ensure that environments, products, and new services will be undertaken in an accessible manner to include as many people as possible (Design for All) and that existing structures will be adapted accordingly.

We must also mention the actions that have been taken by AENOR, the National Institution for the Creation of Standards, in order to develop voluntary standards that help professionals apply accessibility criteria. In the year 2000, the constitution of the Standardization Technical Committee AEN/CTN 170 'Requirements and adaptations of people with disabilities within AENOR' meant a change in the approach – in considering that the use and enjoyment of goods and services for people who are part of society necessarily must be accessible to all, regardless of their disability.

The Committee focused its activity on developing a set of requirements aimed at creating a standardised environment, so users can overcome the limitations of accessibility they can encounter, a concept that has been called 'global accessibility'. Global accessibility can be defined as characteristics that environments have or are known for, where goods and services can be enjoyed under a given context, in order to make them suitable to the capabilities, needs and expectations of all potential users regardless of their age, gender, cultural background or level of ability. These are a series of requirements related to the actions of four wide groups (AENOR, 2007a; 2007b): ambulation, apprehension, location, and communication. These actions, known as DALCO rules, must be satisfied in order to guarantee the global accessibility to environments, products, and services. The global accessibility standards are:

UNE 170001-1:2007 UNE	Universal accessibility. Part 1: DALCO requirements to facilitate accessibility to environments
UNE 170001-2:2001 UNE	Universal accessibility. Part 2: System access management

The list shown below describes each of the actions that are defined in Part 1 of UNE 170001.

- Ambulation: to move from one place to another. It allows the user to get to the places and objects to use, so this action must be possible to perform with ease by anyone. We must be aware that this is to be performed alone or with assistance, using canes, walker or wheelchair, carrying objects or trolleys or baby chairs, etc. Also, that the user can perform the movement in any state, situation, or rhythm, for example, tired, dizzy, quickly, and so on.
- Apprehension: to be able to handle, or use hands, other body parts, or other items, is normally required for the use of components, products, and services, and includes others, such as grasp, grab, seize, and press, and frequently involves the action of transporting whatever handled. Furthermore, it should be possible to approach and achieve the object that must be manipulated.
- Location: to consider within an environment the complex system of elements that serve as a sign or something to raise awareness as distinct from the rest, such as signals, advertising elements, shapes, and volumes of architectural elements and the differentiation of materials and textures and colors of furniture and equipment, lighting, etc.
- Communication: transmission and reception of information supporting the offer of goods and services that take place through both material resources and through staff. It should cover all means to obtain accurate information in order for the environment to be usable by all people in safety and comfortable conditions and as more independent and natural as possible.

The reasons why these standards have been used to conduct our study are:

- With these rules, organisations wishing to demonstrate their ability to provide an accessible environment according to DALCO criteria, can help create a system of global access management that will keep them updated with the moment and technological advances available.
- Universal Accessibility, as mentioned in the First National Accessibility Plan 2004–2012, means overcoming the stigma of difference that has been traditionally associated with people with disabilities and assume that their constraints in relation to the environment are on the same plane as other more common and shared, such as age, the type of activity taking place or any time limitation of function; to assume that the human dimension is not defined by capabilities, or performance measures, but should be viewed more generally; a way of focusing diversity as what is general rather than the exception.
- It should be noted that this provides generic requirements intended to be applicable by all types of organisations, regardless of their size or activity, avoiding the above-mentioned problem of specificity of the tourism standard. In addition, these standards represent a tool with which organisations can develop a management system of global accessibility to the built

environment, whether in places, buildings, establishments or facilities, where goods and services can be enjoyed, enabling their users to overcome the limitations of accessibility they may encounter.

- AENOR and the ONCE Foundation have established a collaboration agreement to promote and communicate among organisations what Global Accessibility is about. Once AENOR verifies that the organisations meets the requirements of the UNE 17000-2:2001, it is granted the Registered Accessibility certificate of AENOR.
- AENOR, conscious of the need in society, has created the Certificate in Management Systems for Universal Accessibility that is provided to any organisation which, having been evaluated, meets the requirements of the UNE 170001-2. This involves not simply passing a test to ensure that facilities have no architectural barriers, but also demonstrates a commitment to help eliminate other social barriers. For example, the organisation trains staff in how to act with disabled customers. And, above all, it commits to improve a little every year on the accessibility of its facilities and, of course, to keep them in perfect condition. Presently, AENOR certifies the managerial aspect more than the installation one.
- The implementation of a management system for Universal Accessibility, also compatible with other management systems, facilitates the law compliance of each Autonomous Community; it helps optimise organisational resources and promotes a positive working environment.

Application of inclusive strategies in the Euskalduna Conference Centre

Conference centres are created to allocate professional meetings and events. PREDIF (Plataforma Representativa Estatal de Discapacitados Físicos) states that, in Spain, such infrastructures are mostly accessible. However, such accessibility is only related to the building itself and its environment: conference rooms, toilets, lifts, parkings, restaurants and bars, etc. This accessibility is basic, so the event can take place smoothly and with the participation of disabled people. This has turned out to be insufficient, since accessibility must be worked on all levels: physical, communicative, and social, as defined above. Because of our humanist conception of tourism, where the human being is at the centre of all decisions, this study focuses its attention on a MICE event attendees' point of view. Furthermore, following the recommendations of the WTO (2015, we will approach the analysis from all the stages of the business tourism value chain, where information about the accessibility of the sites is a determining issue.

This research has analysed the physical and sensory accessibility of the Euskalduna Conference Centre in Bilbao. In 2010, we made a first evaluation of the physical and communicative accessibilities of this venue. In 2011, with the advice of CEIS (Test, Innovation and Services Centre), Euskalduna ran an Accessibility Plan for the period 2011 to 2017. For this reason, at the end of 2017, we have re-evaluated the accessibility of the site, being able to compare and see the evolution of the accessibility strategies of this conference centre. In both cases, the research methods we have used include: 1) direct observation of the site, access, rooms, spaces, etc. and its official web page www.euskalduna.eus; and, 2) in-depth interviews with managers of the Euskalduna, including the Technical Director.

Euskalduna Conference Centre was built during an era when standards of design of this kind of venue were not as strict and demanding as they are nowadays. This fact was registered in our first analysis in 2010; however, the results of the interviews with the managers of the centre were encouraging, as they explained to us how worried they are regarding improving accessibility on their site. This idea became a reality with the Accessibility Plan of the Euskalduna Conference Centre 2011–2017. The Plan was drawn up hand-in-hand with CEIS (Test, Innovation, and Services Centre) and includes:

- situation diagnosis, legal requirements and voluntary requirements (MGLC)
- technical advice on architectural and building projects
- plans improving accessibility, specific measures during the period 2011–2017, including all spaces, even those modified or built from then until today
- awareness-raising courses and specific training for staff
- design and implementation of Accessibility Management Systems (UNE 170001-2).

Regarding the accessibility of the environment, from the observation of the site and its Accessibility Guide, we state that it achieves the highest standards in matter of physical inclusion. The same goes for the website www.euskalduna.eus, a strong component of which is web accessibility, willing to offer its content to as many people as possible, regardless of their disabilities. This is why it uses technologies as set by W3C and it follows guidelines WAI 1.0. The main room of this venue is its Auditorium where Row 6 has been designed to allocate wheelchairs. Even so, surveys measuring satisfaction have brought up the question of people in wheelchairs being able to participate in all rooms of the centre and in all types of settings. An area for improvement has been highlighted in the diagnosis of the Plan regarding internal ambulation of the building. Since 2011, and even presently, the Euskalduna Conference Centre is accomplishing various reforms and works, eliminating architectural barriers, such as stairs and uneven surfaces, increasing the number of elevators, setting hand rails on both sides, creating digital signage, and using colors and contrasts in the walls and floor, etc. Regarding the accessibility of events in the Euskalduna Conference Centre, in our interview with the Technical Director, we have confirmed that the Euskalduna has hosted events with disabled attendees, mainly physical disabilities. Nevertheless, it has not hosted an event of only disabled people. We believe this fact has to be taken in account, as it shows this venue is prepared to have a few attendees with special needs, but we cannot ensure it is prepared to guarantee accessibility of large groups. We must remember that the Euskalduna Conference Centre is just a site where MICE events take place, but it does not promote or organise events by itself. This is the reason why guaranteeing the accessibility of specific events is not part of its responsibility. Even so, it does collaborate with a list of companies that give service to events and are compromised with accessibility standards. One of the challenges the Technical Director explained to us during the interview is how to design all spaces and activities in order that everyone can participate equally. As an example, he described the case of an award-giving event, where one of the awardees might need help to reach the stage, becoming the centre of attention and giving rise to an uncomfortable situation. The number of staff at the Euskalduna Conference Centre is less than 20; the rest are hired to other companies (outsourced) when an event takes place. These employees, because of their profile and functions, do not have a specific training in attending to special needs, such as sign language. Whenever an incident is reported, the maintenance team must fill in a form and check if the problem reported affects accessibility. In this case, this problem will have priority in being solved over others.

Conclusions

MICE tourism is a growing industry, which contributes greatly to a destination in terms of economic, social, and cultural benefits. In the Basque Country, MICE is one of its strategic tourism priorities, but, at the same time, MICE seems to be forgotten when talking about accessibility. Today, the demand for infrastructure and technical means to ensure accessibility is low, and, it is also considered to be expensive and currently non-profitable. Even so, entrepreneurs in the tourism sector should see that in providing accessible services, potential clients can be translated into significant economic benefits. Just as quality and sustainability are indisputable in terms of tourism, the same should happen with accessible inclusion. Finally, as important as achieving full accessibility of MICE venues, it is also crucial to report successfully the special services offered by the centre, since, in many cases, if disabled persons do not know that they can make use of them, those services will not be asked for or used. We therefore propose the development of robust guidelines that can be carried out by conference centres to ensure their use and enjoyment by all. This also includes the training of management and customer service staff to ensure all are able to embrace inclusion fully and welcome guests with disabilities and specific access requirements. If, as event organisers, we want our projects to be accessible, then in the planning and design phase, we need to negotiate with suppliers that meet the regulations and recommendations on accessibility, and this includes choosing sites that have the certification and adopt the principles of accessibility and inclusion.

Questions for discussion

1. Do you think the fact that MICE events are outsourced, which implies the use of different companies, is a problem when working to guarantee accessibility at an event?

2. How can a venue such as the Euskalduna Conference Centre encourage all stakeholders involved in MICE events to adopt accessible and inclusive principles and practices?

3. The main difficulty that has arisen in implementing accessibility in venues located in different countries has been the differences in their legislations and accessibility standards. Therefore, a major challenge is to design a standard that works in all European countries. Do you think the protocol we have used in our research can be used and extrapolated to other venues and conference centres?

References

AENOR. (2007a). *Norma UNE 170001-1 Accesibilidad Universal. Parte 1: criterios DALCO para facilitar la accesibilidad al entorno*. Madrid: Ediciones AENOR.

AENOR. (2007b). *Norma UNE 170001-2. Accesibilidad Universal. Parte 2: sistema de gestión de la accesibilidad*. Madrid: Ediciones AENOR.

Basque Tourism Observatory. (2014). Ibiltur MICE Report 2014. Bilbao: Turismoaren Euskal Agentzia.

Gorbeña, S., Madariaga, A., Rodríguez, M. (2002). Protocolo de evaluación de las condiciones de inclusión en equipamientos de ocio. Documentos de estudios de ocio, 22. Bilbao: Universidad de Deusto.

Ostelea. (2015). *El Turismo de Negocios en España*. Barcelona: EAE Business School.

Theobald, W. F. (2005). *Global Tourism*. Massachussets: Elsevier Science.

World Tourism Organization. (2014). *Manual sobre Turismo Accesible para Todos: principios, herramientas y buenas prácticas – módulo I: turismo Accesible – definición y contexto*. Madrid: WTO. www.tur4all.com/documents/2.pdf.

World Tourism Organization (2015). *Manual sobre Turismo Accesible para Todos: principios, herramientas y buenas prácticas – módulo II: cadena de accesibilidad y recomendaciones*. Madrid: WTO. www.fundaciononce.es/es/publicacion/manual-sobre-turismo-accesible-paratodos-principios-herramientas-y-buenas-practicas-0.

16 Academics in two places at once

(Not) managing caring responsibilities at conferences

Emily F. Henderson

Introduction

> Check that [my son] is OK between the keynote and first parallel session.
>
> (P4)

> During a technical hitch I check my phone. I don't like having my phone on silent as I worry I may miss a call from school/nursery.
>
> (P12)

Conferences are important but neglected research sites in the research field that focuses on documenting and analysing academia and the academic profession (Henderson 2015). As sites where knowledge is constructed and shared, where careers are made and unmade, where important connections are formed, conferences play a vital role in the development of research fields (Basch 2001; McCulloch 2012). The issue of access to conferences is therefore much more than an issue of accessing an event for a few days; it is an issue of access to any number of potential future avenues. There are many factors which determine who accesses which conferences where, including funding, institutional support, and border politics (Henderson 2017); this chapter focuses on the impact of caring responsibilities on academics' participation in conferences. The chapter is based on a research project entitled 'In Two Places at Once: the Impact of Caring Responsibilities on Academics' Conference Participation'[1] (www.warwick.ac.uk/i2po). In this project, access to conferences is framed in two senses, which reflect debates about access to education, where access is understood as access *to* and access *within* (Aikman and Unterhalter 2005). Access *to* conferences refers to an academic's ability to attend conferences, while access *within* calls attention to the possibility of the academic fully participating in the conference while there. As with the equivalent debates on access *to* and *within* education, access *to* conferences has hitherto received more attention than access *within*. This chapter therefore focuses on the issue of access *within* conferences for academics with caring responsibilities.

As can be seen from the quotations at the start of this section, participants in the study were involved in managing a state of being 'in two places at once', between conferences and caring responsibilities. The excerpts are from a time-log data collection tool which I developed for this study, in order to capture some of the minutiae of the 'in two places at once' state. The chapter asks the following questions: (i) what was involved in being 'in two places at once' – which aspects of the conference and care were participants balancing?; (ii) how did the participants enact 'in two places at once', and which mechanisms did they use to achieve this?; (iii) how can we understand 'in two places at once' as a temporal mode of being? The third question builds on the theorisation of academic subjectivity and temporality in relation to conferences that I have previously developed (Henderson 2018). The definition of 'care' in this study encapsulated partners, children and other family members, pets, friends and kin; the findings discussed in the chapter therefore address a range of care constellations. The chapter as a whole argues that issues of access and conferences should be framed in relation to access *within* as well as access *to*, and that paying attention to the harder-to-measure aspects of access provides important insights for both conferences and wider academic practice.

'In two places at once': academics, care, and conferences

The questions that are addressed in this chapter bring together somewhat discrete areas of literature from different disciplinary contexts: care and academia; academic mobility; work-based travel. Indeed we can say that there is no real sense of a body of literature on academic conferences, because of the sporadic and dispersed ways in which they are written about – at times as a site for researching social and academic processes, including academic identity formation (Bruce 2010; Henderson 2015), learning and pedagogy (Burford, et al. 2017; Walkington, et al. 2017) and knowledge construction (Gross and Fleming 2011; Henderson 2016); as a focus for professional development (Becker 2014; Rowe 2017); as a form of tourism (Tretyakevich and Maggi 2012; Yoo, et al. 2016) and a corporate business (Lee, et al. 2012). In social sciences and humanities literature on conferences, conferences tend to be researched as a side or background topic in an author's oeuvre, for example in relation to class (Stanley 1995), gender (Pereira 2017), dis/ability (Hodge 2014), and sexual harassment (Jackson 2017). The implication for conferences research is that there is a lack of consistent interrogation of the inequalities that academic conferences produce and reproduce. The 'In Two Places at Once' project is envisaged as a contribution to this lacuna, by offering a sociologically informed analysis of issues surrounding care and conferences.

Although literature on care and academia tends to predominantly focus on the higher education institution as the workplace, there is growing recognition that expectations of academic mobility demand special attention (Moreau and Robertson 2017). Furthermore, researchers are starting to recognise that, although the direct and indirect career benefits of mobility are difficult to quantify, there is increasingly a mobility imperative in the academic job market (Herschberg, et al. 2016). As Leemann (2010) has indicated, academic mobility has often been constructed as the movement of a lone mobile subject, meaning that mobility expecations and provision operate to the exclusion of caregivers, who are often women (Jöns 2011). In the literature on academia and care, and on gender and academic mobility, there is a clear focus on parenting and children, with care and caring responsibilities associated within a normatively defined nuclear family. In the 'In Two Places at Once' study, in line with Moreau and Robertson's (2017) conceptualisation of care in their study of academics with caring responsibilities, care was understood as often "combining multiple caring responsibilities" and as "fluid and...complex" (p.3). This wider conceptualisation problematises the conception that offering childcare services at conferences is *the* solution, and instead takes into consideration caring responsibilities that are more hidden from the eyes of the institution, such as elderly parents and ill partners (ibid.).

Attending conferences is a form of academic mobility, albeit a short-term form. Due to the scarcity of literature on short-term academic mobility (measured in days), it is necessary to look towards literature on work-based travel more generally to understand the consequences of conference travel for academics with caring responsibilities. The aforementioned patterns of family commitments as a determinant of academic mobility (especially for women) are also reflected in research on work-based travel in the form of weekly travel and overnight trips (Dubois, et al. 2015; Viry, et al. 2015). It is clear from Vincent-Geslin and Ravalet's (2015) participants' accounts, as well as from Ralph's (2015) study of Euro-commuters and Willis, et al.'s (2017) study of business travel, that regular business travellers develop well-honed strategies for managing caring arrangements while away – even if these arrangements are a constant struggle and negotiation. While conferences mirror business travel, as noted by Parker and Weik (2014), there are some important differences. With the exception of elite academics who are "at home in motion" (Fahey and Kenway 2010: 568), conference travel occurs much less frequently than business travel of the kind researched in the aforementioned studies. In the 'In Two Places at Once' study, participants often did not have strategies in place for conference attendance, and previously used strategies were often obsolete by the next conference attended. Secondly, in the work-based travel literature, there is a sense of unquestioned obligation relating to travel. Conferences, however, hold a special status in that academics choose to attend them for their own professional development. This means that they are not understood as integral to the job as such, but are nonetheless clearly associated with career progression (Hickson 2006; Rittichainuwat, et al. 2001). Conference travel, then, is both akin to and distinct from (i) routine patterns of work within a higher education institution, in that it involves a break with routine; (ii) longer-term academic mobility, in that it does not involve relocation in the same sense; and (iii) work-related travel, in that it is less frequent or regular and has more of an 'optional' or 'chosen' status. These differences make conferences a distinctive site for the study of academics with caring responsibilities.

Researching conferences and caring responsibilities: methodological and theoretical challenges

The research design for the 'In Two Places at Once' project drew on studies by Hook (2016) and Moreau and Robertson (2017), which employed in-depth qualitative interviews to focus on the varied care scenarios of doctoral students (Hook) and academics (Moreau and Robertson). In line with these studies, 'In Two Places at Once' is also a small-scale, qualitative, exploratory study, which incorporates a focus on temporality. The specific focus on conferences required a research design that captured the break from routine, rather than the routine. This was particularly important for the issue of access *within* conferences, so as to capture the intricacies of specific conference experiences. In order to do this, participants were asked to focus on one particular conference as a form of case study for the purposes of this research. The conference experience was captured using a time-log data collection tool, that drew on time-use studies such as Wigley's (2017) study of mobile prayer practices. Participants were asked to record on a simple form their interactions with caring responsibilities or co-carers during the case study conference, as well as conversations with others about their caring responsibilities, and thoughts that came into their minds in relation to their caring responsibilities. They were asked to record the time and nature of the interaction/thought, and extra information as appropriate, for example relating to feelings and parts of the conference missed. For example, two entries on P14's[2] time-log state:

> 10:10 Text: I text her Dad to remind him she has a disco with her rainbows group on the weekend.

> 12:08 Thought: My mind wanders from the presentation + I think about my daughter and all the things I have to sort out for her new bedroom as we are moving house in 5 weeks.

Participants' use of the time-log varied from a few entries to several pages, and as such is not interpreted as an objectively comparable quantitative record of time use at conferences. Rather, the data is interpreted as participants' subjective portrayals of the state of being 'in two places at once'. The time-log data was then used as the basis for in-depth interviews both on the case study conference and participants' experiences of conferences more generally; in this chapter the time-log data is considered as a data set in its own right.

Participants for the study were recruited on a first-come, first-served basis, following the issuing of the call for participants on several academic mailing lists and on social media. Due to the flexible, exploratory nature of the study, participants could be based in any country, and were self-defined as 'academics' and as having 'caring responsibilities'. For 20 participants, the UK was the country of residence, but the sample also included Australia (5), US (2), Austria (1), Canada (1). Conference destinations were UK (13) Australia (3), US (3), Canada (2), and one each in Denmark, France, Germany, Japan, Kuwait,

Portugal, South Africa and Sweden; 18 participants attended conferences within their country of residence, and 11 crossed international border/s. Conferences varied from one day to six days; 3 days was the mode (12 participants). Participants included one full-time carer (resuming work as a lecturer later in 2017), doctoral students (6) and doctoral students with parallel roles (5), research associates (4), as well as lecturers/assistant professors (4), senior lecturers/ associate professors (3), readers and full professors (6). Primary caring responsibilities stated on the form primarily included children (25 participants), animals (9 participants), partners (6 participants), parents (5 participants), but also included a sibling, a friend, and a children's club. However, it is necessary to note that many participants added extra caring responsibilities into the time-log and the interview, and that the primary responsibilities declared on the form are a reflection of participants' interpretations of the term 'caring responsibility'. Furthermore, several participants listed as primary caring responsibilities a combination of two (8 participants) or three (5 participants) of the above categories.

The analysis of the time-log data that is drawn on in the following section is based on the theorisation of conference time that is outlined in "Feminist conference time: aiming (not) to have been there" (Henderson 2018). This theorisation is located within analyses of time in contemporary academia, where time is commonly understood as "fast moving and constantly changing" (Harris 2005: 421) and "compressed" (Mountz, et al. 2015: 1236). However, in line with Lapping's (2016) analysis, the theorisation recognises that it is not that time is objectively speeding up, but rather that people's relationship to time is altering (see also Sullivan and Gershuny 2017). Key to this conceptual reversal is the understanding of time as external to subjects, who then react to time in a passive or active manner. In a passive relationship with time, time is understood as "clock time" (Adam 2006; Adkins 2009). This means that "the continuous duration of time [is perceived] as a given" (Lapping 2016: 3). At conferences, this relationship with time is clearly evident in the strictly timetabled conference schedule, where delegates move obediently between allotted spaces at allotted times. For delegates with caring responsibilities, the clock time of a conference can be understood as constructing a parallel timetable for managing caring responsibilities, including when phone calls can be made, or which arrangements need to be in place to allow punctual arrival at the conference. A more active or agentic relationship with time sees subjects develop strategies to manage time, or lack thereof, known as "self-governing technologies" (Nikunen 2014: 120), which give the impression of the "subjugation of time to human will" (Clegg 2010: 347). In relation to managing caring responsibilities while at a conference, this understanding of time was enacted in the adaptation and stretching of the conference 'clock time', where the timetable was adapted to allow for the parallel role of care-giver.

It is important to note that the passive and active relationships with time are not discrete – rather, they are held in constant tension. There is a (subjectively determined) limit to how much the conference 'clock time' can be adapted to fit with managing caring responsibilities – how many sessions and networking opportunities missed, how much attention diverted during sessions; for if this limit is surpassed, 'clock time' – and its inflexibility – wins. The following section explores the interaction between conference and care schedules to further develop the understanding of being 'in two places at once'.

Exploring the state of being 'in two places at once'

The analysis of being 'in two places at once' at conferences that is presented in this section is based on the 100+ time-log entries which explicitly mentioned both the conference schedule and participants' caring responsibilities. The analysis in this section is structured according to the three questions asked in the introduction to the paper: (i) what was involved in being 'in two places at once' – which aspects of the case study conference and care were participants balancing?; (ii) how did the participants enact 'in two places at once', and which mechanisms did they use to achieve this?; and (iii) how can we understand 'in two places at once' as a temporal mode of being?

Balancing conference and care

There were two principal types of care-related contact in general. Firstly, a 'check-up' to establish that all was well with participants' caring responsibilities and to check that scheduled transitions in care (for example, school pick-up) had gone to plan. For example, P10 made a phone call to her mother, who was looking after her three children during part of the conference: "Phone call as I was walking to the conference venue to check in on everyone;" P35 exchanged five text messages in the mid-morning break "to check everything was ok at home". Secondly, participants became involved in communicating about an unforeseen incident. P2 and P23 both experienced issues with their pre-planned childcare plans, as in both cases a child was sent home from school because of illness, and P18's dog had to be urgently taken to the vet.

Participants tended to use the beginning and the end of the day for planned, longer 'check-up' interactions. Breaks and transitions were used for more perfunctory 'check-ups'. For example, P49, who is a full-time carer for her mother, who has a life-limiting condition, notes, "I phoned mum during the lunch break to check she was ok." In another example of break-time activity, P23 makes a mental note about a care transition: "'I wonder if my dad has managed to pick up my daughter and get her to piano class." Her entry continues, "It is lunch time so does not interrupt the conference." This statement constructs just the formal sessions as constituting the 'conference', which omits the importance of social times as the moments where collaborations are formed. The dual status of break-time as time for socialising and attending to care is reflected in an entry in P18's time-log, where she received a care-transition confirmation text from her parents while "in the midst of a conversation with a new contact" and noted that she "lost [her] train of thought/couldn't remember what [she] had been saying to them." Again there is a sense that the social parts of the conference are not as important as the formal sessions; depending on the reason for attending a conference, this time may in fact be the most valuable slot of the day. In general, the formal sessions were seen as the least interruptible, though, as shown in the next section, very few participants were prepared to completely lay aside the 'care' part of being 'in two places at once' during sessions.

Attempting and (not) achieving a state of being 'in two places at once'

This section returns more explicitly to the theorisation of conferences and time, where conference delegates try to stretch and manipulate 'clock time' in order to achieve a state of being 'in two places at once'. Here I refer to two examples of 'winning' and two of 'losing' in this struggle. Firstly, an unexpected break in the formal sessions of the conference is experienced as a 'win'. For example, P1 was attending a conference that was partly in a language that she did not speak; she used this time as a bonus "opportunity to think about what [she] need[ed] to do". This included setting up "a to-do list in [her] online calendar", "buy[ing] [her husband] a birthday present", as well as "reading some research articles". A second 'win' came from actively and creatively sharing the conference with those back home through use of virtual communication. P6, for example, took pictures of "how grand/fancy the facilities and services are" to send to her partner.

In terms of a 'loss' in the attempt to produce and maintain a state of 'two places at once', in some cases the conference was dominated by unforeseen incidents which produced a sense of helplessness, guilt and frustration for participants. These types of incidents seemed to highlight the fragility of the arrangements that participants put into place in order to be able to participate in this type of short-term, irregular mobility. P10's partner was going through a gender transition and their mental health was fragile; they were also looking after the couple's children and pets during part of the conference. P10 became concerned about her partner's wellbeing when she phoned and could not get hold of them; this concern manifested itself in 11 missed calls to her partner's phone, as well as text conversations with her mother and neighbour. P18, whose care arrangements fell through when her dog needed to be taken to the vet, wrote an entry at 9am on the last day of the conference: "I essentially felt like my conference was over, and I was completely distracted by thoughts of what I needed to do when I got home".

The second type of 'loss' that I address here involved missing whole or parts of conference sessions because of care issues. For P23, a phone conversation with her partner about her daughter being sent home ill from school was longer than expected, and led to her "missing a panel"; she then sat for an extra half an hour "still thinking about [her] daughter being ill and what is for the best with her tomorrow in terms of childcare". P9 was "30 minutes late" and therefore missed the summary given by "[his] main collaborator" at the conference because of a "nice easy" Skype conversation with his partner and daughter which became "not easy when it came time to go to work". This moment prompted an emotional self-questioning of "priorities" around "what is the right thing to do"; P9 recorded "Still a bit teary as I write." A commonality in all of the accounts is the prominence of mobile technology – both as a means of staying in touch and a reminder of distance (Willis, et al. 2017) or even of the fallibility and fallacy of actually being 'in two places at once'. The role of technology is explored further in the next section.

'In two places at once' as a temporal state of being

Thus far in this analysis section, 'in two places at once' has been principally represented through actions – calls and messages sent and received. These actions are set against a backdrop of what we might call 'active inaction', that is, a constant state of hyperawareness of caring responsibilities at all times, which is particularly intense because of the distance and changes to usual caring arrangements. This was particularly clear when participants recorded that they were waiting for contact. For example, P5 waited for 1.5 hours for a reply to a "check-up" message she sent at 9am. This waiting period coincided with the time before her presentation, where she was firstly distracted from preparing for her presentation by "feeling upset" and "wondering why no message", and then, when the message arrived "just before...going to present", the relief meant that she was then "not 100% focused on [her] presentation". Similarly, P15 realised at 3pm that the school pick-up that her mother was doing would be complete before her presentation slot at 4:15pm, so she waited for a sign that this had gone smoothly. From 3pm until 3:27pm she "kept an eye on phone for reassuring text from [my mother]". Eventually at 3:27pm she sent a "check-up" text to her mother, and at 3:30pm she received a text from her mother to say "all was fine". This ongoing state is also manifested in entries where participants recorded a specific thought that appeared to rise up into their minds in a session. For example, P7, whose mother had just been diagnosed with cancer, and whose partner was away on a research trip in another time zone during P7's conference, realised that, by attending the keynote, she was "missing [her] chance to speak to [her] partner before she went to sleep", and "found [her]self weighing up whether the keynote was worth it". P13 "switched off" during a "presentation [that was] out of [her] sphere of comprehension" and found herself thinking, "I'd rather be with my dogs." These time-log entries give an entry to the ongoing mental state of managing and thinking about caring responsibilities while at a conference. Here, the relationship between the conference participant and 'clock time' is shown as an internal, everpresent dialogue with self, an interweaving of parallel threads of thought, where a kink in attention paid to the conference leads to the surfacing of the thoughts about care.

Conclusion

Given the almost complete lack of research conducted into the impact of caring responsibilities on academics' conference attendance, this article has sought to provide some foundations for this area of study. In particular, the article has focused on issues of access *within* conferences, arguing that it is not enough to record the enrolment figures at a conference: it is just as important to explore academics' experiences of managing care while at conferences. It is also noteworthy that for many participants contact with home was pleasurable and comforting, and that the care was mutually bestowed on conference participants who had had a difficult day or who were lonely and homesick. As such, caring responsibilities cannot be conceived as simply having a negative impact on participants' conference participation. From the analysis of the time-log data, it was clear however that conferences constituted a challenging environment for maintaining contact.

Combining the data analysis with the theorisation of time and subjectivity resulted in the elucidation of what it means to 'win' or 'lose' against the 'clock time' of a conference. 'Winning' involved finding extra time for care within the schedule, and creatively sharing the conference experience with those 'back home'. 'Losing' involved the conference being dominated by care issues which required practical solutions from a distance and which provoked high levels of anxiety in participants; 'losing' was also manifested when parts of an important session were missed due to the difficulty of managing communication into transition and break times. A common factor of both 'winning' and 'losing' was the role of technology in both managing care and exacerbating anxiety. Moreover, the importance of technology is not only manifested in its use; the time-log data also revealed that, even when not directly using technology, participants were at times waiting in a state of 'active inaction' for a sign that all was well. As such, the state of 'being in two places at once' can be understood as much more than a set of actions – rather, it is a state of mind that is both impossible and yet nonetheless experienced by conference delegates.

Questions for discussion

1. How do events exclude or include people with caring responsibilities?
2. What makes an event 'care friendly'?
3. What does considering 'access within' add to discussions of 'access to' events?
4. What are the different temporalities involved in events, and how can they be researched?

Acknowledgements

Many thanks to Holly Henderson for her comments on draft versions of this chapter; to the editors for initiating this book project; to those who gave their time to participate in the study; and to Julie Mansuy for her invaluable assistance during data collection.

Notes

1 Funded by the University of Warwick Research Development Fund in 2017.
2 The participants (P) are numbered according to the order in which they responded to the invitation to participate, though not all of these participated.

References

Adam, B. (2006). Time. *Theory, Culture & Society*, 23(2–3), 119–126.

Adkins, L. (2009). Sociological futures: from clock time to event time. *Sociological Research Online*, 14(4), 8.

Aikman, S. and Unterhalter, E. (2005). *Beyond access: transforming policy and practice for gender equality in education*. Oxford: Oxfam GB.

Basch, F. (2001). Moulin d'Andé, France 1978–1979, Shaker Mill Farm, USA 1982. *Cahiers du CEDREF*, 10, 33–36.

Becker, L. M. (2014). *Presenting your research: conferences, symposiums, poster presentations and beyond*. London: SAGE Publications.

Bruce, T. (2010). Ethical explorations: a tale of preparing a conference paper. *Qualitative Inquiry*, 16(3), 200–205.

Burford, J., Henderson, E. F. and Pausé, C. (2017). Enlarging conference learning: at the crossroads of fat studies and conference pedagogies. *Fat Studies*, 7(1), 69–80.

Clegg, S. (2010). Time future – the dominant discourse of higher education. *Time & Society*, 19(3), 345–364.

Dubois, Y., Ravalet, E., Vincent-Geslin, S. and Kaufmann, V. (2015). Motility and high mobility. In G. Viry and V. Kaufmann (eds.) *High mobility in Europe: work and personal life*. Basingstoke: Palgrave Macmillan, 101–128.

Fahey, J. and Kenway, J. (2010). International academic mobility: problematic and possible paradigms. *Discourse: Studies in the Cultural Politics of Education*, 31(5), 563–575.

Gross, N. and Fleming, C. (2011). Academic conferences and the making of philosophical knowledge. In C. Camic, N. Gross and M. Lamont (eds.) *Social knowledge in the making*. Chicago: University of Chicago Press, 151–179.

Harris, S. (2005). Rethinking academic identities in neo-liberal times. *Teaching in Higher Education*, 10(4), 421–433.

Henderson, E. F. (2015). Academic conferences: representative and resistant sites for higher education research. *Higher Education Research & Development*, 34(5), 914–925.

Henderson, E. F. (2016). *Eventful gender: an ethnographic exploration of gender knowledge production at international academic conferences*. PhD thesis awarded by UCL Institute of Education.

Henderson, E. F. (2017). Conferences and caring responsibilities – individual delegates, multiple lives. *Conference inference: blogging the world of conferences*. Available at: https://conferenceinference.wordpress.com/2017/03/13/conferences-and-caring-responsibilities-individual-delegates-multiple-lives/.

Henderson, E. F. (2018). Feminist conference time: aiming (not) to have been there. In Y. Taylor and K. Lahad (eds.) *Feeling academic in the neoliberal university: feminist flights, fights and failures*. Basingstoke: Palgrave.

Herschberg, C., Benschop, Y. and Van Den Brink, M. (2016). *Gender practices in the construction of excellence*. Trento: University of Trento.

Hickson, M. III (2006). Raising the question #4 why bother attending conferences? *Communication Education*, 55(4), 464–468.

Hodge, N. (2014). Unruly bodies at conference. *Disability & Society*, 29(4), 655–658.

Hook, G. A. (2016). *Sole parent students and higher education: gender, policy and widening participation*. Basingstoke: Palgrave Macmillan.

Jackson, L. (2017). The smiling philosopher: emotional labor, gender, and harassment in conference spaces. *Educational Philosophy and Theory*, DOI: 10.1080/0013 1857.2017.1343112.

Jöns, H. (2011). Transnational academic mobility and gender. *Globalisation, Societies and Education*, 9(2), 183–209.

Lapping, C. (2016). The explosion of real time and the structural conditions of temporality in a society of control: durations and urgencies of academic research. *Discourse: Studies in the Cultural Politics of Education*, 38(6), 906–922.

Lee, S. S., Park, K. and Khan, M. A. (2012). Perceived importance of ICT-based feature and services on conference center selection and differences among meeting planners. *Journal of Hospitality and Tourism Technology*, 3(1), 32–46.

Leemann, R. J. (2010). Gender inequalities in transnational academic mobility and the ideal type of academic entrepreneur. *Discourse: Studies in the Cultural Politics of Education*, 31(5), 605–625.

McCulloch, G. (2012). The standing conference on studies in education, sixty years on. *British Journal of Educational Studies*, 60(4), 301–316.

Moreau, M.-P. and Robertson, M. (2017). *Careers and carers: career development and access to leadership positions among academic staff with caring responsibilities*. London: University of Roehampton & Leadership Foundation for Higher Education.

Mountz, A., Bonds, A., Mansfield, B., Loyd, J., Hyndman, J., Walton-Roberts, M., Basu, R., Whitson, R., Hawkins, R., Hamilton, T. and Curran, W. (2015). For Slow Scholarship: A Feminist Politics of Resistance through Collective Action in the Neoliberal University. *ACME*, 14(4), 25.

Nikunen, M. (2014). The 'entrepreneurial university', family and gender: changes and demands faced by fixed-term workers. *Gender and Education*, 26(2), 119–134.

Parker, M. and Weik, E. (2014). Free spirits? The academic on the aeroplane. *Management Learning*, 45(2), 167–181.

Pereira, M. d. M. (2017). *Power, knowledge and feminist scholarship: an ethnography of academia*. London: Routledge.

Ralph, D. (2015). *Work, family and commuting in Europe: the lives of Euro-commuters*. Basingstoke: Palgrame MacMillan.

Rittichainuwat, B. N., Beck, J. A. and Lalopa, J. (2001). Understanding motivations, inhibitors, and facilitators of association members in attending international conferences. *Journal of Convention & Exhibition Management*, 3(3), 45–62.

Rowe, N. (2017). *Academic & scientific poster presentation: a modern comprehensive guide*. Cham: Springer.

Stanley, J. (1995). Pain(t) for healing: the academic conference and the classed/embodied self. In V. Walsh and L. Morley (eds.) *Feminist academics: creative agents for change*. London: Taylor & Francis, 169–182.

Sullivan, O. and Gershuny, J. (2017). Speed-up society? Evidence from the UK 2000 and 2015 time use diary surveys. *Sociology*, 52(1), 20–38.

Tretyakevich, N. and Maggi, R. (2012). Not just for business: some evidence on leisure motivations of conference attendees. *Current Issues in Tourism*, 15(4), 391–395.

Vincent-Geslin, S. and Ravalet, E. (2015). Travel time use and place attachment among highly mobile people. In G. Viry and V. Kaufmann (eds.) *High mobility in Europe: work and personal life*. Basingstoke: Palgrave Macmillan, 180–208.

Viry, G., Vincent-Geslin, S. and Kaufmann, V. (2015). Family development and high mobility: gender inequality. In G. Viry and V. Kaufmann (eds.) *High mobility in Europe: work and personal life*. Basingstoke: Palgrave Macmillan, 153–179.

Walkington, H., Hill, J. and Kneale, P. E. (2017). Reciprocal elucidation: a student-led pedagogy in multidisciplinary undergraduate research conferences. *Higher Education Research & Development*, 36(2), 416–429.

Wigley, E. (2017). Constructing subjective spiritual geographies in everyday mobilities: the practice of prayer and meditation in corporeal travel. *Social & Cultural Geography*, DOI: 10.1080/14649365.2017.1328527.

Willis, C., Ladkin, A., Jain, J. and Clayton, W. (2017). Present whilst absent: home and the business tourist gaze. *Annals of Tourism Research*, 63(Supplement C), 48–59.

Yoo, H., McIntosh, A. and Cockburn-Wootten, C. (2016). Time for me and time for us: conference travel as alternative family leisure. *Annals of Leisure Research*, 19(4), 444–460.

17 A tripartite approach to accessibility, diversity, and inclusion in academic conferences

Trudie Walters

Introduction

The overall aim of this chapter is to provoke some introspection amongst conference organisers, leading to conferences that provide better experiences for delegates and are more representative of the field (and not just in academia). This research is based on the author's experiences as co-convenor of the Australia and New Zealand Association for Leisure Studies (ANZALS) conference to be held in New Zealand in late 2019 with the theme, 'The Diversity of Leisure'. This theme was deliberately chosen because the organisers want to encourage a diverse mix of scholars to participate and showcase the wide variety of leisure-related research being carried out across disciplinary boundaries. However, the notion of 'diversity' in the title can be seen to carry a deeper, more fundamental meaning which in turn connotes a significant responsibility on the organisers.

Diversity not only means the diversity of research being carried out in the field of leisure studies and related areas. It also means diversity in the geographic location of that research and giving voice to the diverse range of scholars carrying out that research. The organisers want to create a conference that celebrates this diversity, which signals the need for it to be accessible and inclusive. This raises the questions: how do we set about making decisions to do with conference organisation and logistics in order to achieve this vision? And why is it important that we do so? This chapter adopts a case study approach and is a reflexive examination of personal experience over the first six months of conference planning, highlighting both the challenges and the opportunities encountered by the author. First, however, it is necessary to provide the context for these reflections. The next section will therefore unpack the reasons that academic conferences are important, and this is followed by an examination of the issues experienced by conference delegates, with a focus on accessibility, diversity, and inclusion. The case study and research approach are then discussed, and then the author's reflections are then presented in the form of a tripartite approach to considering accessibility in academic conference organisation: physical accessibility, financial accessibility, and cognitive accessibility. It is argued that adopting such an approach facilitates diversity and fosters an environment of inclusivity, which has benefits for all conference delegates.

The importance of academic conferences

Conference attendance is important for a number of reasons, but especially the face-to-face networking it facilitates (Jago and Deery 2005). The building of networks is recognised as an important component of a career; it may begin or indeed be strengthened at a conference, thus underscoring the significance of conference attendance for establishing a successful academic career (Mair and Frew 2016; Sang 2017). Delegates may also reap other benefits from networking and establishing friendships through regular conference attendance. These include increased motivation and a contribution to the feeling that they belong to an academic community, new solutions and ways of thinking about an issue, future collaborations, and improved productivity, performance, and satisfaction with work (Jago and Deery 2005; Wu, et al. 2008; Hixson 2012; Foley, et al. 2014; Mair, et al. 2018). Furthermore, recent research from Australasia has highlighted the particular importance for women of networking opportunities at academic association conferences to establish their reputations amongst peers and advance their careers (Ramirez, et al. 2013; Mair, et al. 2018).

Conference attendance is vital at all stages of academia career from emerging scholars to professors. For tenured academics, conferences can be part of maintaining a vibrant research agenda and play a valuable role in achieving promotion (Bos, et al. 2017). For postgraduate research students and early career academics, it can be an important means not only of disseminating one's research and getting feedback, but also for beginning to establish one's reputation in a field and meeting potential employers, colleagues, and top scholars in one's discipline. Conferences provide opportunities to present research and to join discussions such as during question-and-answer times that follow presentations. These opportunities enhance one's visibility – others begin to know your name, your work, and your intellectual contributions – and this visibility (arguably a form of social capital) has been shown to be related to success and greater earnings in academia (Kriwy, et al. 2013).

In addition to being showcases for the knowledge leaders in the field, conferences allow attendees to participate in activities that add to the full richness and experience of academic life. These activities can be important factors in achieving a promotion, and failing to make conferences accessible, diverse, and inclusive therefore perpetuates the structural inequalities that disadvantage women and minority groups in academia (Sang 2017).

Critiques of academic conferences

While the preceding discussion has argued conference attendance can be both important and beneficial, delegates may face a number of issues that preclude their attendance or lead to a sub-optimal conference experience. These include gender (in)equality and under-representation of minority groups, along with concerns around the cost of attendance, sexism, and personal safety. Each of these will be discussed in turn, with a focus on their consequences for accessibility, diversity, and inclusion.

Critical event studies research has shown the consequences of unequal power relations in various types of events. For example, in their case study on a UK community festival, Clarke and Jepson (2011) identified an undemocratic exercise of power by the organisers, which had ramifications for both the festival events and the audiences. Despite the original vision for a festival celebrating multiculturalism and diversity, the exclusion of the local community from the planning processes meant attaining the vision was impossible. In a similar vein, Walters (2018b) found that power was a significant factor contributing to the life (decision to establish) and death (decision to discontinue) of a food festival in Australia, with organisers eventually capitulating to the power wielded by stakeholders including local government and sponsors. These studies demonstrate power may both enable and constrain event stakeholders (Clegg 1989; Onyx, et al. 2007). While a direct examination of power plays and imbalances has been largely overlooked in the context of conferences, and especially academic conferences, they have nevertheless been noted in passing (Clark, et al. 1998; Jago and Deery 2005; Mair and Frew 2016) and their impacts can be observed.

In the academic conference context, the exertion of power often sees women and other minority groups excluded from visible leadership and 'expert researcher' roles such as keynote speakers and conference chairs (Munar, et al. 2015; Walters 2018a). Furthermore, it has been found that in some cases conference organisers may say that accessibility, diversity, and inclusion matter to them; yet, this is not reflected in the conference programme itself (Walters 2018a). The behaviour that is being modelled to the next generation of scholars normalises a lack of diversity and inclusion (Walters 2018a), and, as a result, women and minority group delegates are not provided with role models that they can relate to and emulate. Rather, the behaviour suggests that [only] white males are the experts. This devalues the perspectives and knowledge that women and minority groups bring to their fields and excludes their voices from the conversation (McCurry 2017; Biggs, et al. 2018).

One final hurdle faced predominantly by women conference delegates is childcare (and other caring responsibilities) and calls have been made for more family-friendly conferences (Mair and Frew 2016; Bos, et al. 2017; Biggs, et al. 2018). Women, more so than men, have identified family commitments as significant barriers to progressing their academic careers, and this is exacerbated by excluding children from academic conferences either directly (through policies such as not allowing children at some conference venues) or indirectly (holding conference activities after hours when childcare facilities are unavailable) (Bos, et al. 2017).

Unlike corporate conferences, attendance at association and academic conferences is not dictated by the employer; rather, they are discretionary activities and delegates are often faced with a choice about which conference(s) they attend in a given year (Mair and Thompson 2009). In recent years, however, university funding for discretionary activities such as conferences has become more constrained (Mair, et al. 2018). It is therefore unsurprising that cost has been found to be an important consideration in attending conferences, irrespective of whether the employer is funding the employee (Oppermann and Chon 1997; Rittichainuwat, et al. 2001; Mair and Thompson 2009). It is argued here that it is an even more significant issue for staff on zero-hours contracts (also known as casual, sessional, and precarious staff), postgraduate students and early career academics whose conference funding may be more constrained or non-existent. Some universities require a peer-reviewed output or publication as part of funding conference attendance, meaning that conferences that do not provide this option are considered less accessible.

Personal safety, sexism, and sexual harassment are also issues often faced by women at academic conferences (Ramirez, et al. 2013; Mair and Frew 2016). One simple solution to concerns about personal safety is having suitable accommodation near the conference venue (Jago and Deery 2005). Perhaps unsurprisingly, Biggs, et al. (2018) found that women were more likely to perceive sexism at conferences where they were under-represented; and, furthermore, where the women responded with silence (rather than vocally challenging it), they were more likely to express an intention to leave academia. This finding is concerning and serves to reinforce the need to create diverse and inclusive conferences. Research by Kriwy, et al. (2013) supports this: their study found that where there were more women in the audience for a conference presentation, they made longer comments, which then enhances their visibility, an important factor for success in academia as highlighted above.

Unfortunately, as can be seen from this discussion, much of the research to date has focused on the experiences of women at academic conferences and highlighted the issues and concerns they face. The perceptions of other marginalised groups have gone largely unheard (Darcy 2012), but are no less important when striving to organise a conference that is accessible, diverse and inclusive. Indeed, Mair and Frew (2016: 17) state, "conference organisers should be aware of issues of equity and diversity when selecting session chairs, panel members, and plenary and keynote speakers, and, wherever possible, offer these opportunities to junior academics, female delegates, and those from other under-represented groups."

Case study and research approach

As mentioned in the introduction, the focus of this chapter is a case study based on the author's role in the organisation of the 2019 Australia and New Zealand Association of Leisure Studies (ANZALS) conference. It is an auto-ethnography based on personal notes while examining the critical event studies literature and attempting to apply research to the practice of conference organisation. It details her personal thoughts and learnings while reading widely across the academic literature, blogs, and other information about industry best practice and the experiences of academics (and others) with issues around accessibility, inclusion, and diversity at conferences. In addition to reading, opinions were also sought from others in the form of an informal poll of an academic women's group on social media in order to gain an understanding of how best to serve the needs of those who face challenges with conference attendance. It is therefore a personal account, but one that should resonate with others for improving understanding and learning about these issues.

Reflections from an academic conference co-convenor

A conference co-convenor is in a position of both significant responsibility and exciting possibility. Some initial questions arise: how can a conference that is accessible, inclusive, and diverse be created? What would such a conference 'look' like? What do these terms mean for an academic conference? Here, the findings of the auto-ethnographic case study are presented, reflecting upon the challenges, opportunities, and learning experiences within the first six months of conference organisation.

Accessible, diverse and inclusive – what, how and for whom?

During informal investigations into academic conference websites, seeking inspiration and evidence of best practice, the author has unfortunately noticed that accessibility is commonly interpreted to mean access to conference venues for wheelchair users; diversity is synonymous with ethnicity; and inclusive is taken to mean events that cater to these narrow definitions. When considering accessibility, diversity, and inclusion in this way, the obvious groups to which attention is directed are those with physical disabilities (most often mobility issues), women, and ethnic minorities. However, a search of non-academic conference organisers' websites and the social media poll highlighted a number of other not-so-obvious groups who may be overlooked during conference planning processes. These include: students; early-career academics; precarious academics (those on casual or zero-hours contracts); academics with hidden disabilities, such as chronic health conditions, cognitive impairments, or mental health challenges (Sang 2017); academics with specific religious or dietary requirements (Jago and Deery 2005; Sang 2017); or academics with caring responsibilities (Jago and Deery 2005; Mair and Frew 2016; Bos, et al. 2017). There is equally thus a challenge and an opportunity here in asking how a conference can be accessible to such a diverse range of needs and also be inclusive and welcoming? The best way to rise to the challenge is simply to stop making assumptions and ask people what they need, as they are the experts in their requirements (Bos, et al. 2017). To that end, the author has read, listened, and incorporated their advice, and duly presents it here.

Accessibility must be considered to be a broader umbrella concept which includes financial, physical, and cognitive accessibility. Likewise, the notions of diversity and inclusivity encompass more than delegate gender and ethnicity; everyone irrespective of gender, ethnicity, sexuality, [dis]ability, family status, age, dietary requirements, religion, or postcode should be made to feel welcome, valued, and safe. As mentioned earlier, in the case of the ANZALS 2019 conference, the organisers have expanded understanding of diversity further to incorporate the geographic location of the research, the researched, and the researcher, the level of scholarship (postgraduate research student to senior academic), and the subject and type of research being carried out (pushing the boundaries of the discipline and the methodological approach).

If these broader conceptualisations of accessibility and diversity are to be realised in the academic conference context, then inclusive practice must surely try to ensure a welcoming and supportive environment exists for *all* delegates (Kramer 2016). But is this practical and achievable in reality, or is it simply a naïve pipe dream and Utopian rhetoric? What follows is an examination of academic conference organisation from a critical event studies perspective. The frameworks of financial accessibility, physical accessibility, and cognitive accessibility are employed with some examples of how each form of accessibility could be addressed, using the ANZALS 2019 conference as a case study. At the same time, it must be acknowledged that these categories are not mutually exclusive and that there are intersectionalities at work. The author also acknowledges that this is a work in progress, and, with time, there are going to be many more opportunities for learning about how to best embed accessibility, diversity, and inclusion as guiding principles as the work of organising the conference continues, and, therefore, the list of examples here are not exhaustive. Nevertheless, it is argued that by adopting such a tripartite conceptualisation of accessibility, conference organisers may be able to create an academic conference that is by its very nature diverse and inclusive.

Financial accessibility

One significant challenge for conference organisers is creating an event that is financially accessible. This challenge is complex and multi-faceted but relates to diminishing university funds for conference attendance in many parts of the world (Mair, et al. 2018), and the increasingly rigorous criteria being set for applications for said funding such as the need to provide evidence of publications, impact or other forms of output from conference attendance. ANZALS 2019 is being held in New Zealand, and in an expensive 'tourist mecca' part of New Zealand, and it will therefore be expensive for delegates to travel from the northern hemisphere. This is a challenge that southern hemisphere academics regularly deal with when attending conferences on the other side of the world, but is one that seldom seems to be taken into account by conference organisers there. This experience has simply served to make ANZALS 2019 organisers more mindful of the problem. It is also important to acknowledge that postgraduate students, early-career academics, and those on casual or short-term contracts in particular often struggle to find funding to attend conferences.

To that end, the organisers are looking hard at costs and stripping away some of the traditional yet perhaps unnecessary expenses in order to keep the registration fee as low as possible. One of these unnecessary expenses is keynote speakers. While this may be contentious, it has been argued (and personally observed on many occasions) that most keynote addresses are not well attended and that most keynote speakers simply revisit past research ideas rather than presenting anything new and groundbreaking (Lundy 2016). Not having keynote speakers represents a saving of flights, transfers, and accommodation, which can be passed on to delegates. Naturally, group discount for block bookings is being sought from accommodation providers as well as offering rooms in the student quarters at the conference venue. Conference attendees are being urged to make use of the cheap bus service (or walk where possible) to move between accommodation and conference venue. The buses are wheelchair- and stroller-friendly, and the paths from bus stop to conference venue are well-maintained and easy to navigate (Fife Centre for Equalities 2017). The idea of providing delegates with a pre-loaded concession card for public transport has been mooted, but the logistics of this needs further consideration.

In order to encourage student attendance at the 2017 conference, the ANZALS Board implemented a competitive scholarship scheme for higher degrees by research students (Honours, Masters, and PhD students). The conference registration fee was paid for up to five applicants who successfully met the criteria. This scheme was well-received and is to be continued for future conferences, improving the financial accessibility and enabling more participation from the next generation of leisure studies scholars. Welcoming people from less privileged backgrounds, countries, or universities is important, but, again, it is not always possible for them to obtain funding to attend international conferences. At the 2017 conference, one scholarship recipient was unable to obtain funding for flights from Africa and sadly had to abandon attendance; it was disappointing both for them and for what they would have brought to the conference in terms of a different perspective, as their research gave voice to under-represented groups in our field. However, in the course of the author's research into best practice conference organisation, it was found that some conferences have successfully approached sponsors to provide travel grants to support attendance. For ANZALS 2019, university alumni from the three host organisations could be approached in the first instance, or other philanthropic organisations that seek to empower women, minority groups, and other marginalised peoples. Ideally, the goal is to gain funding to offer two grants for international attendees and five or six for domestic attendees.

Being able to include sole parents and families with children is important; therefore, keeping costs low and offering some form of subsidised or free childcare options (for all ages of children) needs to be investigated. This is often something that prevents people (particularly but not exclusively women) from attending conferences (Bos, et al. 2017). At this point in time, there are no firm solutions for the ANZALS 2019 conference, but the challenge is on the agenda, and one idea is for the Trans Tasman Challenge (more on this below) to be a family-friendly social event where children are welcome.

Physical accessibility

As stated earlier, ANZALS 2019 seeks to offer a conference experience that is physically accessible and welcoming to all, irrespective of gender, ethnicity, sexuality, religion, dietary requirements, [dis]ability, family status, or health issues. While this is all very well in terms of rhetoric, how can this be the case in practical terms? What does a physically accessible conference need to 'look' like?

As mentioned above, the notion of accessibility is frequently applied to those who have difficulty with mobility (Richardson 2017). Legislation is in place in a number of countries to ensure that public buildings (including conference venues) are accessible for those in wheelchairs or who use mobility aids (Darcy 2012). Despite this, horror stories (that could easily have been avoided with some forethought) are not uncommon (Dunstan 2017; Sang 2017). Certainly, with regards to ANZALS 2019 conference, it is uppermost in the organisers' minds, not least of all because of sensitivities to colleagues who use wheelchairs and speak openly about conference experiences around [in]accessibility. However, physical accessibility extends far beyond the reaches of the conference venue, and mobility issues can be faced by those who are bringing a baby and need to use a stroller. In a situation where a delegate has a carer accompanying them, that person should not have to pay the conference registration fee (Dunstan 2017).

The conference space needs to be comfortable, safe, and non-threatening for delegates, and particularly for women (whether alone or in groups) and other minority groups. Furthermore, space should be available for a diverse range of specific purposes. For practising Muslims, quiet prayer space is important (McCurry 2017). For those with babies or small children, space for feeding and changing nappies is important (Bos, et al. 2017). For those with food allergies or specific dietary requirements, the ability to have those needs catered to is important and makes the networking benefits of a conference (which often occur over a shared meal) accessible (Sang 2017). For delegates with hearing and sight challenges, wayfaring needs to be easy and conference presentations need to be clear (Fife Centre for Equalities 2017). Resources are available to help conference organisers to communicate best practice when developing presentations (Fife Centre for Equalities 2017; Vocal Eyes 2017), and these are going to be disseminated to ANZALS 2019 delegates via the conference website. The author enrolled in a web page design course in order to be able to edit the conference website. One of the lessons learned has been that visually impaired delegates who use screen-readers need carefully designed web pages that provide in-depth descriptions of images and weblinks to allow them to 'see' what is on the page. Furthermore, when using hashtags on websites and social media, it is important to capitalise each word in the hashtag so that the screen-reader recognises and reads it correctly (for example, #AccessibilityAndInclusion rather than #accessibilityandinclusion).

Cognitive accessibility

This category takes into account cognitive, mental, and emotional wellbeing of conference delegates, which are often hidden but very real barriers to participation. For all delegates, but particularly those with disabilities and cognitive impairments, communicating important information, directions, and instructions about the conference, the venue(s), and the destination in advance helps to minimise stress (Dunstan 2017; Sang 2017). For those suffering from anxiety or other mental health conditions, space for time out from the noise and pressure is important (Richardson 2017). Fatigue is often a problem that is not catered to at conferences, with long days proving difficult for many with cognitive or physical challenges (Dunstan 2017; Sang 2017); shorter days may facilitate attendance and longer breaks between presentations allows for recuperation. To that end, the author has suggested that the ANZALS 2019 conference programme could include shortened presentation sessions and longer breaks in between. Not only will this help with overcoming cognitive overload and fatigue, it will also foster the continuance of conversations started during the presentation question time and provide much-valued networking time. This suggestion has yet to be adopted by the organising committee, but has received positive feedback to date.

The Trans-Tasman Challenge has been an ANZALS conference tradition since they first began and is a well-guarded secret up to the very last minute. We acknowledge that this 'secrecy' may be stressful, as it creates a sense of uncertainly, and delegates may choose to opt out of this social event because of the potential for disaster surrounding such an unknown situation. This has made the organisers acutely aware of the need to create a non-threatening environment of trust in which delegates will be more likely to want to participate, and to communicate this in advance (without revealing the exact nature of the Challenge).

Including the local

One final but important element of inclusivity for the creation of ANZALS 2019 is the ability to include as much local culture as possible. There is a wish to provide delegates with a rich experience of the destination. After all, it seems to the organisers that it is the destination that provides the distinctiveness to conferences, and it is important to include as much of the 'essence' of the destination in the offering as possible. To that end, the organisers are in consultation with local Māori (indigenous New Zealanders) as to the best and most culturally sensitive way of achieving this aim. Investigations are also under way as to the best avenues to introduce other aspects of local culture to conference delegates through devising a social programme of events that allows them to gain an understanding of the local leisure culture (as befits both the association and the conference theme). This remains a work in progress, and there will be a 'slow tantalising reveal' of the social programme over the coming months.

The importance of being explicit

In terms of best practice, it is important that conference co-convenors and organising committee members are explicit about their decision-making. If, for example, when planning a conference programme, the decision is to incorporate half-hour breaks between sessions in order to cater to those who need time out, need to take medications, attend to family needs, or want to continue conversations started during question time, then it is imperative to state clearly these reasons in conference communications. This, then makes the conference transparent to attendees and helps to reassure them that the organisers are genuinely trying to embed accessibility, diversity, and inclusive practice into decision-making and take their needs into account (Dunstan 2017). The author's wish is that by doing so, the ANZALS 2019 conference will also act as a catalyst for effecting change in future academic conferences in multiple discipline areas. It is important that attendees and organisers alike are aware that there are not only things about the ANZALS 2019 conference that make it 'different', but also that there are sound moral and ethical reasons for doing things in that way, and that these should become the norm rather than something unusual.

Conclusion

Academic conferences are important fora for disseminating knowledge, learning, and meeting like-minded scholars in one's field. They provide a platform for vital networking and enhance both reputation and visibility, which are shown to be important for academic success (Kriwy, et al. 2013; Mair and Frew 2016; Sang 2017). However, significant issues remain around accessibility, diversity, and inclusion for many groups including women, disabled academics and those with impairments, students, early career and precarious academics, and those with caring responsibilities. These issues preclude or make attendance difficult, which then limits not only the range of voices presented, but also limits career advancement. Indeed, it is argued here that conference attendance can be thought of as a social justice issue.

In concluding, it is important to note that having an accessible conference brings other benefits to delegates beyond the obvious. For example, Vocal Eyes (2017) mentions that making conference presentations accessible to blind and partially sighted people also helps those who are not fluent in the language and people with different learning styles. In addition, an accessible conference widens delegate understandings of the discipline area that is the focus of the conference, as they are exposed to a more diverse representation of perspectives (McCurry 2017). This chapter has highlighted a tripartite approach to embedding accessibility, diversity, and inclusion in conference organisation, and has provided personal reflections on the challenges, opportunities, and learning experiences that the author has had in the early months of organising an association conference. The author does not pretend to have all the answers, but hopes that by sharing her thoughts she has in some small way contributed to an awareness that accessible conferences are a necessity rather than a luxury, if we are to have a more equitable and respectful academe.

Questions for discussion

1. Think back to your last conference experience. Did you notice any issues with accessibility, inclusion, or diversity, either at the time or in retrospect?
2. Why is the need for accessible, inclusive, and diverse conferences a social justice issue?
3. What was the most important idea you learned from reading this chapter, and why?

References

Biggs, J., Hawley, P. H. and Biernat, M. (2018). The academic conference as a chilly climate for women: Effects of gender representation on experiences of sexism, coping responses, and career intentions. *Sex Roles*, 78, 394–408.

Bos, A. L., Sweet-Cushman, J. and Schneider, M. C. (2017). Family-friendly academic conferences: A missing link to fix the "leaky pipeline"? *Politics, Groups, and Identities*, DOI: 10.1080/21565503.2017.1403936.

Clark, J. D., Evans, M. R. and Knutson, B. J. (1998). Selecting a site for an association convention: An exploratory look at the types of power used by committee members to influence decisions. *Journal of Hospitality and Leisure Marketing*, 5(1), 81–93.

Clarke, A. and Jepson, A. (2011). Power and hegemony within a community festival. *International Journal of Event and Festival Management*, 2(1), 7–19.

Clegg, S. R. (1989). *Frameworks of power*. London: SAGE Publications.

Darcy, S. (2012). Disability, access and inclusion in the event industry: A call for inclusive event research. *Event Management*, 16, 259–265.

Dunstan, V. (2017). *Problems as a disabled academic attending conferences*. https://vivsacademicblog.wordpress.com/2017/08/31/problems-as-a-disabled-academic-attending-conferences/.

Fife Centre for Equalities. (2017). *Accessible Events Toolkit*. https://centreforequalities.org.uk/wp-content/uploads/2018/02/Accessible-Events-Toolkit-DEC2017active.pdf.

Foley, C., Edwards, D. and Schlenker, K. (2014). Business events and friendship: Leveraging the sociable legacies. *Event Management*, 18, 53–64.

Hixson, E. (2012). The psychological benefits of attending conventions. In R. J. Mykletun (ed.) *Advances in event management research and practice proceedings from V Global Event Congress June 13–15, 2012*. Norway: University of Stavanger.

Jago, L. K. and Deery, M. (2005). Relationships and factors influencing convention decision-making. *Journal of Convention & Event Tourism*, 7(1), 23–41.

Kramer, M. (2016). How to throw an intentional, inclusive journalism conference. www.poynter.org/news/how-throw-intentional-inclusive-journalism-conference.

Kriwy, P., Gross, C. and Gottburgsen, A. (2013). Look who's talking: Compositional effects of gender and status on verbal contributions at sociology conferences. *Gender, Work and Organization*, 20(5), 545–560.

Lundy, C. (2016). Free the academic conference. https://theresearchwhisperer.wordpress.com/2016/07/12/free-the-academic-conference/?utm_content=buffer9bdb1&utm_medium=social&utm_source=twitter.com&utm_campaign=buffer#comments.

Mair, J. and Frew, E. (2016). Academic conferences: A female duo-ethnography. *Current Issues in Tourism*, DOI: 10.1080/13683500.2016.1248909.

Mair, J., Lockstone-Binney, L. and Whitelaw, P. (2018). The motives and barriers of association conference attendance: Evidence from an Australasian tourism and hospitality academic conference. *Journal of Hospitality and Tourism Management*, 34, 58–65.

Mair, J. and Thompson, K. (2009). The UK association conference attendance decision-making process. *Tourism Management*, 30(3), 400–409.

McCurry, D. (2017). Why accessibility at conferences impacts academic debate. www.exordo.com/blog/accessibility-at-conferences-impacts-academic-debate.

Munar, A. M., Biran, A., Budeanu, A., Caton, K., Chambers, D., Dredge, D. and Ram, Y. (2015). *The gender gap in the tourism academy: Statistics and indicators of gender equality*. Copenhagen: While Waiting for the Dawn.

Onyx, J., Edwards, M. and Bullen, P. (2007). The intersection of social capital and power: An application to rural communities. *Rural Society*, 17(3), 215–230.

Oppermann, M. and Chon, K.-S. (1997). Convention participation decision-making process. *Annals of Tourism Research*, 24(1), 178–191.

Ramirez, D., Laing, J. and Mair, J. (2013). Exploring intentions to attend a convention: A gender perspective. *Event Management*, 17(2), 165–178.

Richardson, S. (2017). Mental health and conferences: A practical guide. https://richard sonphd.wordpress.com/2017/08/16/mental-health-and-conferences-a-practical-guide/.

Rittichainuwat, B. N., Beck, J. A. and Lalopa, J. (2001). Understanding motivations, inhibitors, and facilitators of association members in attending international conferences. *Journal of Convention and Exhibition Management*, 3(3), 45–62.

Sang, K. (2017). Disability and academic careers. https://migrantacademics.files.wordpress. com/2017/05/disability-sang-may-2017.pdf.

Vocal Eyes. (2017). Guidelines for making your conference presentation accessible to blind and partially sighted people. http://vocaleyes.co.uk/wp-content/uploads/2018/01/Voca lEyes-guidelines-for-conference-speakers.pdf.

Walters, T. (2018a). Gender equality in academic tourism, hospitality, leisure and events conferences. *Journal of Policy Research in Tourism, Leisure and Events*, 10(1), 17–32.

Walters, T. (2018b). 'Power wrestling': The life and [untimely] death of the Real Food Festival. In A. Jepson and A. Clarke (eds.) *Power, construction and meaning in festivals*. London: Routledge, 139–152.

Wu, L., Waber, B., Aral, S., Brynjolfsson, E. and Pentland, A. (2008). Mining face-to-face interaction networks using sociometric badges: Predicting productivity in an IT configuration task. https://ssrn.com/abstract¼1130251.

Index